TWENTY-FIRST-CENTURY
BUDDHISTS IN CONVERSATION

21st
CENTURY
BUDDHISTS
IN CONVERSATION

Edited by Melvin McLeod and the Editors

of *Buddhadharma: The Practitioner's Quarterly*

WISDOM PUBLICATIONS • BOSTON

Wisdom Publications
199 Elm Street
Somerville, MA 02144 USA
www.wisdompubs.org

Library of Congress Cataloging-in-Publication Data
Twenty-first-century Buddhists : over sixty leading figures in conversation / edited by Melvin
McLeod.
    pages cm
  Includes index.
  ISBN 1-61429-086-5 (pbk.)
  1. Buddhism. I. McLeod, Melvin, editor. II. Buddhadharma.
  BQ4055.T94 2015
  294.3—dc23
                        2014020586

ISBN 978-1-61429-086-5   ebook ISBN 978-1-61429-106-0

19 18 17 16 15
5 4 3 2 1

Cover and interior design by Gopa&Ted2, Inc. Set in DGP 10/14.

Wisdom Publications' books are printed on acid-free paper and meet
the guidelines for permanence and durability of the Production Guidelines
for Book Longevity of the Council on Library Resources.

This book was produced with environmental mindfulness. We have elected to print this title on
30% PCW recycled paper. As a result, we have saved the following resources: 16 trees, 7 million
BTUs of energy, 1,332 lbs. of greenhouse gases, 7,288 gallons of water, and 484 lbs. of solid
waste. For more information, please visit our website, www.wisdompubs.org.

Printed in the United States of America.

Please visit www.fscus.org.

Contents

Editor's Preface

THE COMMUNITY OF Buddhist practitioners is said to be the oldest continuous institution in human history. Yet while the outward manifestations of Buddhism—its organizations, culture, and body of teachings—are vital, its essence is a living lineage of practice and realization, transmitted unbroken from teacher to student for 2,500 years. The success of this transmission has never been guaranteed. It has always depended on the realization, skill, and integrity of teachers and on the devotion, merit, and diligence of students. Particularly challenging to the success of this process are those times when the transmission of the Buddha's teachings takes place not just from generation to generation but from country to country.

Transmission across international borders is not something that happens quickly. The establishment of a genuine Buddhist tradition in a new culture can take centuries. As Buddhism moved outward from its birthplace in India—south to Sri Lanka, north to Tibet, and east to Southeast Asia, China, and Japan—it had to adapt to the various traditions, religious beliefs, social structure, and psychology of each place, while always maintaining the essential integrity of the teachings. In every new culture to date, this has been done successfully.

Now Buddhism is in the early stages of perhaps its most difficult transition ever—to find a true home in the West.

Western culture offers unique challenges for any genuine spiritual tradition. Modern capitalism is finely tuned to create and increase materialist appetites. The explosion of entertainments and communications distances us from the present and the natural. Stress, speed, and anxiety weigh on all, and a multitude of spiritual and philosophical systems offer competing promises of relief. The ethics of individualism and egalitarianism pose a challenge to the teacher-student relationship at the heart of the Buddhist transmission.

Yet the basic challenge is the same as it's been in every culture Buddhism has entered: to change what is culturally dependent in order to adapt to the new culture without weakening the timeless and radical truths of the Dharma; to speak in new ways to communicate effectively with the local mindset without giving in to its neuroses; and to create opportunities for serious meditation practice and Dharma study in a culture where none previously existed.

It will take many more decades at least—some say centuries—before the development of Buddhism outside of Asia is complete. I believe there are five markers that will define the successful development of Buddhism in North America, Europe, Australia, and beyond. As committed practitioners, we need to be working toward a Western Buddhism that is:

- *Genuine*—serving only nonego and enlightenment and not corrupted by physical, psychological, or spiritual materialism.
- *Complete*—encompassing the full range and depth of Buddhist practice, philosophy, and ritual.
- *Sustainable*—supported by the institutions, infrastructure, and financial resources needed to establish a religious tradition that will last for generations to come.
- *Integrated*—becoming an accepted and natural part of Western society, not a foreign implant or fringe phenomenon.
- *Successful*—reaching all who would benefit from it.

As daunting as this may seem, the good news is that millions in North America and Europe have already been touched by Buddhist teachings and practice. Hundreds of thousands more are serious practitioners of the Dharma. *Buddhadharma: The Practitioner's Quarterly* is where committed Buddhists come together to deepen their practice and to study and ponder the challenges Buddhism faces in the West.

Reflecting *Buddhadharma's* mission to serve Buddhists of all traditions, each issue features a panel discussion bringing together leading figures from across the Buddhist spectrum. Nowhere else is such an outstanding and diverse collection of Buddhist voices assembled. They include leading Asian-born teachers and many Western Buddhists who are important and insightful teachers in their own right. They are joined by leading Buddhist academics, writers, activists, and sangha organizers.

Buddhadharma's readership is primarily in North America, and almost all of the panelists are based in North America. Naturally, their focus is on the unique challenges they face as practitioners in the West, but the issues they discuss are relevant to Buddhists around the world. In traditionally Buddhist areas in Asia, Buddhists also face the challenges of twenty-first-century global culture and its values. This book offers them abundant experience and insight as they work to maintain or re-establish genuine Buddhist traditions in their own societies.

This book brings together twenty-seven of the best panel discussions from the pages of *Buddhadharma*. More than sixty of today's outstanding Buddhist figures are represented, discussing all the important topics of concern to Western Buddhists today. I have grouped the panels into three sections:

Buddha: The Practice

The future of Buddhism always depends on the sincere and devoted practice of individual Buddhists. This section offers insight and instruction that will benefit every reader's meditation practice. Here we can see one of the unique benefits of *Buddhadharma*: that while we may be practitioners of one particular school of Buddhism, we can always learn from the teachings and experience of other traditions.

Dharma: The Teachings

It is vital to Buddhism's future in the West that practitioners not only meditate but also have a deep understanding of Buddhist teachings and philosophy. In some of these discussions, experts take us deeper into specific teachings, such as the practice of *lojong* and the philosophy of Dōgen. In others, leaders in different traditions debate and analyze questions of importance to all Buddhists, such as the nature of prayer, the doctrine of rebirth, and the relationship between Buddhism and Western psychology.

Sangha: The Community

Here, teachers, organizers, activists, and practitioners discuss the challenges that Buddhist communities face in Western society. Many reflect the difficulty of adapting a religion with its roots in conservative Asian countries to a modern society that values diversity, freedom, and individualism. Others offer thoughts on systemic sexism, racism, and classism that Buddhist communities are not immune to. While progress has been made, there are still many difficulties to overcome before Buddhist communities truly reflect the core value of Buddhism—that all men and women are created equal in their buddha nature.

Twenty-First-Century Buddhists in Conversation makes a unique contribution to Buddhism at this important moment in its history. Nowhere else are outstanding Buddhist figures of all traditions brought together to discuss such a range of important subjects. This book provides a valuable snapshot of Western Buddhism early in the twenty-first century. I hope it will deepen your practice and study and invite you to participate in this extraordinary effort to bring the Dharma to a new world. How fortunate we are to be present, here at the beginning of the twenty-first century, for this important moment in the 2,700-year history of Buddhism.

Buddhadharma is published by the Shambhala Sun Foundation, an independent nonprofit, and everyone at the foundation has helped make this book possible. However, two people are most responsible for this outstanding collection. Tynette Deveaux has been the editor of *Buddhadharma* since its birth. She is a diligent and highly professional journalist who is deeply committed to the Dharma. She is doing it real service. Many of the panels in this book were moderated by Barry Boyce, who brought to them his journalistic skills and deep knowledge of the Dharma. A longtime student of the late Chögyam Trungpa Rinpoche, Barry is now benefiting all sentient beings as the editor-in-chief of *Mindful* magazine.

I would also like to thank our friends and colleagues at Wisdom Publications, whose work I admire greatly. Josh Bartok was the original editor for this book, and he passed the reins to Andy Francis. Both are skilled professionals and a pleasure to work with. On behalf of all Buddhists, I also want to thank Tim McNeill, president of Wisdom Publications, for his lifetime of great work for the Dharma.

Of course, the people truly responsible for this book are the more than sixty teachers, organizers, academics, and practitioners who have offered their insight and knowledge to the readers of *Buddhadharma*, and now to us. They are latest generation of an unbroken lineage that goes back to the Buddha himself, and their commitment and realization is our most hopeful sign for the future. They are the reason we can be optimistic Buddhism will continue to grow in the West, genuine, complete, and successful.

Melvin McLeod
Editor-in-chief
The Shambhala Sun
Buddhadharma: The Practitioner's Quarterly

A Brief Note on the
Buddhadharma Forum Panels

WHEN YOU START a magazine, you need to dream up unique features and departments that will keep readers coming back. Some of them don't make it off the drawing board, a few last for a while and then peter out, and some become well-loved institutions that readers look forward to in every issue. Over a decade ago, when a few of us got together to envision *Buddhadharma* magazine, we thought it might be interesting to hold a regular conversation with Buddhists of many different stripes, mainly teachers, to kick around ideas and concerns. So much wonderful Dharma takes the form of conversation, from the sutras to kōan stories to the free-ranging discussions in a carload of people returning home from a retreat. We hoped it would convey that kind of lively spirit. It would demonstrate that Dharma is anything but dry—that, on the contrary, it's intensely personal.

It's been my pleasure to have been the main convener of these conversations for the *Buddhadharma* forum's first ten years. Every three months, *Buddhadharma*'s editor, Tynette Deveaux, and the editor-in-chief, Melvin McLeod, and I would gather to bat around what the topic could be for the next issue and whom we would invite to talk about it.

In some cases, we delved into something that came out of our own experience of practice (such as working with emotional upheavals), a philosophical topic of contemplation (what is karma and rebirth anyway?), or issues about how the Dharma is being assimilated in the West (diversity, gender, politics, and so forth). In these cases, we always tried to find people from various traditions to keep the discussion broad.

In other cases, we acted as a fly-on-the-wall, listening in on the kind of discussion people of one particular tradition might have—such as Zen teachers sharing their passion for Dōgen, Theravāda teachers talking about applying formal practice to everyday life, or Vajrayanists considering whether Dzogchen has been watered down in its current presentation in the West.

When we called to ask people to take part in these ninety-minute conference calls, with participants calling in from far-flung time zones, they were unfailingly generous in agreeing to take part. When the appointed day and time arrived, we always started with a script of questions that had been shared with the panelists, but once things got rolling, the script usually came apart in my hands.

One thing I can tell you: the Buddhists I had in conversation were very kind about not interrupting others and allowing them to finish their thoughts. Conventional journalistic wisdom would say that such politesse inhibits the free flow of ideas. Not so. The flow was very free, and fun. In many cases, people who had heard about each other for many years had an opportunity to meet and get to know each other in the virtual forum we created.

A painstaking, weeklong process of editing the transcript of these free-for-alls ensued. It was hard work, but it held many rewards, not the least of which was that when you read something over fifteen times, the point would start to sink in. It was also an interesting challenge to try to carry over not just the meaning but some of the tenor of the conversation. I'm happy to see that this book stays true to the liveliness and enthusiasm of these lengthy chats.

There were many times when every one of us on the call laughed out loud as a joke ripped away the skimpy veil that ego uses to obscure reality, or when we fell silent at an especially poignant image or insight. I felt so delighted to be capturing this for our readers—and now for you—because the *Buddhadharma* forum is unique. It's a wide-ranging, decade-long conversation among Buddhists in the West about what dharma means in our lives—and in particular how it could help others. May this conversation continue for many decades to come.

Barry Boyce
Editor-in-chief
Mindful magazine

Twenty-First-Century Buddhists in Conversation

BUDDHA:

The Practice

1

Face-to-Face with the Buddha:
The Teacher-Student Relationship

ZOKETSU NORMAN FISCHER

SHARON SALZBERG

DZOGCHEN PONLOP RINPOCHE

Why is the teacher-student relationship so important in Buddhism?

ZOKETSU NORMAN FISCHER: There is an alchemy that takes place when we put together the teachings, the student, and the teacher. The teachings are not external material that one masters. In the Dharma, the external material is just a tool to effect an inner transformation. That transformation requires a deep spiritual relationship with another person, who in the Zen tradition is understood to be an ordinary human being and is at the same time envisioned as an empowered buddha. It's a human relationship conducted on the basis of Dharma. In Zen, it's not something that's optional or that makes the Dharma better if it's there. It's required to bring about the transformation that is the heart of the Dharma.

SHARON SALZBERG: In the Theravāda tradition, the word for teacher is *kalyāna-mitta*, which means "spiritual friend." The teacher is not a friend in the sense of being a pal, yet the teacher embodies all the qualities, such as trust and comfort, ease and guidance, and a sense of inspiration, that we associate with a very good friend.

There is also a lot of importance placed on one's own effort in working with the teacher. This principle of applying our own effort starts with our relationship with the Buddha, who as the primary spiritual friend points the way and inspires us to follow his example. He asks us to make the same effort he made.

We have enormous regard and respect for the teacher as the one person who, as one text puts it, "is always on our side," the one who is motivated not by self-aggrandizement or a wish to be venerated, but by the wish for the liberation and freedom of the student. The teacher guides us by relying on their expertise both in methodology and the teachings. It is said that the teacher bring us back to a balance of mind, out of which insight, love, compassion, and other such good qualities can arise. We work with the teacher to open to all of those qualities, and the teacher responds directly to our effort, our seeking, and our understanding.

DZOGCHEN PONLOP RINPOCHE: In Vajrayāna Buddhism the teacher-student relationship goes through several levels of development. It is a personal relationship that is directly connected to the Dharma. Because it is based on Dharma, as it becomes more intimate, it becomes more profound and results in spiritual accomplishment. As the student's commitment matures, the teacher invokes the enlightened nature of the student and shares experiences on the path of realization. When this relationship reaches the level of what we call the guru-disciple relationship, the teacher guides the student through all the different experiences they encounter on the path.

Is a teacher necessary or can a beginner learn to meditate from a book?

ZOKETSU NORMAN FISCHER: If you don't have a chance to encounter a spiritual teacher, by all means, learn meditation from a book and begin practicing. But meditation is essentially an oral tradition. It's learned in an apprenticeship model. The written instructions are always generic, and there are no generic people. This is another reason you need a person who can look you in the eye, have some sense of who you are, and provide instructions that are suitable for you.

SHARON SALZBERG: I am forever grateful that I have been able to practice under the direct guidance of people. Words on a page can seem very simple.

The instruction and the methodology can seem very straightforward, but it's not so easy when you get right down to it. It took the kindness, presence, and further instruction of the teacher to guide me through what happened when I actually started to try to follow those simple instructions. Nurturing was very important at that point.

DZOGCHEN PONLOP RINPOCHE: In the Tibetan tradition we have something called "visual transmission." It provides something different than books or online instructions can. The visual transmission takes place even when no words are spoken. Simply being in the presence of properly trained practitioners and properly trained teachers, you learn something you cannot find anywhere else.

As Norman said, meditation is not generic. A person does it, and a person needs the nurturing of a teacher and a sangha. You can share your experiences with the teacher, and when there are uncomfortable experiences or experiences that are too comfortable, the teacher can show you how to overcome that obstacle.

ZOKETSU NORMAN FISCHER: When it's face-to-face with teacher and student, it's not about the information. There may not be any words or any instruction, but a mutual recognition in a face-to-face presence is the bottom line of total transformation in Zen.

What is the particular nature of the relationship that one makes with a spiritual teacher?

SHARON SALZBERG: It's many different relationships, and it evolves over time. Overall, faith in the teacher is critical, and the first kind of faith we have is called, in the Theravāda tradition, "bright faith." You're sitting alone in a dark, constrained room and then the door swings open and you have a sense of possibility you didn't have before. Most often that moment of brightness first occurs when we meet a teacher. It's no longer an abstract sense of possibility—it's a real possibility for us. We have a conviction that our lives can be different. Often it is another human being who wakes us up to the immense potential inside of us. The glimpse they give us has all the elements of falling in love. It can be quite dazzling.

While that's considered a very powerful and potent state, it's just the beginning of a journey of faith, because ultimately that sense of possibility needs to rely on our own experience and practice. When we explore for ourselves, and probe and question, we enter a much more mature stage of the relationship.

ZOKETSU NORMAN FISCHER: The teacher-student relationship is based entirely on the Dharma. Although the personal quality is there, it is only in the service of a mutual commitment to the Dharma. Wouldn't it be nice if, in all our relationships, each person was only concerned for the spiritual well-being and development of the other person? That would be a beautiful world. But it's usually not like that. Usually there's a kind of mutual need, a *quid pro quo*, that is the basis of even the relationships that are most intimate in our lives.

DZOGCHEN PONLOP RINPOCHE: All of the relationships in our lives are based on what we call the interdependent nature. The whole world functions on the basis of interdependence. In the relationship with the teacher, though, we transcend all the usual levels of interdependence in our lives—parents, friends, enemies, what have you. The very fact of having a relationship that is based on Dharma and nothing else is very transcendent, without even adding any specific teachings to it. It is the relationship of all relationships.

Yet working with the teacher is not so easy sometimes. Even though you'd like it to be very Dharmic, spiritual, and enlightening, it also involves a lot of confusion and misunderstanding—and a lot of emotions. It is human. But when you have emotions like jealousy, attachment, or even anger in relating to the teacher, they take place in a sacred context. Having such a relationship becomes the best way of transforming our basic relationship issues in life, which means the whole of samsara.

If you have an attack of emotion (*kleśa*) in regard to the teacher, is that a proper state of mind in which to be working with a teacher?

DZOGCHEN PONLOP RINPOCHE: That's a very common experience. The whole point here is to apply the instructions we have learned up until that point. Then the teachings we have been studying become Dharma in action—not theoretical understanding but applied understanding.

When the emotion is directed toward a teacher or fellow Dharma practitioners, it becomes a sacred object. As a result, we have more opportunity and support to work with our emotions. In ordinary life situations, we don't enjoy that kind of support, but the whole point of being in the presence of a teacher is to work with our emotions. In fact, when the emotion is very powerful, sometimes the guru gives further pointing-out instructions to look at and see the enlightened nature of emotion.

When the relationship has evolved to that kind of intimacy, is the teacher there to pull the rug out from under your ego?

ZOKETSU NORMAN FISCHER: Yes and no. From my own experience, I would say that the rug does get pulled out from under you, but the teacher doesn't need to do that intentionally. If the teacher is working with you on the basis of Dharma, and you're coming from attachment, desire, and the thirst for accomplishment, you will experience the rug being pulled out from under you just by virtue of the teacher's ordinary, unintentional responses. The teacher is not scheming, "How can I pull the rug out from under her?" The teacher is just going about his or her own business, in accord with Dharma. The student will feel the rug disappearing because of the gap between the student's ordinary perspective and the perspective of the teacher.

One will have that experience over and over again, and if the relationship is strong and the student is motivated, that feeling of the rug disappearing will be instructive time and time again. It will be a path of training and understanding. All this is possible because the teacher is not an outside object of desire. The teacher is one's own nature, which is identical with the Buddha. That is the final stage—if we are ever lucky enough to get there— that the relationship is moving toward: seeing the teacher as one's own basic nature.

On the way to that point, we have all sorts of emotions and problems that become a beneficial path of training. This transformation of our normal experiences can occur because it all happens in the context of our Dharma practice. In Zen we would say everything and everyone is your teacher. Your relationship with your Dharma teacher shows you the truth of that.

SHARON SALZBERG: When we take refuge in the Buddha, we are taking refuge in the supreme teacher. By doing so, we're not admiring an externalized being. We are acknowledging something that is obscured within us. We're also seeing something about the nature of all sentient beings. So the relationship with the teacher is never simply about the teacher or ourselves. It is also universal. The teacher doesn't exist to be admired by us, but to point us back to our innate nature.

In order to draw out our true nature, the teacher uses many methods, or skillful means. Can you give us some example of the various ways in which the teacher transmits the Dharma?

DZOGCHEN PONLOP RINPOCHE: One way we begin to bring the Dharma into everyday life is by serving the teacher, which is a unique experience, especially when you have an authentic teacher. Whatever they do accords with the Dharma, so they are teaching all the time, whether they have any spoken Dharma to impart or not.

Serving a meal, for example, involves a lot of mindfulness, and in that situation you experience a lot of compassion and love from the teacher. You can see their mindfulness and how they relate with each and every minute of their life. It's not just serving the teacher, then. It is actually serving oneself, because in the profound moments you spend with your teacher, you learn more about the Dharma of everyday life than you can learn in formal teaching. You see how a great master manifests Dharma in simple situations, like eating or speaking to their friends or working with their emotions.

ZOKETSU NORMAN FISCHER: If we have interactions with the teacher on a more mundane basis, then the teaching becomes concrete. If we simply hear the teacher presenting Dharma from the high seat it can be idealized. I would add that having this kind of relationship transforms all our relationships. So in serving the teacher, we can learn how to serve all sentient beings. We want to be capable of helping people, but it can be hard to do that. If we can start to do that with the teacher, someone whom we respect and admire, maybe we can learn how to relate that way to ourselves and then to others.

SHARON SALZBERG: It's striking to me how many times, in speaking about their teacher, people will say, "She was very kind to me." Usually people are speaking about the less formal, unstructured moments. It's not that we're excluding their brilliant scholarship or eloquent explanations, but there's something about the quality of the human kindness that comes out so strongly in situations that are not set up as formal teachings.

What about when the teacher asks you to do something that you resist, that goes beyond what you would like to do?

SHARON SALZBERG: Every teacher I've had has done that, not only by saying you should do this or that, but by simply taking me beyond my sense of limitation, either explicitly or implicitly sending the message: You can do this!

ZOKETSU NORMAN FISCHER: It's important to note that those commands or directions can only be given when you have given deep permission for the teacher to give them to you, and you are ready to receive them. It's not as if the teacher is going around giving people directions right and left. They are sensing where there's permission for that, and even though the permission might be unknown to the student or might require a stretch, the teacher can see whether the permission is there or not. And if it's not there, there are no directives. The giving and receiving of specific directions can only really occur after the relationship has ripened.

DZOGCHEN PONLOP RINPOCHE: In the Vajrayāna, that permission is called devotion, or confidence. Following the teacher's instructions comes from one's own confidence. It demonstrates how deeply we have attained confidence in Dharma, in the wisdom of the teachings, and in the wisdom of the teacher. The student's confidence arises based on the qualities of the teacher.

Does that sometimes lead to disappointment?

DZOGCHEN PONLOP RINPOCHE: Sometimes our disappointment shows that we have a misunderstanding of the teacher-student relationship. We have tremendous expectations and a sense of never having enough knowledge or enough materials. We mistake the role of the teacher and what we should expect from them. Certainly in the Vajrayāna, teachers will provoke our disappointment in order to shake up our usual dualistic concepts about having and not having.

ZOKETSU NORMAN FISCHER: There is an essential paradox, which presents itself as a problem from the dualistic perspective: How can the teacher be worthy of the faith and confidence we would apply toward a buddha and at the same time be a human being who might be conditioned in various ways? From the dualistic perspective, this dichotomy is really hard to take. We might ask, if the teacher is worthy of our confidence and the teacher is a buddha, how come he or she says this or does that?

But the problem there is a misunderstanding, as Rinpoche has just said. Our expectations for perfection and superhumanness on the part of the teacher are always idealizations. They are a neurotic expectation that a teacher is supposed to be otherworldly. When we can learn to accept and appreciate the teacher for his or her humanness, we see that humanness as an expression of his or her highest understanding. At that point, we are beginning to achieve some genuine understanding. But we have to go through those horrible periods of disappointment, and if we can stay with the Dharma and not leave the teacher or start over again looking for another perfect being, then we can reach that kind of very basic understanding.

There's something magical, as I said, alchemical, about what happens when student and teacher meet face-to-face. Why should this be so? Why would we need another person to transform ourselves or understand the Dharma? You would think we would be able to do it on our own if we're smart and if we work hard enough. Perhaps we need instruction because somebody has information that we don't have. All right, so we need the person for information, but why would a human relationship be necessary for this transformation? In terms of how we usually understand learning and transformation, it doesn't make sense.

Yet there seems to be a magical element involved in this human relationship that carries with it a Dharmic dimension that is a necessity for full transformation to take place. Without a teacher, you can certainly master teachings and learn a lot about meditation and have deep concentration states. A great deal is possible without having a teacher, but for true realization, the magical element of a human relationship with a teacher is what is needed. It may be confusing, irrational, and emotional, but that is very much the point. It is a face-to-face encounter of two people seeing each other's humanness and each other's buddhaness.

SHARON SALZBERG: What seems to be happening is a kind of mirroring. In different encounters with the same teacher, we seem to see many different facets. Even in the same encounter with one teacher, different students will have completely different perceptions of what happened. They will recount the actual words differently, not to mention the teacher's mood. Someone will recall how stern they were, while another will remember them as being very funny.

What we see and hear is based partly on what we're able to see and hear and partly based on our projection. Beyond that there is a kind of magic that is greater than what we're bringing into the situation. There are many layers in any single encounter with the teacher.

DZOGCHEN PONLOP RINPOCHE: We are taught that we have to rely on the guru up to a certain point, and then we have to rely on our inner guru. That wisdom of being able to be your own guru comes from the blessings, the kindness, of your own teacher. Therefore, you are never parted from your teacher. On the other hand, we must go through the pain of growing up, which is like leaving home. There is a sense of loneliness, but it's a valuable kind of loneliness, because we are growing up spiritually. The loneliness is a quite profound experience. You cannot have a babysitter for your entire life.

ZOKETSU NORMAN FISCHER: When you're in the stage of development where you're more independent and you don't see the teacher so much, it's not as if you're by yourself. You're with the whole world. You're with all your other relationships in the Dharma and out of the Dharma. What in the past you were looking to the teacher for, you're finding everywhere around you. It's not as if you're wandering around all by yourself. Your life is full of instructions. Everything and everybody has become the teacher, which is what the teacher truly was in the first place.

SHARON SALZBERG: Perhaps the movement is not from dependence to independence, but rather to interdependence. It's the interdependence that Rinpoche was talking about in the beginning, but now it is in a fuller, more wholesome, and complete manifestation.

DZOGCHEN PONLOP RINPOCHE: I would like to add that this relationship between student and teacher that we have been talking about does not come out of any particular culture. I believe it will develop as a Western type of relationship. It doesn't necessarily have to be exactly the same relationship in every respect as how it was taught and practiced in other cultures. That is already beginning to happen, and it will continue to develop, so that there will be many more profound relationships between students and teachers in the Western context.

ZOKETSU NORMAN FISCHER: The student-teacher relationship is something very valuable that Buddhism brings to our culture. If our culture ever had the idea or the practice of working with a spiritual teacher, we've largely lost it. We know we need to go to the doctor, and we know we need to have teachers in school, but we don't know that in the deepest part of our lives we require helpers and guides. Most people do not know they are lacking that. They don't know that there is a greater dimension to their experience that needs to be taken care of.

As time goes on, this will become something that people recognize they need. As the number of qualified teachers and spiritual guides increases, ordinary people will begin to realize that we all need this in our lives. It's important because we live and we die. Life is fleeting. We need this kind of connection and guidance to make sense of our lives.

SHARON SALZBERG: People need the sense that an ordinary person can actualize spiritual teachings if they practice and work at it. If that kind of confidence becomes more widespread, people will seek the appropriate kind of teacher, and the teachers will be there in whatever form is appropriate.

2

The First Awareness:
Meditating on the Body

CYNDI LEE ▪ **PHILLIP MOFFITT**
REGINALD RAY ▪ **TENZIN WANGYAL RINPOCHE**

Meditation is most often thought of as a mental or psychological practice. In what way is it also a body practice?

CYNDI LEE: To me, starting with the body is a no-brainer. If you can't sit upright, if you have bad digestion, if you don't sleep well, that makes it pretty difficult to have mental clarity and stamina. It's essential to have strength and stability in your body if you want to cultivate it in your mind.

PHILLIP MOFFITT: In the Theravāda tradition, the *Satipaṭṭhāna-Satipaṭṭhāna Sutta* presents mindfulness practice in the form of the four foundations. The Buddha lays out the spectrum of awarenesses in this teaching, and the first awareness is "awareness of the body in the body." This becomes the foundation on which the other awarenesses of your experience are to be understood. We come to understand how our awareness of the pleasant and the unpleasant in the body controls the mind. Then we move to awareness of the mind states themselves, but these utilize the body as well.

I've found that students who don't have the ability to stay aware of what's going on in the body are much less likely to develop in their practice. They get stuck.

What does "awareness of the body in the body" mean?

PHILLIP MOFFITT: It means orienting toward direct, nonconceptual experience. Not staying in your head. I use the term "dropped attention," which comes from *Aikido*. We drop out of our head and into direct experience, which is often called the "felt sense." We are talking about knee pain as a direct experience, not our view and opinion about knee pain. There are so many different awarenesses that arise out of that.

In modern terms, we are deconstructing phenomena. We are looking at moment-to-moment phenomena as they arise. The Buddha was the original deconstructionist, and the body is a great laboratory for practicing deconstruction. We can experience phenomena, rather than the soap opera of our lives that goes on up in the old coconut. "Oh, my knee hurts. What's gonna happen to me in the future? I'm not going to be able to walk!" We get outside that story and start to see the phenomena in deconstructed form. We start to see the nonself aspect and the *dukkha*, and we see that it's always changing.

REGINALD RAY: The question of the role of the body in meditation assumes there's meditation and there's a body. What is it that meditates, though? In a sense, it's the body that meditates. As Phillip said, awareness is not localized in the head. It pervades the body, and when we tap in to the fundamental awareness of our person, we are completely contained within our somatic experience.

The reason we ask this question is that we objectify the body as somehow separate from our awareness, separate from our minds, but that's incorrect from a Buddhist standpoint. We can rephrase the question as, "Who or what is meditating?" The answer is that our whole being is meditating. The body is the locale of that awareness; it is the one and only gateway for the meditative state.

Engagement with the body is at the heart of spirituality. It may be at a coarse level at the beginning, but if you go far enough in working with your body, you discover your fundamental being beyond time and space.

TENZIN WANGYAL RINPOCHE: In our tradition, we often talk about practice from the perspective of the body, the flow of the wind (*prāṇa*), and the arising awareness of the mind. The average person can deal with the body much more easily than working immediately with the flow of wind, energy, or the subtleties of awareness of the mind.

So it's good to start with a good sitting position such as the five-point or seven-point posture. The moment somebody is sitting in one of those positions, all the channels and the chakras align. That supports the good flow of the wind, which supports awareness. The mind requires much less effort to be in the state of awareness.

The role of the body, then, is to help the wind, and the wind helps the mind. It would be almost impossible for someone to bypass the body and the wind, to directly force the mind to achieve sudden awareness. We can avoid trying to force the mind to be quiet by working with the body. When you try to tell the mind to sit quietly, it often does the opposite. When you're trying to tell mind what to do, mind never listens. But if you create the right causes and conditions with the body, mind will follow.

Why are so many people interested in yoga? Because it's easy to follow. Of course, it's not necessarily easy to do, but it's much easier than dealing with a lot of complicated stages of mental practice. The popularity of yoga is a wonderful thing because it can become a door to Dharma. It can start as an interest in fitness, well-being, and health, and gradually become the door to higher understanding.

CYNDI LEE: I agree. For most people it's easier to start with the body. You can feel it. You can touch it.

People come to yoga for a variety of reasons, but stay for different ones, which usually have some relationship to Dharma. In the yoga tradition, the very first two limbs are *yama* and *niyama*—how we behave in the world and how we interact with other people. After that comes *āsana*, the codified physical system of aligning muscles and bones to promote radiant health—this is what most people associate with the term "yoga." The limbs after āsana—*prāṇayama, pratyāhāra, dhāraṇā, dhyāna,* and *samādhi*—are subtler and take us into the meditative realm.

Yoga is definitely a door to the Dharma. Processing takes place. Even when people aren't aware of the four foundations of mindfulness, the experience still happens to a certain degree. It isn't magic, though. People need to be taught how to relate to what they're feeling. For example, how to be aware of the intricacies of the knee pain they're experiencing, as Phillip was describing, rather than being caught up in their story line about it.

PHILLIP MOFFITT: In fact, every āsana is a form of meditation. There is a one-pointedness to every single āsana, and if you find that one-pointedness within the practice, it changes the practice. Even if you're not informed about a particular map of how energy moves in the body, you discover blockages, and the awareness itself starts to open up the channels.

CYNDI LEE: I would add that there is not only the one-pointedness of the āsana—what I would call the *śamatha* aspect—but also panoramic awareness. You feel the energetic circuitry in space in a room with other people. It becomes a template for how we are with other people in the world.

One of the early instructions many of us received was not to focus or "central-ize" on the body. We were told to go beyond thinking of ourselves as our body. How do you understand this teaching in relation to the strong focus on the body you've all been speaking about?

REGINALD RAY: When we're instructed not to focus on the body, we're being taught not to focus on our idea of the body, the body as we currently experience it. The more you explore your physical body, the more it dissolves into energy, and you realize that even the idea of having a physical body is mistaken. The body is an energetic phenomenon onto which we have super-imposed the idea of solidity.

PHILLIP MOFFITT: The body is the way to get into this moment, and to develop a continuity of presence, of being.

REGINALD RAY: At a very deep level, we can talk about experiencing the Buddha's body, the three *kāya*s. The *nirmāṇakāya*, or "created body," is the flesh and blood physical body, but it's understood as pure. The *sambhoga-kāya*, or "body of enjoyment," refers to the energetic world, the invisible world of symbol and magic. The *dharmakāya* is the ultimate body, the body of reality itself.

All those kāyas manifest within the body, so when we talk about not focusing on the body, we are not suggesting that spirituality is elsewhere. That just puts you back up in your head.

How is something as rarified as the sambhogakāya and the dharmakāya still "body" in the sense that we understand body, as the thing with ears and nose and toes?

REGINALD RAY: We have a cultural understanding of what the body is, but we have to realize that lots of people in different cultures look at the physical body and see very different things. Some look at a body and all they see is physical phenomenon defined by modern biology, but a meditator can look at the body and see that as a conceptual overlay.

What the body actually is, as Phillip said, is a continuous flow of sensations, none of which is solid. At a further level, someone could look at this body and see pure energy. They literally don't see anything physical. An enlightened person would see space. From our literal, modern viewpoint, it sounds very ethereal to talk about the body's energy, but that's actually what the body is for some people. We can deconstruct our ideas of the body as a definitive phenomenon. It isn't one solid, predetermined thing. It's an open field for investigation.

TENZIN WANGYAL RINPOCHE: In my tradition, we refer to body, speech, and mind as the three doors. The body is a doorway into the nirmāṇakāya, speech into the sambhogakāya, and mind into the dharmakāya. If we engage these well, they become gateways to enlightenment, to buddhahood.

In the *Satipaṭṭhāna Sutta*, the Buddha asks us to delve further into the body—to explore its many parts and subparts, the fact of its decay, the fact that it is a bag of guts. What is the benefit of this teaching?

REGINALD RAY: Those teachings work with the way we hang on to the body as a reference point. They're trying to help us let go of that process of hanging on. This frees the body to be itself. It doesn't deny the body. It doesn't put it down. It just frees it from our grasping and fixation, our trying to use the body as a source of security, which obviously blocks us and locks us up.

PHILLIP MOFFITT: If we grasp one way, it's eternalism. If we grasp the other way, it's nihilism. And neither of those lets the body be what it is.

Do people who have stayed with a body discipline a long time begin to let the body be what it is, just by continued exposure to working closely with it?

REGINALD RAY: There's a lot of potential experience in working closely with the body, but without some sort of spiritual mentoring we really can't go anywhere. That might be one of the main dilemmas in our culture. So many people are working with the body, but if the spiritual outlook isn't there, the full extent of what's possible in working with the body doesn't come to fruition.

CYNDI LEE: At OM Yoga, people are trained with that kind of orientation. So when they get more advanced, they get more interested in the experience rather than the story line about the experience—what they can and cannot do anymore, for example. Instead, they consider: What am I feeling? What am I experiencing right now? How is it changing? It becomes an immediate meditation in the body. We teach people that kind of immediate attention from day one, but it takes a while for people to sustain intense interest in what's going on with the body at an intimate level.

PHILLIP MOFFITT: I start guided meditation by saying, "Bring attention to the body—not your body, the body. I'm pointing to a phenomenon occurring right now." I continue by saying we are not judging, comparing, or fixing the body. Those three tend to be our primary relationships with the body: Do we like our body? How does it compare to our body before, or to others' bodies? What's wrong with it that we need to repair?

If you're judging, comparing, and trying to fix your body, you're in duality: it's the body you want vs. the body you have. This separation is creating solidity, and it happens on some very subtle levels. So one of the teacher's major jobs is to facilitate students becoming present for their own experience, as opposed to saying to them, "This is what you should notice about your experience." At that point, life is teaching them, life is leading them forward.

Fixing in general seems to be a big hang-up in our society, but it's particularly the case when it comes to the body.

CYNDI LEE: That's a big challenge in yoga. You're in downward dog and your hamstrings are too tight and your stomach is too big. Then you hate yourself. But after a while, your hamstrings loosen up. The body is an incredible venue for shifting our paradigm of attachment and aversion. We start out objectifying ourselves, objectifying each other, but as we go on, there's really no problem to be fixed.

REGINALD RAY: All of what we've been talking about—respecting the body, making room for it, not exiting into mental judgment—is what we call *maitri*, love of our own personhood. And that is the basis for compassion for other people. Working with the body in a deep way is the ground of generating genuine compassion. It's based on acceptance of one's own experience, not just an idea of doing something nice for someone else. With such close attention to what's happening in our experience of being human, it's unavoidable that we're going to take the same attitude toward other people, welcoming, accepting, and being with them in the same way.

3

Space and Stillness:
Varieties of Formless Meditation

PATRICIA DAI-EN BENNAGE ▪ **TENZIN WANGYAL RINPOCHE**
GAYLON FERGUSON ▪ **VEN. AJAHN SUMEDHO**

I'll begin by asking each of you to speak about your understanding of formless meditation from the point of view of your tradition. In Zen, for example, formless meditation often goes by the name of *shikantaza*, or "just sitting."

PATRICIA DAI-EN BENNAGE: Yes, we say "just sitting," but the "just" in "just sitting" doesn't mean "just" in the usual way. It means thoroughgoing, total sitting. It's like the feeling you would have if you were riding a horse at an incredible speed and you fell out of the saddle and found yourself between the saddle and the ground. What kind of state of mind would you have there?

Shikantaza is thoroughgoing, total attention to everything, a tremendously powerful practice. It's like a huge gymnasium opens up in front of you in which there are no lines of demarcation, no markers to go by. You don't know what to do with that immense space, but you can learn to have deep trust.

The abbot I trained with in Japan talked about allowing ourselves to be babysat by the universe. Since the universe is good, it takes no effort to be babysat by it. We simply allow ourselves to be present. In Zen, we have a recitation: "Abandon myself to breathing out and letting breathing in naturally still me. All that is left is an empty cushion under the vast sky, the weight of a flame."

Abandoning ourselves to breathing out means *no effort*. It means allowing the causes and conditions of where we are in the universe to do the breathing for us. All that's left is the great emptiness and the vivacity of who we are.

TENZIN WANGYAL RINPOCHE: In the Dzogchen tradition, we introduce people to form practice precisely in order to introduce them to formless practice, the nature of mind. In formless meditation, we abide in the boundless view, without any judgment, without observer and observed.

Spontaneous meditation and flexible action is what formless meditation really is, and in the process of doing it, we experience emptiness, clarity, and bliss. However, if we grasp at these, it does not work. We have to be aware but not grasp. We call this "self-liberation."

Formless meditation is ultimately about self-liberating the observer. No one is grasping, because there is no observer to grasp. Everything is effortlessly self-liberated into space. This is the experience of emptiness, which in turn leads to fearlessness. With nothing there, there is nothing to fear. Yet there is also unceasing clarity: the flow of life never stops, experiences never stop. Everything is lively and fully there, without anybody doing anything.

This kind of clarity offers a deep experience of hopelessness—not in a bad sense, but in a positive sense of having no need to go anywhere or get anything. When the emptiness and clarity, the hopelessness and fearlessness, are inseparable, the experience of bliss—happiness with no reason to be happy—is produced.

GAYLON FERGUSON: Formless meditation might appear more mysterious than it is. There's a sense in which the attitude of formless meditation, which is not to manipulate whatever arises in our experience, is there whether we're doing practice with form or without form. There's continuity between the two. Appreciating them both is a matter of understanding the view of the teachers of the lineage—namely, that one could practice without any gaining idea, without pushing anything away, but nakedly and directly experiencing the vividness of whatever arises in one's experience, whether it's emotional or perceptions of the world. Nowness is really the essence of formless practice as well as practice with form.

Formless practice is the simplest of all, but we could complicate it by talking about it. Although it is fundamentally uncomplicated, within formless practice, there is still progression. The Mahāmudrā tradition of formless practice speaks of four stages: one-pointedness, stabilizing the mind in its own essence; simplicity, where there are no further complications to deal with; one taste, the seamlessness of nonduality; and finally, nonmeditation, not manipulating the sacred world in any way. These are simply further levels of spaciousness and vividness.

VEN. AJAHN SUMEDHO: In the Vipassanā tradition, you begin by examining the impermanence of conditions. After your practice deepens, the sense of personal identity lessens and attention is awakened. Once you realize the state of awakened attention—what we call the unconditioned, stillness, or the still point of awareness—you gain perspective on the conditions of the present. You witness rather than grasp and identify. With this insight into the truth of cessation, you have direct insight into emptiness and nonself.

At that point, we no longer seek identity in and attachment to worldly conditions—the sense of ourselves as a personality and the illusory world that most people need for identification. This reality doesn't need an object for its existence. It's a natural state of being that isn't created or dependent on conditions.

Once there is realization of awareness and nonattachment, then there's no need to use form anymore, because the path of awareness is very clear. Awareness does not require an object. Its natural state is not a created state. Most people are always looking for something they conceive of or that they imagine. Awareness—what we call the gate to the deathless—is learning to realize this natural state of being. Then we don't need a form any more. We can just be present with the existing forms as they rise and cease. We can use form, but we don't need it anymore, because our insight embraces form rather than depends on form.

Would you describe this as a practice or as an attainment?

VEN. AJAHN SUMEDHO: When you're talking about attainment and meditation, it sounds like you've got to get something you don't have. The Buddha was pointing to something quite obvious, suffering, which is a very banal human experience. In investigating that truth, we let go of the causes rather than attain anything. It's a matter of relinquishing, letting go—of nonattainment really. Wisdom isn't an attainment. It's a natural state we begin to recognize and access through our awareness of existence as it manifests.

Some students get to this quickly, others take much longer. In either case, I don't let people delude themselves, thinking they have to do something in order to become something. But obviously, they need meditation retreats and formal practice to realize the natural state of awareness that needs no object.

How do meditation with form and formless meditation work together?

PATRICIA DAI-EN BENNAGE: In order to have formless practice, the forms around it are essential as a support. Therefore, we put extreme emphasis on the quality of the seated posture. We are not invited to allow ourselves to be more comfortable. We are asked to deal with what comes up sitting in that position and to see how often the pain is not physical but comes from the mind. One needs to understand this or formless experience will not be possible.

All of the myriad forms support the formless experience, especially in the monastery, where I lived a cloistered life for twelve years. We didn't have interviews often, only if we really felt we had something to discuss with a teacher. But our teachers never took their eyes off us—where we were, the sound we made with our slippers, the way we reached for something, the way we passed something to someone else, the tone of our voice, our body language in standing at a distance or near to other people. What we do on the cushion should be manifest in sitting, standing, lying down, and walking.

TENZIN WANGYAL RINPOCHE: In Dzogchen, we refer to form and formless meditation as meditation with attributes and meditation without attributes. It's very traditional to do meditation with attributes before going into meditation without attributes. The usual style of meditation with attributes is "calm abiding" (*gzhi gnas*). One begins with effortful calm abiding, which develops into natural calm abiding, and finally into ultimate calm abiding, which is essentially the beginning stages of formless meditation.

At the effortful stage, one is dealing with all the external problems that dominate us—sounds, discomfort, movement of the thoughts, and so forth. One might also have internal obstacles, such as falling asleep or becoming extremely creative, having many ideas and projects. Working with all of these requires effort.

We usually need to practice calm abiding for a long time and follow strict rules, but it all comes down to being alert in the moment and focusing on an object. Gradually we begin to develop stability. We find the calmness more inside of us than in the object of meditation. Eventually we feel the same calm even when the object is removed. That is natural calm abiding. The mind is clear, sharp, and stable, and those characteristics are still there when the objects are removed.

Once we achieve the ultimate calm abiding, there is no sense of observer or observed. We abide in ultimate stillness. When you are finally able to rest there, that's formless practice.

VEN. AJAHN SUMEDHO: Naturally, you start out from the point where you are, which for most people is attachment to objects and ideas. So your teacher directs your attention to the impermanence of conditioned phenomena—their arising, presence, and absence.

When you see the nature of conditioned phenomena and mental formations as impermanent, that which is aware of the impermanence takes refuge in transcending the conditioned realm. You are now at the gate to the deathless realm, the unconditioned. Allowing things to cease in your mind, you have insight into the Third Noble Truth of cessation. With this perspective on human existence, you have insight into the Fourth Noble Truth, the path of nonattachment, or nonidentity, with conditioned phenomenon. At this point, there's no need to use form anymore because the path of awareness is very clear.

GAYLON FERGUSON: In the Kagyü and Nyingma lineages of Vajrayāna, we begin with calm abiding and insight (śamatha and *vipaśyanā*). The student begins with mindfulness of body and breathing as objects, and then moves to insight into the nature of reality and some experience of spaciousness or egolessness. At that point, one begins to work with compassion practices to awaken the heart. Those mind-training or lojong (*blo sbyong*) practices often involve resting the mind in its basic nature, in its fundamental goodness, as the basis for compassion practice.

The full development of the formless aspect of this path is called Mahāmudrā in the Kagyü lineage and Dzogchen in the Nyingma lineage. In those advanced meditation practices, the essence of mind is itself taken as the formless object of meditation. Alongside those techniques, Vajrayāna uses visualizations and mantras as part of what's called the development stage of *sādhāna* practice. This is accompanied by a completion stage, in which you dissolve the visualization. You no longer rest your mind on visualizing something or saying a mantra, but rest in the essence of what you've been connecting with through the mantra recitation and visualization. The completion stage of sādhāna practice, then, is another instance of formless practice.

Are there different kinds of formless meditation experience?

GAYLON FERGUSON: To answer that, one would need to have practiced in all those traditions.

PATRICIA DAI-EN BENNAGE: Correct. To actually taste each of those— that's a rare person. How can we open our mouths to make a judgment about a style in which we have no experience, no guided training?

TENZIN WANGYAL RINPOCHE: It's very important to define more precisely what formless meditation means here. Does it simply mean meditation without an external object? Does it refer to a feeling in the body? Does it refer to whether you are focusing on the emotions in the mind or not?

As far as Dzogchen is concerned, formless practice does not have much to do with emotions or feelings or external objects. Ultimately, it's about the observer. At some point you have to get beyond that. That's real formless meditation. Everything else is an approximation of formless meditation. You might experience bliss, but there's definitely somebody who wants that bliss and does not want to let go of it. You cannot say the experience is not bliss, but it's not real formless meditation. There's no "object" *per se*, but meditative experiences become objects.

GAYLON FERGUSON: This comparison of experience across traditions applies not just to formless meditation, but to meditation altogether. Is all Buddhist meditation in essence the same? Certainly it's all a matter of the wakefulness of the Buddha. There's an essence of wakefulness that is the nature of mind and it is inseparable from the nature of reality. That understanding is held by all the traditions. At the same time, there's undoubtedly a different flavor of practicing satipaṭṭhāna, the Theravāda tradition; shikantaza or zazen; or formless meditation within a Vajrayāna sādhāna. I'm sure the experience of a specific tradition has its particular flavor.

PATRICIA DAI-EN BENNAGE: I believe that the fruits of practice come in many flavors, but that there is some commonality that manifests as growing spaciousness and acceptance over time. This commonality covers not only Buddhism but also any practice of giving up ego for the greater good of sentient beings. The flavors are important, but I'd like to hope that there is commonality that runs through numerous traditions.

TENZIN WANGYAL RINPOCHE: There are a few issues we are mixing here. In essence, formless meditation has got to be the same, because formless is formless. What makes the difference is the form, how one is introduced to the form, the development of the form, and how one enters into the formless from there. These are the things that create the differences.

When it comes to the formless, every tradition has different ways to do it. I always encourage students to listen to other teachers and learn from them, but it's always important to have one thing that you follow completely. That's not a question of one being better than another, but if you're focusing on too many things, you might not have anything in the end.

All sorts of forms in all sorts of traditions support formless meditation. Not only that, everyday human experience supports it. Imagine carrying a big weight, walking for many miles, and then setting it down. Imagine that moment. You say, "Aah," and in that very moment you can have a great life experience that does not belong to any tradition. It needs no label. A moment of physical or emotional exhaustion can give you great access to stillness. Everybody has that, even if they haven't heard one word of Dharma.

Is that a Dzogchen experience?

TENZIN WANGYAL RINPOCHE: Yes, definitely. Dzogchen is unique in engaging less with the conceptual mind and emotions. We need to engage them to some degree because they are within our experience, but we engage them minimally in achieving formless experience.

GAYLON FERGUSON: Formless meditation is ultimately about nonconceptual wisdom; the fruit of all of these practices would not be a matter of the technique or the practices themselves. We would look for fewer fixations on self, more gentleness, and more compassion. That would be the proof in the pudding of formless meditation.

4

All Part of the Practice:
Obstacles and Their Antidotes

JUDITH SIMMER-BROWN

EZRA BAYDA

KAMALA MASTERS

What do you see as the biggest obstacle in meditation practice?

JUDITH SIMMER-BROWN: Two immediately come to mind. One is the obstacle of not getting to the cushion regularly in the first place. The other, faced by more mature practitioners, is becoming addicted to meditation experiences that masquerade as the fruition of the path but cause a dead end in one's practice. But perhaps the most haunting obstacle to practice is the way we try to use meditation to fix ourselves rather than to connect with our fundamental humanity and goodness.

EZRA BAYDA: Resistance is an inevitable part of practice life. It comes in many forms, such as not wanting to sit, choosing to spin off into our thoughts, and not wanting to stay with our experience for more than a few moments at a time. A more subtle form of resistance is talking and thinking about practice rather than actually doing it.

The root of all resistance is wanting life to be other than it is. It's something we have to be honest about—there's a really big part of ourselves that doesn't want to wake up, that doesn't want to be present, that would rather hold on to our habits and illusions and beliefs than do what's necessary to make us happy. Until we recognize the extent of our resistance, it's very hard to get beyond it.

KAMALA MASTERS: Meditators often think that practice is all about achieving states of calm and tranquility, and when the opposite comes up, they find themselves wanting something that isn't happening. Many people also think practice is about sitting still or just getting to the cushion, which is a very low expectation. So one of the obstacles is low expectations and not understanding what the practice is really all about, and the other is having too high expectations about practice. Students can feel inadequate and disappointed in their practice and think they're doing it wrong.

We tend to think of obstacles as problems rather than as a normal part of our meditation experience. Is that part of the problem?

JUDITH SIMMER-BROWN: Such a big part of our human nature is rejecting who we are and feeling that there's something fundamentally wrong with us—that's what's called *dukkha* in the Buddhadharma.

The core of the Buddha's genius was seeing that our struggle to live life as we think it should be, as opposed to how it actually is, is our fundamental dilemma. And of course we can use practice the same way—as a means of rejecting who we are and trying to create an ideal world instead. It's difficult to see that all of our turbulence occurs within nonturbulence and goodness. It takes time to understand the totality of our experience. That's why practice is so subtle and a lifelong journey. It's not just a challenge for beginners; it's a challenge however many years we've been practicing.

KAMALA MASTERS: As we go deeper, we learn to become more present with subtleties in our practice. We also tend to develop an awareness that's like a magnifying glass, so obstacles may feel even bigger than what we've experienced before. So as our practice matures, we still need people to remind us that this is a natural part of the unfolding of our practice.

EZRA BAYDA: One of the major obstacles in practice is our universal, deep-seated desire to feel a particular way. I think all of us begin with the illusion that if we practice hard we'll feel better. So when obstacles arise, we automatically see them as impediments and don't understand the pivotal point that practice is not about feeling any particular way. As long as we view obstacles as obstacles, as something to oppose, we're going to stay stuck.

One of the most crucial things for students to learn, at any point along the path, is that obstacles are the path. We have such an instinctual aversion to discomfort that when an obstacle arises, we forget to ask the simple question, Can I see this as my path? Whatever comes up is our exact path to freedom, no matter how much of an impediment it seems to be.

What are some of the other obstacles that come up?

JUDITH SIMMER-BROWN: The six classical obstacles outlined in ninth-century Indian texts are exactly the obstacles I face in my own practice, so that really is testament to the universal experience of meditators. I find it very enriching to realize that meditators from the beginning of time have struggled with falling asleep, with wild, intense, angry, and lustful thoughts, and with dullness of the mind.

KAMALA MASTERS: In the Theravāda tradition there are the five basic hindrances—attachment, aversion, restlessness, doubt, and sloth and torpor. My grandfather teacher, Mahasi Sayadaw of Burma, taught that there are over a thousand defilements. Of course, I can't remember them all, but they include arrogance, pride, ingratitude, extolling oneself, disparaging others, and indulging in pleasant experiences in our practice.

Once when I was cooking for one of my teachers, Munindraji, I noticed he got a bit annoyed at me because I wasn't putting in the right herbs. I said, "Munindraji, are you annoyed? Are you upset?" He looked back at me and said, "My path is not yet finished." I was so relieved when he said that; he was honest about the fact that he was still working to free his mind of greed, hatred, and delusion. That was very reassuring.

EZRA BAYDA: Human beings spend the vast majority of their time in a state of waking sleep, lost in their thoughts, activities, and emotions. Waking sleep is our default position. We walk around asleep, but through conscious efforts we can become more awake.

No matter how strong our aspiration or understanding of practice may be, if we don't become familiar with the power and magnitude of waking sleep, it will blindside us again and again. So we must learn to see waking sleep in all its forms, in all the ways it manifests within us. The more we see it, over a long period of practice, the less it blindsides us and dictates our behavior. We're born with our buddha nature intact, but the paradoxical truth is that we live a life of complete sleep unless we're able to see the nature of that sleep and begin working with it in an intelligent way.

KAMALA MASTERS: Delusion is a kind of baseline; it's what lies underneath, holding up all other hindrances, fueling our misunderstanding. The potential to be awakened is always within us, but in order to awaken fully to our potential we must be conscious of all the ways delusion manifests.

Doubt can also be a serious obstacle even for longtime practitioners. People who've been meditating for decades sometimes confide that they don't know if it's doing them any good.

JUDITH SIMMER-BROWN: In the Shambhala teachings, doubt is considered the greatest obstacle, more so than ignorance, because it makes us fundamentally doubt our own buddha nature, or basic goodness.

According to the Shambhala tradition, we live in an age when people have lost track of that fundamental goodness at the core of who they are. So when people take up practice, they often use it as some kind of self-improvement campaign, as a way to further reject themselves. If meditation becomes a way to express harshness and negativity toward oneself, a sense of hopelessness can creep in. In our Judeo-Christian culture, we have been so shaped by a belief in original sin. People can practice for a long time and feel they're not benefitting from it because that fundamental obstacle has never been addressed.

EZRA BAYDA: I think self-doubt is a natural part of the path; you can't enter a practice life without doubting yourself on occasion. But there's another kind of doubt that I want to mention. In Zen it's called "the dry spot," which is when we lose all connection with the aspiration that originally brought us to practice. Usually people hit this after a number of years of practice, when they realize that all the expectations they brought with them, like wanting to become calm or enlightened, haven't been fulfilled. Discouragement creeps in, and we lose connection with our genuine wish to wake up.

The dry spot is probably the deepest form of doubt because we're not only doubting ourselves, we're doubting practice. It's as if none of it makes sense anymore. But the interesting part is that the doubt itself is the solution. When we are able to see doubt as the path and stay present with it, a much deeper renewal can take place.

Thomas Merton said, "True love and prayer are learned in the moment when prayer has become impossible and the heart has turned to stone." So it's really important to understand that dry spots are a very natural part of practice and that they don't mean we're a failure on the path.

KAMALA MASTERS: I have experienced doubt as a place where things have broken apart. It feels like something whole has shattered, like a glass dropped on the ground. I have come to realize that this signals a new stage in my practice, a place of crossing a threshold into the unknown.

What about the experience of doubt for someone who's new to practice?

JUDITH SIMMER-BROWN: I find that my newer students deal with doubt as if it's doubt about something in particular—they doubt whether they have found the right teacher or the right practice, or they may doubt some aspects of themselves or the teachings.

EZRA BAYDA: I think the doubt that new practitioners experience is quite different from the kind that long-term practitioners get caught by. What's really unfortunate is when new practitioners get so caught up in doubting the practice or the teacher or themselves that they leave the practice. They don't understand that having periods of insecurity and doubt and believing the things that go through your mind is part of what practice is.

I think that when people have practiced long enough, and have gone through a few periods of dry spots, doubt doesn't impact them in the same way. At some point along the path we can actually welcome the experiences of doubt because we understand them as an opportunity to go deeper. We do not really doubt in the same way. We're asking ourselves, "What is this?"

KAMALA MASTERS: I've found that seasoned practitioners are more spacious around what happens in the terrain of their bodies and minds. There's usually more flexibility and more ability to see doubts as passing thoughts and not to believe them. Seasoned practitioners have that ability to see everything as more impermanent and impersonal. You see that nothing is going to give you lasting happiness, or unhappiness, so why hang on to them or why push them away?

Let's look more specifically at how to work with obstacles that arise. Let's start with dullness. If there's not much life energy in our practice, what should we do?

JUDITH SIMMER-BROWN: Dullness is one of the hardest obstacles to work with because it tends to defeat any momentum to do anything about anything. The classical texts say that people who have this kind of dullness need to be around death—to lean into the urgency of life and death as a way to wake themselves up.

But Trungpa Rinpoche said that getting heavy-handed with our dullness will make us retreat into dullness even more. So he advised using a light-handed approach. For instance, if you keep falling asleep on the cushion, just let yourself fall asleep. Eventually you'll jerk awake, and that kind of natural return to wakefulness works best.

EZRA BAYDA: If someone is experiencing dullness, I don't think they're going to want to go out to a cemetery and contemplate death because they're not motivated at that point—there's dullness in their motivation as well. So what we recommend is to have the curiosity to study dullness itself. We tell people to just let themselves fall asleep and to study as best they can what it feels like to be dull or tired. How often do we spend time honestly studying what dullness or sleepiness or boredom feel like? When you're sleepy on the cushion, feel what it's like in those last few moments before you close your eyes. When you wake up, maybe just a few seconds later, feel what it's like to wake up from sleep. In doing so, even though there may still be residual dullness, you're actually being present. I think that's the best solution, rather than trying to push yourself into a "better experience."

KAMALA MASTERS: According to the Theravāda tradition, what causes dullness is a lack of investigation. One thing that's helpful is to ask yourself what other conditions are present. Is there heaviness, lightness, or confusion? Just be aware of whatever the experience is. Also dullness often has a physical component. Standing up helps because we tend to be more alert in that position.

JUDITH SIMMER-BROWN: In the Mahāmudrā tradition, the approach to practice is to sit for very short sessions, as short as five minutes, to keep the mind engaged and fresh. There's something wonderful about using really short sessions as a way to reinspire the mind. Making sure that you never sit long enough to get dull begins to ignite a new kind of freshness in your practice, so even if you go back to longer sessions, the quality of freshness remains.

What would you say to practitioners reading this who may feel like their meditation practice has stalled or gone off the rails in some way?

EZRA BAYDA: Life itself is our best teacher, much more so than any living person. Life has a way of constantly putting us up against ourselves, and if we're fortunate enough to have the desire to keep learning, this adversity is where our deepest awakening takes place. There are certain qualities that we learn on the cushion, like the ability to persevere, to be curious, and to be present, but the deepest learning takes place off the cushion, in learning how to deal with life itself and understanding that adverse circumstances are the path.

JUDITH SIMMER-BROWN: We need to remember that meditation practice is not a self-improvement project that is going to proceed according to our plan. When we really step inside our practice, we begin to tune in to who we are underneath it all. The most powerful thing I've learned in practice is to tune in to how I actually feel. Our tendency is to either bury or act on feeling but not to actually feel feeling. Here I don't mean a particular feeling but the felt sense that is underneath all feeling: our beating heart, our humanity, our buddha nature, or basic goodness. The most important thing is to connect with that, and then everything else is just our life. Our path is not a project; it's life. It's so powerful to realize that practice is fundamentally choiceless. It's about being able to connect with our humanity on a more complete level.

KAMALA MASTERS: It's important to remember to be patient with the unfolding of our practice. When we practice mindful attention, along with honoring the precepts of nonharming and developing the wholesome qualities of the mind, the seeds of liberation are being nourished. In their own time, these seeds will sprout, break ground, and bear fruit. We really can't rush the process.

Sometimes patience can sound like a command, so it's helpful to gently remind ourselves to relax around whatever is arising. If that can happen, then clarity, compassion, and liberating wisdom come naturally.

5

The Wisdom of Energy:
Bringing Emotions to the Path

DZOGCHEN PONLOP RINPOCHE ▪ SHARON SALZBERG

JOHN TARRANT, ROSHI ▪ JUDITH SIMMER-BROWN

When people hear about things like nonattachment and mindfulness, they may think they'll have to give up their emotional life when they become Buddhists.

DZOGCHEN PONLOP RINPOCHE: Losing our emotions or thoughts is not something we need to worry about. When we meditate, they're still there. They don't go away. We couldn't lose them, even if we wanted to!

When you enter the Buddhist path, the point is not to get rid of emotions or thoughts. The important thing is to be mindful of the emotions arising—whether they're good or bad, or however you might choose to define them. As we progress along the path of meditation, the key point becomes developing a stillness in which we find freedom from the disturbing elements of emotions.

SHARON SALZBERG: The Thai meditation master Ajahn Chah said: "As you meditate, your mind will get quieter and quieter, like a still forest pool. Many wonderful and rare animals will come to drink at the pool, but you will be still. This is the happiness of the Buddha."

I love the image of the wonderful and rare animals. The stillness is not holding down or repressing any experience. Everything still arrives, but what makes the difference is how all of those wonderful and rare animals are greeted.

Intention and motivation are what's vital. Why do we act the way we do and how do we relate to our emotions? Do they subsume us? Do they overcome us? Are we propelled into actions we later regret? Do we try to hide emotions or do we denigrate ourselves for our emotions?

So can we find a place in the middle, where we are neither overcome by emotion, which often leads to negative actions and consequences, nor repressing and avoiding our emotional states? That place in the middle, which is mindfulness, is a place of discovery, exploration, and enrichment.

Is the full range of emotion, from rage to passion, included?

SHARON SALZBERG: By practicing mindfulness, we are changing the conditions that will affect what might arise. But it wouldn't be realistic to say that we assume control over what will arise in our experience. Control *per se* would not even be desirable, because in the space of rage or passion we can be free nonetheless, and perhaps utilize the energy within those emotions for something more positive in our lives.

JOHN TARRANT, ROSHI: Freedom is just freedom, and it's either there or not. It doesn't matter what you're feeling. In the long arc of a practice, most people do find that they have less intense aversions and so forth. They have less of what you would call disturbing emotions. But it's also true that when it comes to so-called disturbing emotions, we can ask, who is it disturbing and why is it disturbing? The disturbance is measured against a framework that is illusory. Your disturbing emotions have buddha nature—just as much as your nice calm ones do—and they may actually be more likely to lead to a deeper level of awakening than your nice, calm ones.

In evolutionary terms, biologists talk about emotions as necessary and adaptive, and many psychologists regard emotions as central to who we are. Yet emotions in Buddhism seem to be regarded as a problem.

JOHN TARRANT, ROSHI: It's true that when people talk about emotion in the Buddhist context, usually they're talking about something that creates a problem. But what's wrong with emotion, anyway? An emotion is something that arises because we have a body, an incarnation, and in that realm everything is a little bit imperfect. We can't get anything quite the way we want it to be, and emotion is the indicator of that. Having an emotion is different from having an emotional problem, which is usually caused by fighting with the emotion, not exploring or having curiosity about it.

JUDITH SIMMER-BROWN: There's an enormous science in Buddhism devoted to recognizing the experience of emotion. This is quite different from the practice of psychology, which has tended to be heavily interpersonal and management-oriented. However, some psychologists are beginning to appreciate that we can work with the direct experience of our state of mind. That's a very fruitful way to appreciate that what we call emotion is, at its heart, an energetic experience that doesn't have to be painful.

SHARON SALZBERG: Emotion is an element of relationship. It is how our awareness relates to anything that presents itself internally or externally. As a manifestation of relationship, emotion can be quite distorted, based in ignorance, so we misconstrue what we're actually encountering. On the other hand, it can be based in something more truthful and wise and clear, and therein lies the tremendous variety of emotions we experience.

DZOGCHEN PONLOP RINPOCHE: From a classical Buddhist point of view, there's not really a separate topic we would call emotions. Emotions would appear to be part of the wider topic of *kleśa*s, the mental states or experiences that make the mind unsettled. Emotions can be disturbing and destructive when not experienced with mindfulness and compassion. But if we are able to see clearly what the true nature of the experience is, emotions can have tremendously powerful wisdom and compassion.

JOHN TARRANT, ROSHI: Psychology takes the approach of fixing an emotional problem in order to make a person function again. That may be the goal of a society or a culture, but that is not necessarily the goal of a wisdom tradition. Anybody who has been in any tradition of depth has noticed that people who have what look like pathological emotions might be taking a positive step toward disassembling their old way of being, so that a new, greater possibility can come through. If you're always fussing at and fixing your mind, you don't get that journey.

There's also a kind of voluptuousness about what's given by the psyche, which at some level is what's given us by the universe. We can take a housekeeping attitude toward the emotion or we can take the ride and see what discovery is happening. Not a thrill ride, but more of a quest. The problem is not the emotion; the problem is being at war with the emotion or acting out the emotion.

Does Buddhism make a distinction between good emotions and bad emotions?

SHARON SALZBERG: In Buddhism, we think more in terms of what is skillful and unskillful. Skillful refers to those states that, when cultivated, lead to the end of suffering. Unskillful refers to those states that, when enhanced and nurtured, lead to more suffering.

That's a powerful shift for people to make. Instead of falling into the old, conditioned habit of regarding anger or fear as bad, wrong, weak, or terrible—or considering ourselves bad, wrong, weak, or terrible people for having such emotions—we see them as states of suffering. This is a profound transition. It elicits the possibility of responding to ourselves, and to others in the grip of emotions, with compassion rather than rejection or hatred.

JUDITH SIMMER-BROWN: What we might label in the language of morality as "good" or "bad," Buddhists would consider as what is more or less conducive to awakening or to compassionate relationship with the world. It is not an external moral judgment of the kind we so frequently encounter.

Emotions themselves become problematic for us because of what we do with them. They can develop into karmic thought patterns that cause greater pain for us or lead us into negative actions. The activity of the emotions has the potential to cause greater confusion, turbulence, lack of clarity, and suffering—or not. Good and bad are clunky words to describe what the meditation experience tells us about emotion. The moral judgment doesn't fit.

DZOGCHEN PONLOP RINPOCHE: How skillfully or unskillfully we work with emotions determines whether the experience of that emotion is what we call bad or good. It is not about emotions but about how you experience them and handle them. When you experience emotion without skillful means or wisdom, it can be destructive.

The Buddhist teachings present three basic ways of working with emotions. The first approach is mindfulness, which can prevent the destructiveness of the emotions and make them beneficial and useful. The second approach is to bring the emotions to the path of wisdom, by transforming them into something that helps bring benefit to ourselves and others. The third approach, the Vajrayāna approach, is to look straight into the essence of the experience of emotion, where we will find tremendous energy and the power of awakening wisdom.

JUDITH SIMMER-BROWN: One of the things I've found most valuable about Buddhist practice is discovering that we don't really feel our emotions all that often. When there's an emotional impulse that arises—and I'm talking particularly about the painful ones, the kleśas—we tend to either indulge in it, acting out some kind of catharsis or building an intense storyline around it, or we suppress and bury the emotion. One of the tremendous benefits of Buddhist meditation for me has been to be able to sit with an emotion and experience it, rather than feel I have to do something with it or get rid of it.

DZOGCHEN PONLOP RINPOCHE: The act of releasing and expressing emotion is very temporary. It gives brief relief and a sense of freedom, but the root of your emotions is still there. With meditation, one can get to the root of all the emotions and see the true wisdom within them.

JUDITH SIMMER-BROWN: Our tendency to act on emotions comes from the fact that we're afraid to feel them. Mindfulness cultivates the ability to fully experience emotions. Emotions are painful when we feel them. The kleśas are genuinely painful. But when we truly feel the intensity of the painful, obsessive, destructive emotions, we deepen our capacity to understand how habitual patterns work in our lives. We get to see how our acting out of anger has caused incredible pain for us and others. Being able to experience my anger fully, and feel the pain before I act, gives me the opportunity to let go, without repeating the habit of releasing the emotions in some kind of fit. The real relief is in letting go.

When we act on our anger, we are actually practicing anger, training in anger. We are deepening and reinforcing the patterns and tendencies by impulsively acting. With mindfulness, we can see the chain we're caught in, and we can also see the purity at the root of the emotion. To see the alternative is a fantastic relief, not at all like the temporary relief of getting your emotion out.

JOHN TARRANT, ROSHI: I don't experience expressing emotion as relief. Paying attention is what leads to a transformation. Paying attention is actually the best form of love we have to bring to our lives. If we pay attention, we find freedom, rather than relief. Relief is erecting an alternative fantasy world to live in, until it breaks down too.

DZOGCHEN PONLOP RINPOCHE: And it will!

JOHN TARRANT, ROSHI: Freedom is freedom. Full stop. Freedom can be edgy and scary and surprising and wonderful and all that, but it's freedom, which is ultimately a more loving and interesting thing than just unloading an emotion.

What about feeling bad and guilty about our emotions, and keeping them bottled up for fear of the negative consequences?

SHARON SALZBERG: When I first learned meditation with S. N. Goenka, I experienced tremendous anger, which I was very uncomfortable with. I marched up to Goenka at one point and said, "I never used to be an angry person before I started to meditate." But when I got through the distress of facing this newly discovered wealth of anger, I found out that freedom was in recognizing it without shame, without falling into it, without identifying with it.

That's what real kindness is. We can get caught in thinking that kindness means that we should be complacent and passive. But we're confusing action and motivation. We cultivate kindness as the basis of our intention, but finding the best action in a particular situation demands mindfulness in a bigger context. That means we could come from a genuinely kind place but have an intensity or fierceness in our actions if the context invites it.

Often our strongest emotions come up with the people we're closest to.

JOHN TARRANT, ROSHI: It seems you can't raise a child without making an idiot of yourself. For that matter, you can't love without making an idiot of yourself. It's a perfect joining of things. It's not a mistake.

JUDITH SIMMER-BROWN: I was in a Buddhist-Christian dialogue once, and one of the longtime Trappist monks said with great pride that he couldn't remember the last time he was angry. I muttered under my breath that he obviously didn't have a family.

If you create a bubble around yourself and think that having or expressing emotions is a problem, that's a sad life. Our emotions carry our very best features and they are fundamentally wisdom. Chögyam Trungpa once said that emotions are like a game we started because we just enjoyed them so much, and then they got out of hand. We became afraid of them. But at bottom they are a vivid display of our fundamental wisdom and brilliance. We forget that we created them in the first place, because of all the extra baggage they carry.

It's a blessing to be in situations that drive you crazy, because it helps you develop a deeper heart. Being a wife and mother has forced me to take greater responsibility for the games I started. These people in my life who push my buttons are my greatest teachers and dearest friends. I'm grateful that I can remember vividly the last time I was angry.

JOHN TARRANT, ROSHI: You meet the surprise and wonder of life as it arises, finding out what instructions life has for you, rather than what instructions you have for managing life.

What is the relationship between mindfulness and Buddhist practices that cultivate positive emotions like loving-kindness?

SHARON SALZBERG: Mindfulness and loving-kindness are so clearly reciprocal and mutually supportive. There are many people whose mindfulness is challenged by a corrosive habit of self-judgment, criticism, and self-hatred. For people like that, loving-kindness or compassion practice actually creates the ground out of which they're more able to do mindfulness genuinely.

JOHN TARRANT, ROSHI: In *kōan* practice you find mindfulness practice at times, but also kindness. In the beginning, when somebody starts hanging out with a standard kōan like "The whole world is medicine. What is the self?" they will go through all the usual concentration phenomena, but then they might have some sort of transformation, which is wisdom (*prajñā*), emerging. At the same time, they may also find themselves kinder. It's based on wisdom, but sometimes the transformation can start happening in the darkness in a nonrational way. It's a kind of creative move by the universe that happens when you expose yourself to it.

The truth is that, as you keep going deeper into the meditation path, the categories—mindfulness, awareness, loving-kindness—just slide around. There are fewer boundary lines and categories. Your feet find a path, and the path rises to meet your feet.

JUDITH SIMMER-BROWN: These various elements are mutually supportive. Clear seeing reveals the contrast between habitual patterns and a fresh emotional life, and that allows us to act with loving-kindness in our relations with others. Kindness and attention work so closely together it becomes hard to separate them.

JOHN TARRANT, ROSHI: Loving-kindness is a practice, but if you really pay attention you might find that kindness starts coming up from below. You suddenly find you have a loving attitude toward life. That happens because kindness is not something added to awareness. It's fundamental to the nature of awareness. The opposition between paying attention and cultivating loving-kindness ultimately falls away.

JUDITH SIMMER-BROWN: The distortion of our clear seeing is part of the painfulness of emotion. We are removed from the direct experience of the way things are. The painful way we experience emotions and our distorted view of reality are completely intermingled.

So if you lose the distortion, you wouldn't necessarily lose the intensity of emotion, but you experience it differently?

JUDITH SIMMER-BROWN: The energy is completely different without the distortion. Practice helps you see just how much you are caught in your own little house of mirrors, how totally you distort your perspective in the midst of intense emotion.

DZOGCHEN PONLOP RINPOCHE: From the Vajrayāna point of view, we work mostly from the wisdom side of things, but at the same time we employ special skillful means to see the true energy of emotions. Even in the moment when you experience the most destructive emotions, such as rage, if you can penetrate to their essence you find tremendous space and energy, luminosity.

Many of the Vajrayāna practices suggest that we not abandon the emotions but rather work with their pure energy. The pure energy will lead us to a complete state of awakening, because emotions are primordially free. The intensity of emotions has a quality of sudden awakening, right here within the very moment of samsaric experience. From the Vajrayāna point of view, all the practices are directed toward seeing the essence of emotion rather than working with the conceptual or judgmental aspect of mind. We can go beyond that and see the power of the raw and naked state of emotions.

When a surge of emotion comes up, then, it always presents the possibility of awakening?

DZOGCHEN PONLOP RINPOCHE: It's already in the state of awakening. We just have to discover that. From the Sutrayāna perspective, we think in terms of transforming, whereas in Vajrayāna we don't need to transform anything. In Sutrayāna, you work with emotions in a more conceptual way. In Vajrayāna, you go straight to the naked state of the emotions, within which we find tremendous space, emptiness, clarity, luminosity, and vividness—what we call the clear light mind. The naked and raw state of emotions has the quality of bliss and emptiness inseparable, which is beyond joy versus agony. It's self-liberation, self-freeing. Emotions free themselves. We don't need to free them.

JUDITH SIMMER-BROWN: So there's nothing to be done?

DZOGCHEN PONLOP RINPOCHE: The problem is, you're trying too hard. Just relax and enjoy the wild ride.

When we have a strong upsurge of emotion, are there one or two things we can do at that moment to recall the wisdom you've all been talking about?

SHARON SALZBERG: One of the first things to do is notice the add-ons. There's the arising of the emotion, which is its own state, but on top of that we add a future. Or we add a reaction, like shame or exaggeration. Or perhaps we add comparison, by holding ourselves up to an ideal we're not attaining. So probably the first thing to do is to release some of those add-ons, so we can come back to the original experience. Then we can maybe let ourselves be with the basic emotion in as mindful a way as possible. That will open up a little space, and in that space, we see can options.

6

Off the Cushion:
Theravāda Practice in Daily Life

GIL FRONSDAL

MARCIA ROSE

MICHAEL GRADY

Theravāda Buddhism is renowned for its formal meditation practices, such as mindfulness and insight. What is its' approach to Buddhist practice in our lives off the meditation cushion?

GIL FRONSDAL: People are looking for how they can bring Buddhist practice into all aspects of their lives. Meditation and mindfulness are elements of that, but there is much more to a Buddhist spiritual life than mindfulness alone. Theravāda Buddhism is a very rich and profound spiritual path with many elements. Meditation and mindfulness are key, but I think they get overemphasized at times. I like to think of the path as a pyramid, and if your pyramid is upside down, it gets wobbly. It's very important to help people create a strong foundation for their practice, and part of that foundation is the practice of the the transcendent perfections (*pāramī*). They are intertwined with the mindfulness practice and supported by it.

MARCIA ROSE: At our centers we encourage people to take the foundation of their practice of Buddhadharma—mindfulness—into their daily life. Their life is their practice, and it happens on and off the cushion. Of course, people are able to accomplish that to varying degrees.

MICHAEL GRADY: Even though we talk a lot about practice in daily life, we stress heavily how important it is to keep the basic practices of sitting and walking going. Silent practice is essential. It's a worthy aspiration to be mindful and wise and compassionate in your daily life, but without a formal practice it's very hard to genuinely do so.

Can you say more about the perfections and other practices that extend mindfulness into everyday life?

GIL FRONSDAL: There are ten transcendent perfections in the Theravāda tradition: generosity, ethics, renunciation, wisdom, energy, patience, truthfulness, resolve, loving-kindness, and equanimity. They don't appear very much in the Pali canon, but they are prominent in the *Buddhavaṃsa*, the story of the Buddha's previous lives. One of the best later sources is *A Treatise on the Paramis* (*Cāriyapiṭaka Aṭṭhakathā*), by Ācariya Dhammapāla. It's technical in places but very inspiring and profound.

The pāramīs became more and more important in the evolution of Theravāda Buddhism. They're not so much connected to the early tradition as they are to the mature Theravāda as it developed in Sri Lanka, Thailand, and Burma. The transcendent perfections are not mentioned in many of the popular books on Theravāda Buddhism, but if you go to these countries, you will find that they're deeply integrated into how people understand their Buddhist practice.

MARCIA ROSE: The perfections are the practice of life; they apply to the situations we encounter every day. If we take the Dharma into our lives, the pāramīs become the practice of our lives unfolding.

MICHAEL GRADY: They're aspects of insight practice and not separate from it.

MARCIA ROSE: The perfections, the precepts, the *brahmavihāra*s, and other such foundational elements are not meant to be thought of simply in an intellectual way but actually brought into daily life. In every single realm of our life, the perfections show up in the mirror of our relationships.

GIL FRONSDAL: One thing I find beautiful about the perfections, as with the eightfold path and other aspects of the path as described in the early tradition, is that the foundation is our relationship to other people, our interrelational world. We're not just doing our practice for ourselves. We're also doing it in a field of other people. We can practice generosity in relation to ourselves, but mostly it's something we practice in relation to others. Ethics and precepts are also practiced mostly in relation to other people. The foundation of the path is establishing healthy relationships with the people around us, Dharma relationships. Such relationships inform the deep contemplative practice that we do in a more solitary way.

MARCIA ROSE: For example, we can take one of the brahmavihāras, such as loving-kindness (*metta*), and practice it anytime, in any circumstance. If you're in a traffic jam, instead of laying on the horn or swearing at somebody or engaging in unkind speech, send metta and see what happens. See what goes on internally.

MICHAEL GRADY: If you were in a meeting and someone intimidated you and made you fearful, you could use a calming practice, like working with the breath or being aware of touch points in the body, as a way of settling the energy. You could also do metta practice toward yourself or toward the person you're afraid of. You could be mindful of how fear expresses itself in the body, noticing the different sensations that arise, and their impermanent nature. That leads to the insight that fear is an energy that arises in certain situations beyond our control, expresses itself in certain ways, and passes away. This is the basic methodology we use in vipassanā meditation, but we're taking it off the cushion and bringing it into a situation where we are actually experiencing fear on the spot. When you can apply the methods you've been practicing to real-life situations, you develop confidence in yourself and confidence in the practice.

GIL FRONSDAL: One of the most useful practices is mindfulness of speech—paying attention to what we're doing when we speak. There's also an ethical aspect to paying attention to speech. It helps us learn how not to cause harm and to take care of our relationships in a healthier way.

When we bring mindfulness to speech, what we speak tends to become a window into what makes us tick, our deep motivation. Often we don't see our own motivation clearly. By paying attention to why we say what we're going to say, a phenomenal amount of self-understanding and self-purification can come about.

MARCIA ROSE: The teaching of no self (*anattā*) can be liberating and powerful off the cushion. It's a misunderstanding that this fundamental teaching can only come to be understood during formal practice. We can always be mindful of ways that we create, or recreate, a separate self. We can begin to notice that "self-ing" taking place in our daily life. We can notice how we exaggerate our speech and make our self up in the way we speak. We tell tales, exaggerating what we've done, what we've said, who we think we are, who we think we aren't.

The bottom line is looking at our motivation for speaking, and for acting in general. We can look at whether in a relationship we are creating another self, or not. We can see whether we are connecting directly or reacting to life by having to make our self again. We do a nonresidential weekend retreat on that subject alone, because people want to take a deeper look at the process of creating the self in a more concentrated setting. Then they can take what they learn into their lives.

Can you say something about the precepts?

MICHAEL GRADY: The precepts are crucial in the Theravāda tradition. How one holds them varies from teacher to teacher, but holding them is the foundation of the practice. It is also an awareness practice. Laypeople are encouraged to follow the five basic precepts, and we talk a lot about why we think it's important to follow them and take them up as a practice.

The idea is not to hold the precepts as commandments but to treat them as guidelines. The core principle of the precepts is the practice of nonharm, which is based on the recognition that we're all interconnected. Ethics provide a very wise guide for living in relationship with others. Whether it's refraining from harming somebody, practicing generosity and kindness, not taking things that don't belong to you, or exercising wise action in sexual relationships, the precept are a guide for how to relate to others.

How is that different from the commandment approach?

MICHAEL GRADY: Everybody needs to cultivate their own relationship to the precepts. It's important not to see them as something imposed on you. A good example is taking intoxicants. Some people define that as never having a glass of wine at a meal, and other people would say that's fine. What we say is, "Don't take things that cloud your mind." If drinking a glass of wine clouds your mind, affects your behavior, or affects your thoughts, then consider restraining that impulse. But you take it as a practice—you use the precepts as a framework for evaluating the consequences of what you're doing in your life.

Sometimes our own wisdom is limited, and the precepts give additional support and guidance. If you're moving into a relationship and you're getting close to having a sexual relationship with somebody, the precepts ask you to step back and see if it's a wise thing. If you're pursuing self-interest at the cost of somebody else's well-being, that's not a good thing. That would not be living that particular precept. It's a process of investigation, using wisdom and compassion. Mindfulness is involved in all the precept practices, which ask us to recognize that if we engage in harmful activities it inhibits liberation and causes suffering.

MARCIA ROSE: When we use the precepts to take an investigatory approach to our life, we discover that harm goes in both directions. It's never just harming the other person and it's never just harming oneself. Using the precepts as practice requires one to be very honest, and it develops a lot of humility. With humility and honesty come learning. It's about learning, not about obeying a commandment.

GIL FRONSDAL: I find that the cutting edge of people's practice is not always on the cushion. It could be in parenting, at work, or in relationships. I see people growing a lot when they begin applying Dharma principles of mindfulness and practice in all these areas. The spiritual growth that's available in parenting, for example, is just phenomenal.

7

Poison, Fuel, or Medicine?
The Sense Pleasures

**BHANTE PIYĀNANDA ▪ SOJUN MEL WEITSMAN, ROSHI
REGINALD RAY ▪ MIRANDA SHAW**

Bhante Piyānanda, in your book *Saffron Days In L.A.*, you quote this verse from the *Dhammapada*:

From lust arises grief,
From lust arises fear.
For him who is free from lust
There is no grief, much less fear.

This describes the desire for sense pleasures as a central cause of our suffering. How central is the problem of lust to Buddhist philosophy?

BHANTE PIYĀNANDA: In his first sermon, called the *Dhammacakkappavattana Sutta*, the Buddha explained the middle path. He said the search for happiness through sense pleasure is low, common, and unprofitable—the way of ordinary people. He said we cannot understand things as they are through indulging in sense pleasure. On the other hand, Buddha said, the search for happiness through self-mortification is not good either. Buddha avoided these two extremes and followed the middle path.

SOJUN MEL WEITSMAN, ROSHI: The ideal is to find the middle way, and then there's the actual playing out of Dharma in our lives. We are all, every one of us, sensual beings. We have five senses, and we have the mind sense and the ego sense and various levels of consciousness that look for satisfaction. We need to take into consideration the world in which we find ourselves and look at how we deal with this problem of attachment. That's especially true nowadays, when sensuality is being sold to us without limit.

Where does attachment to the sense pleasures come in the process of the twelve *nidānas*, the chain of dependent origination?

BHANTE PIYĀNANDA: In terms of dependent origination, we start with ignorance (*avijjā*) as a cause. Then we have three roads, greed (*lobha*), hatred (*dosa*), and ignorance (*moha*). It is due to these three that all of our suffering started, and if we can begin to remove our greed, hatred, and ignorance, we can begin to end our suffering. It all begins with ignorance, though. We have traveled continually in samsara due to this basic ignorance.

REGINALD RAY: Sometimes attachment is confused with experience. It's interesting that attachment really only arises at the eighth nidāna—it comes along very late in the evolution of our experience. This helps us to see that sense experience itself is not considered a problem in Buddhism. The problem is the attitude we have toward it. Attachment—embodied in passion, aggression, and ignorance—represents attitude and that evolves pretty late in the chain.

The whole problem of ego is that we attempt to maintain a continuous monologue that confirms our identity and security. We use sense experience to reinforce our sense of ourselves. Rather than taking sense experience in and of itself and appreciating its possibilities, we try to co-opt it.

MIRANDA SHAW: From the beginning Buddhism has balanced two seemingly opposing tendencies. First, we have the need for detachment—the need to renounce our greed and dependence on sense experience as a source of happiness. At the same time, there's a profound impulse to affirm the world and a sense that the goal of the practice is not to escape it. The most popular way of representing the Buddha is in the earth-touching gesture, in which his hand is held to the ground. This portrays the idea that enlightenment is not something that is going to remove you from the world of sense experience. Instead, it involves a profound groundedness in reality and on Earth—an enlightened participation in life. The paradox is that we detach from our attachments but not from the world itself.

Is the challenge just our attachment to the sense pleasures, or do we simultaneously have to work with our aversion to pain?

SOJUN MEL WEITSMAN, ROSHI: Pleasure and pain are pretty subjective. Within pain there's pleasure, and within pleasure there's pain. Pain is a natural element of living in this world. We can't avoid pain, but pain is not necessarily suffering. Pain can either liberate us or bite us, depending on how we approach it.

Pleasure may be the same. It is not necessarily something bad or good. Pleasure is simply pleasure. The problem is with our attitude and how we become caught by something. It is about liking and disliking. We habituate ourselves to something we like and avert something we dislike. As we investigate this, we come to the question, *What is really the source of the problem?* The problem is maybe not with objects of pleasure or pain but with our attitudes and attachment.

BHANTE PIYĀNANDA: At the same time we have to ask, How does it come to be? How does it die away? Just as we can see that the leaves fall from the trees in autumn, wise ones must understand that everything is subject to change. If we understand impermanence, then we will be able to handle pain as well as pleasures. That is how to develop the habit of renunciation.

If we look at things as impermanent, we can release our grasping. For instance, if I have a lustful character that I cannot control, I must practice meditation on death or impurity. When I do that meditation on death and understand its nature, then gradually I'll be able to remove my desire. It is a tool to get rid of attachment.

REGINALD RAY: If we have an intellectual understanding of impermanence, it does undermine our tendency to grasp after sense experience. If you actually see the sense experience arise and disappear within your body, there's nothing to hang on to. Attachment doesn't really come up as an issue, because there's such a sense of movement and groundlessness that the mind simply doesn't go there.

MIRANDA SHAW: One of the key differences between the Theravāda and tantric approaches came up in Bhante's comment that when one understands the impermanent nature of things one will automatically detach from them. In tantra a different conclusion is derived. When one understands the essential nature of phenomena as empty of intrinsic reality, the appropriate response is to go to the heart of experience—to immerse oneself in experience and find there the treasury of wisdom and bliss that each experience holds.

The tantrikas called themselves heroes and heroines because they saw themselves as fearlessly diving into the ocean of the passions in order to gain the pearls of enlightenment. For them, turning away from sense experience contained a danger that one may be inadvertently repressing or avoiding experience. Therefore, one should place oneself in situations that will arouse all kinds of attachments. Instead of withdrawing, perhaps one would immerse oneself in relationships, which can arouse our most profound attachments and fears and passions, and use them as a stepping-stone.

What are they a stepping-stone toward?

MIRANDA SHAW: To discovering that sense experiences are intrinsically pure and blissful. The description of reality-as-it-is shifts somewhat. On the one hand, it is empty of intrinsic reality, but it is also inherently blissful.

The way to realize the intrinsic pleasure of being is to immerse ourselves in experiences and not get caught up in our ego-oriented interpretations. Instead, the sense experiences themselves become the objects of our most focused and fearless attention. Attention to music, dance, yoga, to bodily disciplines generally, could all be ways to gain access to the inherent blissfulness of embodiment. Tantrikas are careful to distinguish between ordinary pleasure and this kind of transcendent pleasure.

Is there a specific way of working with sense pleasures in Zen?

SOJUN MEL WEITSMAN, ROSHI: Desire is the key word in this regard.

Desire is not necessarily good or bad. It is a life force working in the world. We have our necessary desires—getting enough sleep, getting enough food, maintaining ourselves. But that's not what we mean by desire here. Desire in this case is something extra, something more than what's needed.

Instead of using desire for self-gratification, we could turn desire in another direction. When desire is turned toward practice it's called "way-thinking mind." Desire is still there, because it's the desire to seek the way. When the desire to seek the way becomes pleasurable, the desire for gratification through other pleasures can diminish. One can work with the tension between self-gratification and the desire for freedom within the Dharma. The Dharma is pleasurable for us.

We have a chant we sometimes use when we have an informal meal: "We venerate the three treasures and are thankful. Now as I take food and drink, I vow with all beings to partake in the pleasure of Zen and fully enjoy the Dharma." This means we have pleasure and enjoyment in the Dharma. This is where enjoyment comes from. The more we seek pleasure and enjoyment from practicing the Dharma, the less interesting sensual pleasures from outside sources become.

REGINALD RAY: We think there's only one kind of pleasure and pain: pleasure that feels good and pain that doesn't. But there's a kind of pain and pleasure that operates outside of the five *skandhas* and the nidānas. That kind of pain and pleasure is what the Vajrayāna is dealing with, and nobody likes that kind of pain and pleasure because it's undomesticated and it destabilizes the ego.

The Vajrayāna picked up on the fact that, in rejecting pleasure, many of the more conventional Buddhist schools were throwing out the transcendent pleasure of great bliss along with the pain. They realized that there is an implicit fear involved in an approach that throws out both ego pleasure and transcendent pleasure. They felt that somehow the people who were taking that more conventional view had not really achieved liberation, because there was still this underlying antipathy to pleasure in all forms, including those that operate beyond ego. The Vajrayāna took the notion of transcendent pleasure as a final stepping-stone toward complete liberation.

Bhante, do you recognize any distinction between conventional pleasure and transcendent pleasure?

BHANTE PIYĀNANDA: Pleasure, conventionally or in any form, is pleasure. However, we do have a desire to practice meditation and a desire to attain *nibbāna*. In the *Rathavinīta Sutta*, Sāriputta asks, "Is it for the sake of purification of virtue that the holy life is lived under the blessed one?" The answer is no. Virtue is only the means to a higher end. If we're clinging to any desires, we may not be able to attain enlightenment. We could even cling to something good. If I have too much faith, I may not be able to meditate well unless I balance it with wisdom. If I have a lot of energy without concentration, I might not achieve a good result. We have to balance, rather than cling; that's the most important thing.

REGINALD RAY: This might be an interesting difference in the way the traditions speak. In the Vajrayāna it would not be said that we need to cut clinging, but rather that we need to take it as an object of meditation. In Mahāmudrā practice, the more disgusting and dirty the kleśa is, the more appropriate it is for meditation. For example, if we feel a tremendous amount of clinging toward a certain person or a certain experience, rather than reject the clinging we make it the object of meditation. Through penetrating and understanding it, not only does its emptiness become a matter of experience but the energy of the clinging is transformed into great bliss and compassion. It becomes fuel for the journey and for relating to other people.

MIRANDA SHAW: This points to a genuine shift in the terminology of the tradition. Whereas in the earlier Theravāda tradition attachment and desire are genuinely regarded as a danger, in tantra the emphasis shifts and passion is seen as a great treasure. It becomes our guide to wisdom, because each of us has deep sensitivities and places where we're very open, where we're vulnerable to the depth of experience and reality. Instead of turning away from those places, they become the focus of our meditation and the fuel for our practice.

BHANTE PIYĀNANDA: I think all Buddhist traditions accept what the Buddha said in the *Kālama Sutta*: When you know for yourself that certain things are unwholesome, give them up. When you know that certain things are wholesome, follow them. Some desires are wholesome, and those we can accept for the progress of meditation and enlightenment. But whatever is unwholesome, whatever is harmful to us and society, we must give up. I think all of Buddhism agrees on that basic doctrine.

SOJUN MEL WEITSMAN, ROSHI: All of our passions, all of our drives, are meaningful. It's not a matter of getting rid of this or getting rid of that. It's a matter of balancing, so that everything works together harmoniously. Harmony is the key, in the mind, in the heart—and in the ego. We think we can get rid of ego, so we won't have any more problems, but ego is not something that we can get rid of, really. In the hierarchy of consciousness, ego has a function. Ego is the sense of self, and the sense of self seems to be the problem. When the self arises, there's clinging and attachment. When there's no clinging and no attachment, we can say there's no real self there. Nevertheless, ego has a function, and when the ego is functioning in a harmonious way with the head and the heart and the emotions and the senses, it's much easier to sort out what is attachment, what is worth taking up and what is worth letting go.

Theravāda and Vajrayāna offer very different, even opposed, methods of working with attachment. Does Zen offer some middle ground on this?

SOJUN MEL WEITSMAN, ROSHI: I could approach that with an example from the life of my teacher, Suzuki Roshi. In general, he didn't smoke and didn't drink; he took care of himself. When he went to a party, however, he allowed himself to have one drink. He would take one drink of champagne or whatever was offered, but he would say no thank you for the rest of the night. He would participate and be with people, but he would participate only to the point where he was not given over to attachment or indulgence.

Learning how to participate, how to flow with things, how to move with society, how to move with the people around you, without being attached to it, is the method. But I would rather talk about it as attitude rather than method, because it's the attitude that makes the difference. We keep precepts through our attitude, not simply by following them by rote.

We have looked at the sense pleasures from the point of view of the path. How would someone who is enlightened handle sense pleasures?

MIRANDA SHAW: I'd like to echo Sahajayoginīcintā, an important Indian female Vajrayāna teacher, who said that for one who has attained buddhahood, all the sense pleasures and all activities become like jewels in the palm of their hand.

An enlightened being can use all situations to liberate sentient beings, and that is done artfully and mindfully but with tremendous flexibility. In tantra, there's no one type of display, or no one way of working with the sensory world, that will be liberating for all sentient beings. Some people may be inspired by the example of someone who is very restrained and modest and detached. Others may be inspired by the example of someone who commands vast resources and uses them in ways that nourish, nurture, heal, and inspire others. Some people need to be liberated by the example of someone who is in no way intimidated by the whole of the senses, someone who can freely enjoy and engage all sense pleasures and yet retain a mind that is untrammeled and free. Such a person could be very outrageous or appear to be a self-indulgent sybarite.

There is no limit to the possibilities. There is no one way. Enlightenment involves the artistry of devising means that will liberate all sentient beings.

REGINALD RAY: We would call this seeing the sacredness of experience. We could talk about each experience—however it may be judged by conventional standards—as empty of inherent essence, and luminous, splendid, striking in its appearance. But there's also a kind of unfolding quality to experience, which is something the Vajrayāna also attends to. It sees that our experience, as it unfolds in our lives in accordance with the laws of karma, is actually the unfolding of wisdom and compassion.

An enlightened person has a tremendous amount of trust in what happens in his or her life and in the world. Such a person sees that each occurrence is an opportunity to connect with other people and help them. At the same time, each thing that happens is a moment of awakening to ourselves as practitioners. The enlightened person exhibits an ultimate trust in life and in what occurs. But it's not a blind trust—it's a trust that emerges out of direct insight into how things really are at the deepest level.

SOJUN MEL WEITSMAN, ROSHI: I definitely agree with the importance of trust—to have intrinsic trust in our practice and in the fact that the practice supports us when we support the practice. I've seen that trust work over and over again. There are two tracks. One is how we deal with ourselves, how we take care of ourselves and practice for our own enlightenment. The other is how we take care of others.

These two go hand in hand. To try to understand people is the best way we can let go of our clinging and our attachments to desires, anger, and ill will. We see what is behind it all; it gives us space and nonattachment to whatever comes up. This is basic Buddhist meditation: simply to notice how things arise and how they cease to arise, and to be with them when they're there. When we allow this process to unfold, we gain some freedom.

Sometimes we also have to step into a situation where there's some attachment and we have to be able to accept that as well. Sometimes that's the skillful means for helping people. There are many ways in the Dharma and I can't criticize any way of the Dharma. I think each school and each discipline has its own approach and each approach is wonderful and interesting and works.

8

A Quiet and Secluded Place: Going on Retreat

GUY ARMSTRONG

ELIZABETH MATTIS-NAMGYEL

GEOFFREY SHUGEN ARNOLD, SENSEI

What is the value of doing a long retreat, meaning at least a week or ten days devoted completely to practice and silence?

GUY ARMSTRONG: It's important to the evolution of Dharma in traditionally non-Buddhist countries to make retreat opportunities available to people, because it seems that's where the deepest understandings of the Buddha tend to get realized. When people make that kind of commitment and put that much time into retreat, it permanently shifts something in their worldview.

ELIZABETH MATTIS-NAMGYEL: I've seen incredible transformations take place in retreat. It's common at our center to do one-hundred-day retreats, and when people come out, I see noticeable shifts in their understanding and in how they are as human beings.

I don't think I really understood what practice was until I went into retreat. When you meditate, you get an incredible flood of thoughts, emotions, and experiences. It can be quite intimidating. Retreat allows you to be with that mind longer, to really get to know it. In retreat, I started to understand my mind, to understand how to work with my experience. Above all, I learned how to find pleasure and enjoyment in my own mind.

GEOFFREY SHUGEN ARNOLD, SENSEI: What retreat means can vary widely—in terms of the container, what's being asked of the student, the amount of guidance they're getting, the challenges they're encountering, how those are handled, and so forth. Retreat encompasses a wide spectrum of experiences, but what comes to mind for me is the Buddha speaking of going to a quiet and secluded place. That's so important.

Though retreat is often discussed as an advanced practice, certain types of retreat are a helpful way to encounter the Dharma in the beginning, when everything is so restless and agitated and we're so easily hooked by things. Stepping away from that helps us to genuinely encounter the Dharma and get some sense of what practice actually is—to encounter our own mind in a way that's a little bit more naked and transparent. Then as we continue with our practice, retreats become even more important, because we're able to practice more deeply, more effectively. So the retreat time is better utilized.

In retreat, what you may have been suppressing in your daily life begins to bubble up to the surface and puts you in a position to process it. Can you get to that deep place without doing retreat?

GUY ARMSTRONG: A lot of people feel they've had transformative experiences just from meditating on a daily basis. I do believe that's true, but there is another level of understanding and realization that comes from the silent retreat experience that isn't available to most people in daily practice.

GEOFFREY SHUGEN ARNOLD, SENSEI: For most people, stepping out of worldly life for a while is essential. The unceasing, moment-to-moment experience of practicing is precious. Often when people are ambivalent about what their motivation is and what their practice is about, intensive retreat clarifies that. It helps them to come back into direct contact with what is important to them and why they began practicing in the first place.

ELIZABETH MATTIS-NAMGYEL: You come to the point where you're able to bear witness to experiences you would continually distract yourself from if you weren't in retreat. There is no substitute for immersing yourself in that kind of intensity. Consistent daily practice is important and wonderful, but the deep silence of retreat takes practice to another level.

GEOFFREY SHUGEN ARNOLD, SENSEI: It's interesting to compare what we mean when we refer to an intensive retreat. Elizabeth is talking about something longer than what we do. The *sesshin* is a unique form of intensive retreat, though. It is completely in silence, but it is a group retreat that follows a unified schedule that includes a work period and meetings with a teacher. They are generally a week long. Since we do them every month, people in residence at Zen Mountain Monastery would do a full week sesshin every month. In our tradition, though, we don't do the kind of lengthier group and solo retreats you see more often in Vajrayāna and Vipassanā communities.

What is the difference between doing a long solitary retreat and a series of sesshins?

GEOFFREY SHUGEN ARNOLD, SENSEI: In the sesshin approach there is a kind of pulsing back and forth. You have a very demanding week of sitting within a very strict container. Then that releases a bit and people have to return to daily life, and then once again they return to sesshin. The moving back and forth can be quite awkward and troubling in the beginning. For me, it felt like everything would come apart after sesshin, but over time those boundaries begin to fall away and there's continuity, a dissolution of the difference between retreat and not retreat.

Retreat, then, is not an escape from the world, because you have to go back.

ELIZABETH MATTIS-NAMGYEL: I find that perception very humorous because retreat is the opposite of escape. It's about no escape. When you go into retreat, everything you've been trying to avoid surfaces. So often we don't have a very sane relationship with our mind. It's all about what you want and what you don't want rather than being there. Practice is about seeing that for what it is. And that is a challenging prospect.

GUY ARMSTRONG: It is. You get into a retreat setting, and you go through a period of homesickness. You're missing your partner, your children, the comforts of home. You spend some time adjusting to the schedule and your body being unaccustomed to so much stillness.

There's a pressure-cooker effect. You have nothing left to deal with than the mind at that point. While that simplicity is a kind of escape from the hassles of daily life, you are plunged into the maelstrom of the untrained mind, working with each kleśa as it arises.

GEOFFREY SHUGEN ARNOLD, SENSEI: Those early experiences of struggle get settled, and then there is a comfort we can develop within retreat, which is not altogether a bad thing. We're learning how to practice more effectively and in a more relaxed and refined way. Intensity is no longer necessarily grueling. But there is a danger in that refinement. Once the surface frictions no longer affect us, we need to discover a deeper level of motivation to genuinely practice rather than just stay on for the ride.

GUY ARMSTRONG: The quality of one-pointedness, which is hard to generate in daily life, is so strong in retreat that when something new comes into the present moment—such as a flash of anger or loneliness or despair—we can fully recognize it and form a relationship to it. Samādhi gives the mind the strength to form that relationship in a positive way, whereas in daily life the force of it might just overwhelm us.

When we become accustomed to retreat, can ego subvert retreat at that point?

ELIZABETH MATTIS-NAMGYEL: The ego is extremely adept at holding on to experiences and thinking that that's the practice. After I had been on retreat a while, I started to realize that the postures and the methods support practice, but the actual practice has much more to do with how I'm responding to my experience. How much of mind can I bear witness to? In the beginning it might be very little, but as we go on, it could become much more if we choose to really practice rather than cling to results. It's not about an answer. It's about the question keeping practice alive.

GEOFFREY SHUGEN ARNOLD, SENSEI: Each of our traditions has forms, rituals, and liturgies, and it's very easy, if not inevitable, to think it's going to automatically do something to you. But it's the subtle fabric of the mind, the nonmaterial aspects of spirit and motivation and all the habits of mind, that are the real stuff of retreat. A teacher can help us to penetrate to that, but it is up to us to notice whether we are actually getting to depth. That's an ongoing process, because we're really quite adept at fooling ourselves, even when we have the best of intentions.

ELIZABETH MATTIS-NAMGYEL: I find it helpful to simply ask myself, "Am I practicing?" It becomes easier to discern whether we were there or not, because we become familiar with the quality of struggle and grasping, and the free and courageous quality of being with the mind. One of the beauties of retreat is being able to clearly discern that.

GUY ARMSTRONG: Once we get somewhat comfortable in doing the physical schedule, the hard part is staying alive to what's happening in the mind—and that involves a lot of investigation, inquiry, and deep listening. I've been working with a suggestion from a Burmese teacher named Sayadaw U Tejaniya. He says to ask, "Is there greed, aversion, or delusion in the mind at this moment?" It's all about how I'm relating to my experience in the moment. He says, greed is present if you want something else to be happening, aversion is present if you want something to stop happening, and delusion is present if you're not in touch with what's happening. If greed, aversion, and delusion aren't so strong, then some of the factors of awakening are going to be there.

How do you avoid becoming unstable and terrified in retreat?

GEOFFREY SHUGEN ARNOLD, SENSEI: In sesshin we're doing everything together, but there's silence and no eye contact. Within this deep solitude is a real experience of Sangha, which provides a grounding so that you don't become freaked out or spacey. If somebody is getting into trouble, throwing themselves into a pit, the teacher can help them.

We also have hermitages and people do solitary retreats that generally last a week. But we reserve those for people who have more experience, because you don't have the Sangha there to direct you and you don't have the access to the teacher. The Zen tradition has many stories of teachers and practitioners living in solitude and practicing for a long time by themselves, but that usually came after a period of communal practice.

GUY ARMSTRONG: It's nothing out of the ordinary for fear to come up in retreat. In fact, it's something we value, because normally in daily life people feel overwhelmed by their fear and don't know how to find any space in relation to it. Seeing fear as another emotion is very liberating and an important part of retreat.

If at any point we feel someone's fear is pushing them too close to the edge, we back them off the intensity of the schedule, encourage them to take more walks, have them interact with staff a bit more, and make sure that a teacher sees them every day for fifteen minutes or more.

GEOFFREY SHUGEN ARNOLD, SENSEI: It's important to determine whether someone has the stability to enter retreat. We only allow people whom we feel are ready to go deep with themselves to enter. No one should be pushed overly hard into retreat, by themselves or by others.

ELIZABETH MATTIS-NAMGYEL: As retreat master, I am there to support somebody to work through extreme difficulties, which we've all experienced in retreat. These experiences are incredible opportunities to develop a new relationship to suffering.

In retreat we have the space to ask ourselves what it really is that we're experiencing before we immediately close down around it. As you learn not to react with greed, aversion, and delusion, you start to see that maybe what you fear is something different than what you thought it was. Freaking out is an opportunity to let your attitude shift. If you can go into retreat with that in mind, it will help you. Otherwise you may take the approach of simply trying to manage your experience, as we so often do in our outside life.

Ironically, the restrictiveness of the retreat container provides the space where a question mark can leak in.

GEOFFREY SHUGEN ARNOLD, SENSEI: Stravinsky said that within discipline we find spaciousness, liberty, and freedom. But that discipline must be held in a way that's based in wisdom.

GUY ARMSTRONG: Retreat places us in a position to work with the painful parts as well as the sublime parts, and working with the painful parts is really what opens the door to compassion. You see the full impact of negative states on yourself, and then you look around and realize everybody is going through the same thing. Compassion emerges naturally.

GEOFFREY SHUGEN ARNOLD, SENSEI: At a certain point, the realization may dawn that although you've left so-called regular life and entered a seemingly artificial environment, you are doing nothing more than living. It's in a slightly more concentrated way, and there's more emphasis on zazen, but it's actually teaching us how to live our normal lives. It's about actually living retreat as just another day of life.

ELIZABETH MATTIS-NAMGYEL: The challenges turn out to be the same. Seeing this helps us to be more ordinary about our retreat and daily life.

Yet there is not a lot of encouragement to do this sort of thing. It's seen as exotic and impractical. Do you have any advice about how to carve out time and money to go on retreat?

ELIZABETH MATTIS-NAMGYEL: It depends on what your focus is. If your intention is to wake up, then you do have time to do it. If that's not your intention, then you won't.

GUY ARMSTRONG: Motivation is the central question, and it usually builds in a series of steps that begins with learning to meditate and progresses through lengthier and deeper periods. Most people, apart from parents with small children, seem to find the opportunity to do retreat once the motivation sets in. Even people who have a busy work life tend to get at least two weeks of vacation a year and can carve out some time.

Helping people find the time is mostly about helping them discover their own motivation and then letting it develop to the point where retreat seems like the sensible next step. And in terms of cost, a retreat can be pretty modest compared with most vacations.

GEOFFREY SHUGEN ARNOLD, SENSEI: I've also been inspired to see people with small children, with full careers, with partners who aren't practitioners—the whole gamut—find time to do retreat not just once but repeatedly throughout the year. And they do it in such a way that they find balance with their families. In fact, retreat can help us to establish priorities in our lives. You may learn to be more discerning about what you take on. You may become clearer about what the most important things are and give them the time they need. You understand why the great spiritual traditions regard simplicity as such an important virtue. I live in New York City, so I know what an uphill battle that can be in our culture, but living simply is always a choice.

The transition from retreat back to daily life can be challenging for many people. Is returning from retreat also an important part of retreat?

GUY ARMSTRONG: We often say at the end of retreats that the first half of your retreat is over, and the second half begins as you make the journey back home. It isn't an easy journey most of the time, especially for people who are going through it early in their meditation career. You've slowed down but the world has maintained its fierce and brusque and often unkind pace. But the bumpiness tends to smooth itself out after a bit of time.

How do you not only survive the transition but also maintain continuity with the quality of the retreat?

GUY ARMSTRONG: We long for the beauty of the retreat experience and that reminds us of the potential of our human nature. It builds motivation, even urgency. It may cause us to adjust our life to make the qualities we cultivate in retreat have a bigger place in our lives. It may also cause us to go into retreat more often.

ELIZABETH MATTIS-NAMGYEL: The longing is quite beautiful. It's an expression of buddha nature. We may judge ourselves harshly at times for not being as connected to it as we would like, but when we feel that longing it shows how truly connected we are. As retreat begins to mature, our feelings of being isolated can decrease. We feel more engaged with life itself, so returning to everyday life from retreat has less contrast—it's just living your life, as Shugen said. And yet there is some difference. Dudjom Rinpoche said that while it's good to do solitary retreats, it's also really important to mingle in the world.

GEOFFREY SHUGEN ARNOLD, SENSEI: It's necessary to leave retreat so we can dissolve the duality. An old master said we need to test our understanding against the sutras. We also need to test our retreat against life itself, where the messiness will challenge our composure and compassion. The retreat is the extraordinary in some sense; we need to bring it to the familiar, and vice versa. As Master Dōgen said, we need to harmonize the inner and outer. Gaining insight on the cushion is the easy part. Harmonizing that with how we actually live our lives is the hardest part. There's always a lag, it seems, between what we've understood to be true and what we're able to embody.

9

Transforming the Kleśas:
The Main Work of Meditation

ZENKEI BLANCHE HARTMAN

RINGU TULKU

GUY ARMSTRONG

To start with, perhaps we could talk about what people expect will happen to their defilements when they start meditation practice.

ZENKEI BLANCHE HARTMAN: Most of the people I meet come to meditation because they are experiencing a lot of pain and confusion, which of course arises from their karmic activity. So in the beginning they need to see what's happening before they can start to relinquish any of it. They need to see how completely unruly their mind is. It takes a while before they can effect any reduction in the disturbances.

RINGU TULKU: It helps to appreciate how difficult it is to uproot defilements, or kleśas, and just how long it could take. To totally uproot the kleśas takes a very long time, according to the Buddhist tradition. Sometimes it is said that to become totally enlightened takes countless eons. On the other hand, the main purpose of meditation is to uproot the defilements. If nothing happens to the kleśas, the practice isn't working.

At the outset, perhaps it is best if we don't think in terms of the defilements but more simply in terms of making our mind a little calmer. After all, when we first start to practice, we experience our mind like a waterfall, which can be overwhelming. We might feel we are worse off, but we are actually better off, because we are aware of the waterfall. For once, we know what's going on.

GUY ARMSTRONG: Most people do come to meditation because of disturbances in the mind. Over the first few years of practice they feel a lot more confident working with those disturbances and perceive an actual reduction in them. Yet at other times in practice, they can feel the kleśas increase and get stronger. That seems to result from having greater awareness of the kleśas and paying more attention to them, because you see more clearly what was covered up.

ZENKEI BLANCHE HARTMAN: Suzuki Roshi used to call this "the instant age." We expect instant everything. We come with all kinds of expectations, and one of the things we learn early is that with expectation comes disappointment. Some people, not finding instant results, or quick results, wander off and look somewhere else. But those who stick around for a while begin to notice some relief.

GUY ARMSTRONG: The true sense of equanimity is not that the emotions go away, but that when we meet any emotion, we find that we have the capability to be with it—without being afraid or running away, or without letting it force us to do foolish things.

RINGU TULKU: If at first we cultivate that kind of relaxation and refrain from creating too many negative situations, we get into less trouble. Then we can try to cultivate the opposites of the defilements a bit. The Buddha said do no evil and try to do positive things, and then tame the kleśas in your mind. Although the defilement is that which generates the negative actions, it has to be worked on gently, step by step.

It seems helpful to understand kleśa activity as a continuum, from the first moment a kleśa arises to full-blown action.

ZENKEI BLANCHE HARTMAN: The karmic results of a thought arising and of punching somebody in the nose are different. The resulting stress and the resulting disturbance are much greater if you act it out. It's very important for us to notice there's no way we can act without experiencing a result. When we become very clear about that, it helps temper our actions.

GUY ARMSTRONG: When kleśas are directly experienced, the energies that they bring up are quite frightening to the untrained person. To feel that we are is in the grip of anger, or in the grip of fear or strong desire, scares us. Our culture hasn't trained us how to be with them, so we need a lot of guidance and support in opening and softening, in realizing that we can feel these energies without their actually damaging us. Little by little, we can become more comfortable with feeling the energies directly. Therefore, the mind can remain undisturbed even when the kleśa is present.

ZENKEI BLANCHE HARTMAN: Not buying into them is a very key point. In the *Mahāsatipaṭṭhāna Sutta* it says, "When anger arises, the monk says, 'Anger has arisen.'" Generally, that's not our experience. Our experience, before practice, is that when anger arises, we erupt. To begin by being aware—"Oh, this is anger"—can give us space so we don't erupt and cause all the karmic consequences that involves.

There's a great bumper sticker, "Don't believe everything you think," which I pass on to all my students. We have a lot of thoughts that could get very destructive if we believe them to be true. If we can just see them as thoughts, they don't cause as much distress.

RINGU TULKU: Looking at the three kleśas, ignorance is the ground of the other two. As long as ignorance persists, we cannot get rid of kleśas and get out of the samsaric state of mind. But while its effect is clearly negative, it is neither dramatic nor tragic. It is in the background. Therefore, it is something you work on slowly, step by step.

Attachment is like water. Our life is filled with attachment and it adapts itself to whatever situation we are in. It has negative aspects—it creates lots of suffering and pain—but it also has some positive aspects—it is associated with love and compassion. It will not dry out very quickly, but it doesn't have the immediate and fearsome destructive energy of anger.

Anger is like fire. It burns you and it burns other people. It has the most negative effect of all. At the same time, it flares up quickly and can quickly die. Therefore, it can be a little easier to deal with, but because of its strong negative effects, it is also the most emergent of the defilements. Therefore, the sutras say anger is the first and most important thing we need to work on. So if we work with anger right from the outset, we can have an immediate effect for the good.

GUY ARMSTRONG: From the Theravādin point of view, the practice of discipline (*sīla*) is a way to safeguard our actions. By exercising restraint through the precepts, right speech, and so forth, we inhibit the action of the kleśa, and we stop spreading suffering around so much. That limits the karmic impact on ourselves and others.

At the same time, it can be very humbling to see that as much as we try to meditate and keep our good intentions, our words and actions do get away from us. In that case, we simply have to make space to realize we're human. Learning in meditation how to relate with these states inwardly gives us a little more space when they arise in daily life. We start to develop the fine art of letting go inwardly while being restrained outwardly. It's quite a dance to do both of those at the same time, but that's how the inner silent work and the work on the outer relationship operate together.

What about the chain reactions you set off when your kleśa activity manifests? Suddenly you have people responding with their own kleśa activity.

ZENKEI BLANCHE HARTMAN: That's how you learn it's not a free ride. If you relieve tension by blowing off steam, you're going to get burned too. It's going to bounce back. That's why Zen training occurs in a close group situation, where you live, sit, chant, and work together. You're always bumping into each other and that brings up stuff that could stay buried for a while if you didn't have constant interaction.

Suzuki Roshi's son used to call it "potato practice." You dig up some potatoes and they've all got dirt on them. But you don't have to pick up each one and scrub them. You put them in a bucket with some water and you stir it, and they bump into each other and clean each other up. Bumping into each other really helps you to deal with things in your everyday life.

RINGU TULKU: Once we see the kleśas, it is very important that we stop thinking they are good for us. Usually we think a kleśa is something useful.

For example, if we get angry, we think we are being righteous and protecting ourselves. We need to see very, very clearly that that's not the case. If I am angry, it's neither good for me or for others. If we don't have this basic understanding, we will not have the incentive to really work on the defilements.

So far we have been talking about kleśas as something to get rid of. Can they also be seen as an opportunity?

GUY ARMSTRONG: When we look honestly at the impact of the kleśas, we feel them as a burden. We sincerely wish it were otherwise, but for the time being they are definitely there. Given that situation, how can we keep a right attitude toward ourselves and toward these states as they arise?

It's helpful to realize they can actually strengthen our Dharma practice. By working with the kleśas, we develop lots of beautiful qualities, like humility and patience. The forbearance we practice to be with a kleśa without doing anything with it strengthens our compassion. We see how the kleśas make us suffer, and therefore we understand the impact they have on others, which strengthens our determination to purify our hearts further. As we have success in doing that, it gives rise to faith and confidence as well.

RINGU TULKU: The kleśas can never be seen as something good from the Buddhist point of view, because they create trouble. Nonetheless, they do present an opportunity. A kleśa can be transformed, and from the Vajrayāna point of view, they are in essence wisdom. But that does not mean that the kleśas are good.

Our basic nature is the enlightened state of our mind, and its natural quality is wisdom. Kleśas occur when we are not able to express that natural quality. They are a reflection of not being able to understand or express our pure wisdom mind. Yet they are not other than that wisdom mind. There is merely an obstruction, and when we clear that obstruction, the kleśas arise as wisdom. In Vajrayāna, we talk about three methods for dealing with kleśas: abandoning, transforming, and transmuting. In the end, they are not something we "get rid of."

ZENKEI BLANCHE HARTMAN: Suzuki Roshi often said a bodhisattva should be very happy about having difficulties, because difficulties give you a way to practice. Whenever you have a problem, there is where your practice is. When you see yourself getting caught by a kleśa, there is where your practice is.

RINGU TULKU: Seeing the problems caused by the kleśas also helps to generate compassion. If we don't see problems, we find no reason to have compassion.

If we measure success in working with defilements in terms of outward behavior, do you think there is much difference between people in Buddhist communities and the average person on the street?

RINGU TULKU: Many people come to a Buddhist center with very big expectations. They hear Buddhists talk about compassion, understanding, loving-kindness, peace, and things like that. So they expect that everyone there will fully embody all those virtues, and when they walk in, they get the shock of their lives. Yet this is a little bit like going to a hospital and being surprised that there are so many sick people. Those who come to Buddhist centers are not people who are already perfect. They are people who feel there is a big need for them to work on the negative things.

We find it very hard to work on our deep-seated attachments, and yet I see students who make lots of progress, and there are even some extraordinary stories. A woman I know who was dying of cancer practiced very intently until she was too weak to do formal practice anymore. In the hospital, in the presence of her mother and friends, even though she was very weak, she was lighthearted and cheerful. She said, "I am not afraid. I have complete confidence in the practice," and she died with a clear smile on her face. Everybody was impressed, including her mother, who was not a Buddhist. I see many such incidents that demonstrate the effects of practice.

GUY ARMSTRONG: There are beautiful people in many walks of life. But rather than compare myself to them, I would rather ask the question, where would I be today if I hadn't taken up this practice thirty years ago? I think I'd be a cynical person working in the computer industry somewhere. Looking at who we are and where we might have been is maybe a better comparison.

It's also true that some of the fruits of practice may not be visible for years, or possibly lifetimes.

Many renowned Buddhist teachers have exhibited bursts of anger or passion, or had habits that seemed on the surface like kleśa activity. How do we account for this?

ZENKEI BLANCHE HARTMAN: On a couple of occasions, I recall Suzuki Roshi getting angry. It seemed to me to be frustration at how slow we were to catch on and how little time he had.

I recall one sesshin when someone rang the bell one hour early. He realized his mistake and went running, saying, "Go back to bed! I rang it an hour early. I'm sorry! I'm sorry! I did it an hour early."

Only two students and Suzuki Roshi came down to the zendo. When everybody else finally came down, he said in this terrible voice, "You're all badgers and foxes sleeping in your zazen caves." And he jumped down and started hitting everybody, going around the zendo saying, "When the bell rings, come to the zendo," and a variety of other things, while he was going whack, whack, whack, all the way around the zendo.

It sure looked like anger to me, but it was actually a very effective teaching as well. I think the anger came first and the teaching came second. There were certainly other occasions when he had strong reactions like that. I think we could be pretty frustrating.

GUY ARMSTRONG: I think it's true that people are able to share Dharma teachings effectively well before all their kleśas have been removed. Occasionally, the teacher's kleśas will break out just as much as they would with an ordinary person. Part of the problem is that the role of the teacher makes it difficult for them to speak honestly about their own level of development. It may not seem appropriate to reveal to students the areas in which they're not fully developed yet.

That's why I think it's very important that teachers have a peer group within which they can talk honestly about their own practice and the things they're working with. In the absence of their peer group, where they can share honestly, teachers can get too identified with their role and what they are teaching. As a result, they can believe they're farther along the path than they really are. That's when it gets dangerous. Some degree of honesty and sharing about one's own imperfections is necessary to keep teachers on an even keel.

ZENKEI BLANCHE HARTMAN: Whether we share them or not, our students see them. So we may as well share them.

RINGU TULKU: It's also true that the exercise of compassion is not always so soft and nice. It can be expressed in a very rough-and-tough fashion. Out of compassion, the teacher may have to be a disciplinarian, be stern, offer punishment, and even show anger toward students. It's not necessary that the teacher actually be angry but that the teacher shows the anger.

Not every teacher is at the same level. I have had the opportunity to train with very great masters. You could really see and feel how realized they were, but all teachers are not at that level. This has to be understood very clearly. Students might assume that whatever problems the teacher has are being handled. They might project that the teacher is highly realized, beyond their actual ability.

You cannot be a perfect teacher unless you are completely enlightened. But when you have something to share—and there are not many people who can share this kind of thing—you should teach. Even though some of my students are not very advanced, I encourage them to share whatever they understand with people who understand less. A problem only arises if you become too proud and start to think of yourself as a teacher, not a student. I never think of myself as a teacher. I think of myself as a student who is sharing my little bit of understanding.

So you experience the occasional kleśa, would you say?

RINGU TULKU: Of course. Why not? Constantly.

10

At the End:
The Practice of Old Age and Death

DZOGCHEN PONLOP RINPOCHE ▪ FRANK OSTASESKI
JAN CHOZEN BAYS, ROSHI ▪ VEN. AJAHN AMARO

Why do we have such difficulty understanding that we're aging all the time? Is it possible to embrace this notion without becoming debilitated or depressed?

DZOGCHEN PONLOP RINPOCHE: In general, we lack an understanding of impermanent nature. Culture and religion can reinforce that. In many religions, we seek eternal existence. We keep looking for methods to enable us to go against the law of nature, which is impermanence.

Aging can be appreciated. As you age, your ego-centered and unreasonable impulses start to mellow; you can become tamer, calmer, and more compromising. Relationships age in the same way. In the beginning, you start out fighting for your own agenda, and at some point you mellow into a more cooperative approach.

FRANK OSTASESKI: Getting old isn't easy, and neither is sickness or death. One of the inevitable experiences of getting old is loss, which leads to grieving. For most of us, our self-image is tied to the physical. When it starts to change, we fight against it, and some of us in spiritual communities try to use spiritual concepts as a bypass that actually avoids facing the loss. Instead, we could just feel the loss.

JAN CHOZEN BAYS, ROSHI: Many of us have had a to-do list for a long time, things to get to later. But at some point we realize we're not going to get to those things later. We have to jettison some of those projects, and they can be hard to let go of. One woman I visited recently who was just days away from dying of liver cancer told me, "I always intended to practice later, and now there is no later."

Are there any instructions for young people to help them begin to appreciate aging as early as possible?

VEN. AJAHN AMARO: One of the standard daily recollections in the Theravāda tradition is: "I am of the nature to become sick; I am of the nature to die; all that is mine, beloved, and pleasing will become otherwise, will become separated from me."

That may sound like an extremely depressing thing to think of, but for young people particularly, it's helpful to bring that into consciousness. It helps them to realize that this is the deal, the contract we all sign, the rules of the game. Bringing that into consciousness helps illuminate our presumption that we should not decline or experience grief.

FRANK OSTASESKI: One of the improvisational methods we used with students we were teaching to do hospice work was to ask them to act old. They all hunched over and mimicked being weak and fragile.

Those of us who are getting older need to speak of the beauty of being older. I just went through a series of heart attacks, and the greatest gift that's come out of that for me is a deeper appreciation of vulnerability. That is usually seen as weakness, but I'm experiencing it as a kind of porousness, of feeling less defended, less armored. If we can impart to younger people the gift of that vulnerability, it may help them to embrace aging.

No matter how much we may appreciate the beneficial qualities of aging, old age brings some definite diminished capacity. Is there any practice advice that can help us deal with this difficult time?

JAN CHOZEN BAYS, ROSHI: In our practice communities, I feel that we need to make adjustments so that people who are older can continue to hear and practice the Dharma. We may have to amplify talks more and provide some less rigorous schedules and ways of sitting. The loss of your spiritual life can be a great sorrow, and we ought not to hasten that for people.

And when the time comes that we need help, we can accept it. One student asked me, in great anxiety, "How will I practice if I get Alzheimer's?" I responded, "At that point, you'll be somebody else's practice." We can release our desire to always be in control.

VEN. AJAHN AMARO: In the United States, the culture of independence is enormously strong, and needing to be helped by another represents a state of weakness and diminution. But if we see the illusion of control, if we see that we're never really in control, then as our faculties diminish, we can appreciate giving others the opportunity to practice generosity.

DZOGCHEN PONLOP RINPOCHE: It's interesting to see how our labeling mind works. When does old age begin? Retirement age? When we first get really sick? When we lose our childhood friend? From the day we're born, we're aging and getting old. There's no benchmark we can precisely define.

We need to have a sense of humor and not take our labels so seriously. It's also important to loosen the strong sense of needing to be independent. Everything is interdependent. Even buying something at the grocery store with our own money is not an independent act. It's connected to so many other people and factors, so many causes and conditions that come together to make it possible. Once we have that understanding and appreciation of interdependence, it won't be difficult to accept help from other people when we need it.

JAN CHOZEN BAYS, ROSHI: When my mother was in a retirement home and then an assisted care facility, I saw a lot of old people. Those who were still relying on the mind, the discursive mind, and dredging up old stories again and again, struggled. But the people who had a warm heart, who could only sit there and couldn't carry on a conversation, those were the people you wanted to be near, like a warm fireplace. It's important to cultivate the heart as we get older, because that's what will last.

FRANK OSTASESKI: When I'm holding the hand of someone very old, I notice that their skin is almost transparent, and it's as if their being becomes that way as well. It's as if the wind could blow right through them, and there isn't much that's obscuring who they actually are. In the aging process, we can't sustain the energy that's required to maintain our self-image. It can't be propped up anymore. So aging, sickness, and even death are conducive to our opening. It's vital that we reflect on this and reflect that back to the person who's aging, not in some imposing way, but simply by appreciating it.

JAN CHOZEN BAYS, ROSHI: Cherry blossoms in Japan are appreciated for their transient quality. The poignancy of the briefness of their bloom and their falling is what is beautiful. The very fading of the beauty we want to hold on to is the beauty.

What's important to emphasize in the dying process, whether our own or someone close to us?

DZOGCHEN PONLOP RINPOCHE: We're all dying. Whether you're enlightened or confused, rich or poor, you will die. That's the number one thing we need to completely accept. Secondly, we need to see how we cling to this life, and how we can let go of that clinging.

At the time of death, it's important to have a peaceful environment and a calm and gentle mind. There are many teachings and practices we could do, but the heart of the matter is keeping the mind clear and peaceful. It's said that your last thought is the most important, because that is what will join your mindstream from this life to the next.

FRANK OSTASESKI: In the chaos of illness, one calm person in the room can make all the difference. When we help a sick person, moving them from the bed to the commode, for example, we lend them our body, the strength of our arms and legs. But we can also lend them the concentration and stability of our minds, and the confidence and fearlessness of our hearts. We can open and expand our hearts, which can inspire the other person to open theirs in a similar way. We become a refuge, a presence that restores trust in the patient's capacity to heal, to come to wholeness.

In our hospitals and care facilities, we're so ready to problem-solve and fix things that we often encourage the person who's sick or dying to see himself or herself as broken. When we attend to dying people, we need to help reflect their intrinsic wholeness. Through grace and love, we can help them with the obstacles in front of them. We can be a portal through which they travel to what they feel most disconnected from. Above all, we can love them when they cannot remember to love themselves.

VEN. AJAHN AMARO: What really seems to help is just to be a simple, pure, caring presence and let go of all the stuff we think we should be doing.

Sometimes people, including Buddhists, can be quite doctrinal about how to approach dying.

FRANK OSTASESKI: It's a kind of fundamentalism. I ran the first Buddhist hospice in America, so believe me, I saw Buddhists many times trying to impose their idea on a poor dying person. Everybody who is dying has a story about how one dies, and that story shapes the way they die. It helps to discover more about the story someone is holding and to work with it, rather than to try to change it or impose some other story.

JAN CHOZEN BAYS, ROSHI: It's helpful to remember that whatever your idea is of a good death, there's no guarantee you're going to have that. Yes, preparing is good. If you prepare for a natural childbirth, chances are better that you'll have a natural childbirth, but there is no guarantee. It's the same with death. If you prepare in a sane way and do practices around it, chances are higher that you will have a death that is more serene and involves less anguish for people around you. But we must never forget that the next moment is unknown. If we practice stepping into the unknown, moment by moment, hour by hour, year by year, millions of times, then death is just the next step into the unknown. It loses its terror.

We must also learn not to run away from the inevitable pain but to move into it. We need to take apart the sensations of pain and discover that pain is not a solid object. The confidence we get from knowing the impermanence of pain, from seeing how interesting it can be, replaces anxiety, which makes for a much better time when you're sick or dying.

DZOGCHEN PONLOP RINPOCHE: The greatest fear about dying is the unknown. It helps to see that this unknown territory is something we should be interested in exploring. Like pioneers, we need to explore this new, unknown territory of mind. When we open to that, we lessen the fear and preconceptions we have about unknown territory.

Are the Tibetan teachings about death primarily about what happens to us after we die, or are they about the fact that we are going through birth and death all the time?

DZOGCHEN PONLOP RINPOCHE: The *bardo* teachings are about both of those. These teachings, however, are frequently misunderstood. People take the descriptions of this deity and that deity appearing very literally, but these teachings that come out of a particular framework of symbols. In each manifestation, the deity described is connected with an expression of the enlightened nature of mind, such as transcendence, compassion, wisdom, and love.

One of my teachers, a Dzogchen master, told me that it's not true that all sentient beings experience these deities. That is not the fundamental meaning of these teachings. The bardo teachings are about relating with the nature of mind. In deity meditation, the most important thing is to connect the symbolism with the pure nature of the world. We call this practice "remembering the purity." It is a practice of recalling the pure nature of the aspects of mind that are represented by the deities.

According to Vajrayāna, at the moment of death and after death we have tremendous opportunity to experience the enlightened nature of mind. This nature can be experienced in many different forms and in the form of different types of light, as has been described by people who have had near-death experiences. What is described in the *Tibetan Book of the Dead* (*Bar do thos grol*) is a symbolic representation of this process. I've tried to clarify that in my book *Mind Beyond Death*.

The bardo teachings also tell us that having a meaningful and good process of dying depends largely on having a meaningful and good process of living. If we have lived our life fully in a wholesome way with virtuous and compassionate and loving practices, our rebirth will be positive, if there is such a thing.

What do other Buddhist traditions say about what happens after death?

VEN. AJAHN AMARO: In the Theravāda texts, it's less spelled out than it is in the Tibetan texts, but there is the recognition that the faculties fade out one by one at the moment of death, with hearing being the final one to go. Another principle we recognize is that what the mind fixates on at the end has a strong effect on what the future destination might be. In his teaching on "reappearance through aspiration," the Buddha says if you really want to gravitate to a particular realm, you can do that through the power of your mind. But this kind of activity is for the virtuous, not the unvirtuous. You have to have done your homework and not have too many outstanding debts, as it were.

FRANK OSTASESKI: Most of the people I've worked with have some notion of what is sacred to them, whether they live within a religious or nonreligious context. I try to discover what is sacred for them. The sacred is not something separate or different from other things. It is rather hidden in things, so dying becomes an opportunity to discover the sacredness that is hidden all around us. It becomes this process of gradually removing obscurations that block our capacity to see the truth of what was already there. This process can be facilitated by a good relationship between the person giving care and the dying person.

VEN. AJAHN AMARO: Sometimes the doctrine of rebirth can be threatening, particularly if it's coming from an authority figure. It can be encouraging but it can also be threatening. The more applicable teaching is to focus on the sense that when we meet the unknown from a perspective of self-view, from the ego-centered perspective, what arises is fear. But when we meet the unknown with heart, we experience wonderment. So I try to encourage letting go of self-centered perspectives and instead coming more from the heart, which makes us open to the mystery of what will unfold, rather than feeling we must have a defined image of what's out there to look forward to. All that does is compound self-view.

What is the most important element in the relationship between the dying person and the caregiver?

FRANK OSTASESKI: Compassion doesn't have an agenda. It doesn't have judgments or "shoulds" or a concern for what's "right." It expresses the kindness that's necessary for our hearts to open, and for the heart of the dying person to open. Without that compassion, the heart won't open to its suffering. It just simply won't open to the pain, in the way Chozen was talking about earlier. As a caregiver, my task is to attune myself as closely as possible to where the other person is in that moment and not to try to lead them anywhere, and certainly not try to lead them away from their suffering. We don't really serve a person by taking them away from their suffering. We serve them by helping them come into contact with it.

Dying is a matter of relationship—to ourselves, to those we love, to God, spirit, buddha nature, however we frame our image of ultimate kindness. This process is characterized much more by mystery than mastery. Of course, when we're dying, it's good to have mastery, somebody who knows what they're doing, but that won't be enough. When I'm dying, I'll want somebody there who can help me explore the territory of meaning, to help me understand what's had value and purpose in my life. But there's a point in the dying process where meaning falls away completely. At that point, I'll want somebody who's comfortable in the territory of mystery, of unanswerable questions. I'll want somebody who's comfortable in not knowing.

DHARMA:

The Teachings

11

More than Just Sitting:
The Importance of Study

BHANTE GUNARATANA ▪ **JOHN DAIDO LOORI, ROSHI**
GEORGES DREYFUS ▪ **CHRISTINA FELDMAN**

Buddhism is known as a tradition that places great value on meditative experience. How important is study to the practice of Buddhism?

BHANTE GUNARATANA: Our ideal situation is to have good knowledge of the Dharma and a good amount of practice, combined together—there must be a balance. We cannot do one at the expense of the other.

That being said, the problem in the West is that many people don't study the Dharma. They think that they can learn Dharma by focusing the mind on breathing and doing nothing else, and they have no knowledge of what the Buddha taught. People who are neglecting study are not that spiritually mature, though, and until their perfections are complete, they need to know what the Buddha taught.

When we start learning meditation, we all come across situations where we get confused. We don't really know how to solve the problems we encounter. So then we have to look at the texts and see how Buddha solved those problems. Before he had any enlightenment, he was very much like us. He always had problems, just like we have, and whenever he had problems he found a solution. Since we are not enlightened, when we have a problem we must go to see the way the Buddha solved his problems. This is how knowledge of Dharma comes in handy when we do the practice.

JOHN DAIDO LOORI, ROSHI: The Zen tradition is probably the one best known for special transmission outside of words and letters, a direct realization of buddhahood derived from Bodhidharma, around 500 CE. That special transmission has for the most part defined Zen in both China and Japan. In fact, I've actually studied in Rinzai monasteries where the library was locked most of the time, and people were discouraged from putting too much emphasis on words and letters.

However, we're not in a Buddhist culture in America, so it is necessary to include a pretty comprehensive training in academic study. At Zen Mountain Monastery, our Eight Gates of training includes a good dose of what we call "academic study." This is not only for the monastics but also for lay practitioners.

The tendency of students in the West has been, when they hear certain words and terms in Buddhism, to equate those with the Judeo-Christian tradition, which is what we're familiar with. As a result, they can come to conclusions that aren't accurate. So in addition to studying the sutras that are important to Zen training, we also study the Abhidharma teachings and some of the sutras from Theravāda Buddhism, because these are sutras that were taken up by some of the ancient Zen masters, such as Dōgen.

In Zen Buddhism there was a traditional saying that "painted cakes"—that is, words—"do not satisfy hunger." Dōgen, in the thirteenth century, said painted cakes do indeed satisfy hunger, and aside from painted cakes there's no way to satisfy hunger. So he took a very different point of view from that normally found in Zen.

GEORGES DREYFUS: In the Tibetan tradition, one can distinguish two main approaches: one where establishing the view precedes meditation practice (*from the view looking through meditation*) and one where the view arises from meditation practice (*looking for the view through meditation*). The first is a classical, scholastic approach in which one first studies and then one practices. The second one is reserved for a few people who, under the guidance of a teacher, practice meditation without extensive study and then attempt to gain realization in that way.

Contrary to what is often thought, the more scholastic approach is found in all four traditions of Tibetan Buddhism. In fact, the dominant approach has been the one laid out by Bhante—studying extensively and from there trying to meditate and gain realization.

There are, however, people who have resolutely attempted to gain realization without much study. The point that Daido Loori Roshi made is very relevant. It's quite misleading to take these rare examples of people from traditionally Buddhist cultures gaining realization without extensive study and apply these to Western practitioners. In the Tibetan tradition, the dominant model by far is the first one, where one first studies and then practices. This would also be a good model for us.

CHRISTINA FELDMAN: My experience is drawn mainly from two traditions. When I first began to practice in the Gelukpa tradition of Vajrayāna Buddhism, I anticipated being immediately introduced into great tantric initiations and so forth, but my teacher at that time didn't encourage much meditation practice at all. The emphasis was much more on the academic understanding of Buddhist philosophy. Meditation was introduced slowly.

After a time, I began to train more in the Theravādin meditation community, where there was something of a reversal going on at that time. The emphasis in Theravāda was more on direct, intuitive experience. I found these to be quite radically different approaches. Having made my home more within the Theravādin tradition, and particularly the meditative tradition, it's been interesting for me to see how the question of the relationship between practice and study has been evolving. I guide students based on an intensive meditative tradition, but within that context, there's a great deal of teaching of Buddhist philosophy—*sīla, samādhi, paññā.* I sense a thirst for understanding in many people who began with intensive meditation experience. They seem to want to put that experience into a meaningful context.

Do you find some resistance to study among Western students?

BHANTE GUNARATANA: Things have changed from forty or even twenty years ago. Those were the days when people were tired of going to university and getting degrees. Many of them were the ones who became interested in meditation. They were also the ones who wanted to attain enlightenment very quickly, and who therefore did not think academic study was that important.

Of course, when it comes to Buddhist learning, we are not talking about secular academic degrees or qualifications but rather simple learning. More than ever before, it is true that people have begun to realize the importance of learning Dharma. Though there still are some students who think all they have to do is meditation, among the students who practice with us, most are very interested in learning the Dharma.

JOHN DAIDO LOORI, ROSHI: I haven't experienced resistance to academic study. Most students these days are professionals of one type or another. They're college-educated. They're accustomed to studying. They tend to want to intellectualize things. That's why the balance is so important. So at Zen Mountain, academic study is just one of eight gates. Zazen, sitting meditation, is the core of the whole thing. Liturgy is an important gate. Ethical teaching is an important gate. Body practice is an important gate. Face-to-face teaching with the teacher is also important. These things all balance themselves out.

Academic study is a required part of the daily routine during our ninety-day intensives, but people both in residence and at home can do academic study or not. By and large, they choose to do it, because they're much more comfortable with it than they are with the mysterious realms of sitting meditation, where they don't have any kind of reference system. With study, it's something they can nail down.

CHRISTINA FELDMAN: Twenty or twenty-five years ago one encountered a lot of resistance to study. There was a belief system that valued transcendent mystical experience above everything else—as a kind of fast track to enlightenment. That kind of thinking has changed considerably over the years. Many who are practicing now have a great deal of respect for investigation as a means to awakening. They have found that investigation is not just about having an experience; it's a much broader, much deeper, much vaster way of coming to understand the Dharma.

I do sense there are two schools of thought, although I would acknowledge some convergence between the two. One we could call the "meditation" school. People sit on a cushion, they walk, they practice, and this is essentially what they're looking for. It fulfills their expectations. The other school is the "Dharma" school, in which meditation is a part of a larger picture, which is sīla, samādhi, and paññā. My sense at the moment is that the "dharma" school is becoming more prominent than the school that only values inner experience.

Since there are many more lay practitioners than monastics, is there a different course of study that is appropriate for laypeople?

BHANTE GUNARATANA: Whether people are monastics or lay practitioners, there are three levels of development: learning what is taught by the Buddha (*pariyatti*), putting it into practice (*paṭipatti*), and realizing it (*paṭivedha*).

We can do these three at the same time. We don't have to spend a great deal of time studying first, and then start practicing, and then go on to realizing. As we learn, we practice and we realize. This is the Buddha's scheme, and it is good for both monastics and householders.

Some people are so busy, however, that they become impatient. They want to achieve something very quickly; therefore, they overlook the first two steps, learning and practicing. They want to realize very quickly. That is the problem most people face, whether Western or Eastern, so I have been suggesting to monastics and some laypeople that they must follow a curriculum of very rigorous book study. There also has to be ongoing daily practice that can be followed by anybody without too much academic or rigorous book study.

Contemplation itself is meditation, because we incorporate the message into our life. The Dharma must be kept alive in our daily life, in our thoughts, words, and deeds. In my upbringing, long before we even knew our alphabet, we knew a lot of Pali chanting and Dharma verses from our tradition. The very first thing we heard when we woke up in the morning was our parents reciting something very beautiful, very peaceful, wishing goodwill, peace, solace, and comfort for the world.

The teachings of the Buddha are very practical. The noble eightfold path is not a theory; it is practice. We have to learn to put the teachings into practice. Somebody can philosophize about the teachings, can psychologize about the teachings, but what Buddha taught is a real and practical.

JOHN DAIDO LOORI, ROSHI: Because most people lead very busy lives, many of them will gravitate to the kind of training that just requires sitting fifteen minutes a day or visiting a center once a month to sit or listen to a talk. For example, we have a Sunday program, and it fills a niche in many people's lives, replacing the Sabbath. That's the only time we see them, though. They never really enter into training.

There are other lay practitioners who are a lot more serious and decide to become students. They're required to make a commitment not only to meditation practice but also to engage in our program, the Eight Gates of Zen. We track them and we keep student records. After a period of time, we can tell just by reviewing the records what they need to give more attention to. If we find out that they're just paying dues and not being active, we tell them to save their money and not continue.

There's a whole spectrum of students, then, from monastics, who have made a lifetime commitment, to lay practitioners who have families and jobs, and everything in between. A realistic training program has to address the needs of this very diverse group. We try to do that by using many different venues, so the training doesn't only take place at the monastery. It's on the Web, it's in journals and books, and it's available through affiliate groups around the country.

Whether the students are lay or monastic, they need to be clear about what they are committing to. If people are looking for psychological counseling, they should see a psychologist. If they are looking for physical well-being, they should go to a health spa. If, however, they come with a question—Who am I? What is life? What is death?—then they're asking religious questions, and that's what we do. That's what we're trained for and that's what we can help them with. Physical and psychological well-being may be byproducts, but the initial force for studying and practicing Buddhism must be religious.

CHRISTINA FELDMAN: Historically, a dedicated, vigorous religious life was considered to be the territory of monastics, those who had renounced the world. Currently we have a different paradigm. We have a large community trying to find a way to lead a dedicated spiritual life in the midst of a busy lay life. There has never been a blueprint before for how to do this.

My sense is that there is a very powerful link between rigor and inspiration. If people feel inspired, a great deal of effort and commitment comes out of that inspiration. So the role of meditative communities is not merely to teach people how to sit on the cushion. It's about how to nurture and cultivate the necessary level of inspiration, so that people find the way to be rigorous and dedicated. In our study program, we mentor people throughout a two-year period. They also have homework that does not simply test knowledge; it is reflective, applied homework. The reports we are getting from the mentors tell us that this study process is nurturing inspiration. People are making far more effort in their practice and the application of the practice than they did when they were only attending meditation retreats.

GEORGES DREYFUS: The Tibetan tradition is in transition. It is a very complex tradition and it was moved pretty abruptly from a very traditional Buddhist society to the modern West and exile in India. The various Tibetan Buddhist groups are trying to deal with this transition by developing curricula for this new kind of mostly-lay student, but this is still a work in progress. Even how Western monks should be educated is still not a completely clear and settled question.

Do you believe that a philosophical tradition as complex as Vajrayāna Buddhism can be adapted without being "dumbed down"?

GEORGES DREYFUS: It is adaptable, but it's not going to be easy and it's not going to be quick. Until recently, Westerners have dealt mostly with people who were completely steeped in a traditional culture, who have had less sense of what is required in a modern context. The transition we are talking about does not just involve Tibetans and Westerners, it's also among Tibetans, who have gone through the trauma of invasion, destruction, and exile. How is the Tibetan tradition of learning going to survive and transform as Tibetan society modernizes and changes? I guess we have to be optimistic. Buddhism is, after all, an export product. It remakes itself in very different social and cultural contexts.

Finally, how does study, as opposed to meditation practice, contribute to realization?

CHRISTINA FELDMAN: People tend to transfer their habitual patterns both to how they meditate and how they study. There are different ways of approaching study. There are different ways of approaching meditation. They can be approached in a materialistic way, as a way of accumulating more concepts or more meditation experiences. They can be approached in a greedy way.

Meditation and study are both means to transform those habitual patterns of mind. Though our initial approaches may not be so skilled or even so wholesome, they can be transformed through the simple willingness to begin. Then both meditation and study can be approached in a very reflective way. Approaching study in a very reflective way, sitting with some teaching as one would with a kōan, can bring the mind to great stillness and receptivity. At the same time, approaching meditation in a very reflective, investigative way can open us to levels of understanding not previously accessible.

GEORGES DREYFUS: A great deal depends on how one studies. It's very important that the study remain connected to practice. When I was in the monastery I remember our teachers constantly emphasizing that, because it's so possible to go astray.

It's also important to be clear about what study means. Study traditionally means hearing, reflecting, and meditating. Different people gain different things from different aspects of the tradition. A great deal of insight can be attained in study and a great deal of understanding can be developed through practice. Once again, it is important to balance study and meditation, while recognizing that individuals, based on their particular dispositions, may benefit more from one aspect or the other.

12

How Does Suffering End?
The Meaning of the Third Noble Truth

ANDREW OLENDZKI

ZENKEI BLANCHE HARTMAN

GAYLON FERGUSON

Since the Third Noble Truth is about the cessation of suffering, we should first discuss what suffering really means.

ANDREW OLENDZKI: Suffering (*dukkha*) covers a wide spectrum, from physical pain, aging, and getting ill or injured up through the suffering that comes from change and on to the psychological suffering that results when we don't get what we want or when things go the way we don't want them to. Finally, it includes the suffering occasioned by great existential issues, like the fact that we're all going to die. Suffering is primarily the resistance to the truth of those things.

ZENKEI BLANCHE HARTMAN: We all experience old age, sickness, and death, which are classical categories of suffering. No one is free from those. The Buddha says that suffering is simply present in our life. It's not right or wrong or good or bad. It's just our experience.

GAYLON FERGUSON: Traditionally, we say there are three kinds of suffering: the suffering of suffering; the suffering of change; and fundamental or all-pervasive suffering.

The suffering of suffering means that if we burn our finger, it hurts. The suffering of change is the alternation from one condition to another, and the change can go both ways: from a pleasurable condition to something painful, or from something painful—that we nevertheless get accustomed to—to a happier state. That instability alone is suffering, which leads us to the third kind of suffering, our struggle against things as they are.

So the fundamental suffering, the suffering of fixation, one could say, has to do with the fact that we are attempting to solidify what is a fluid and impermanent situation. That happens even in moments of apparent happiness, if we are holding on to those moments. Traditionally, it is said that with practice one becomes more sensitive to this basic suffering. Initially, it might be like a hair touching the hand, but for the wise, this fundamental suffering is like a hair touching the eye.

Why is the first kind called the suffering of suffering?

GAYLON FERGUSON: The original phrase is simply *dukkhadukkha*, the pain of pain.

ANDREW OLENDZKI: When these words are put side by side, they're being used in two different ways. The first just means pain, as in pleasure (*sukha*) and pain. That level of pain is never going to go away. Even on his deathbed, the Buddha said, "My body is wracked with pain right now." Pain is a feeling tone, which is one of the aggregates. It's hardwired into the mechanism of the human mind and body, you might say.

But when you put the second word after it, *dukkhadukkha*, then it's used in the other sense. Pain is inevitable, but the distress caused by that physical pain will go away when you're enlightened. So in the phrase *dukkhadukkha*, the first dukkha is simple pain and the second dukkha is the resistance to that pain.

GAYLON FERGUSON: In fact, these kinds of pain are intertwined; we can't actually separate out a given physical pain from the resistance and struggle with it. If there were less struggle or no struggle, what would that original pain be like? We don't know what an enlightened person experiences in terms of so-called physical pain.

ZENKEI BLANCHE HARTMAN: The famous kōan of Baizhang's Fox indicates that an enlightened person doesn't ignore pain. I recall when Suzuki Roshi was dying with cancer, I was with him and noticed that he grimaced as if he were having some physical pain. When it subsided he said, "Hmm, my karma is not so good" instead of "Oh my god, this is so terrible! Why me?"

Yet even fledgling practitioners can transform their relationship to pain to a certain degree, can't they?

GAYLON FERGUSON: Of course, mindfulness-based stress reduction has shown that when mindfulness lessens the struggle with chronic pain, the pain is somehow lessened.

ANDREW OLENDZKI: Dharma practice is intended to help us to stop stabbing ourselves with the second arrow, rather than concerning ourselves with the arrow that has already penetrated us, as the traditional analogy goes. The physical pain is inevitable, but as we resist it or feel sorry for ourselves or wish it were different, we continue to jab ourselves. That's the emotional suffering we experience in the face of the pain.

Having discussed the nature of suffering and of conditioned existence, how do we understand cessation in that context?

ANDREW OLENDZKI: The idea of cessation does obviously invite the question, "Cessation of what?" There's a lot of confusion and misunderstanding throughout the Buddhist tradition about what we mean by that. For example, you have the issues that came up in China at the time of the founding of the Zen tradition when the Northern School of Chan essentially said that if we empty our mind of thoughts, we'll be free of suffering. The Southern School said that if you empty your mind of thoughts, you're just like a rock or a stone. This led to the distinction that there is an emptying of the mind, but what is emptied is the resistance to what is happening, rather than what is happening itself.

The Buddha was very clear that cessation of suffering is not being without consciousness and perception and all the rest of it. What happened to him under the Bodhi Tree, as I understand it, is that he became an altered person.

He still had a body like the rest of us; he still had the five aggregates. What ceased was wanting things to be different than they were, which is craving.

GAYLON FERGUSON: In the *Heart Sutra*, Śāriputra gives a pithy synopsis of what the Buddha taught: "Regarding dharmas that arise from a cause, the Tathāgatha taught their cause and also their cessation." That's a lion's roar proclamation that we are not doomed to struggling and fighting with life. There is another possibility.

ZENKEI BLANCHE HARTMAN: David Brazier talks about cessation (*nirodha*) as originally meaning an earthen bank. He offers the image of being down behind a sheltering bank of earth or putting a bank around something so as to both confine and protect it, like containing or controlling a fire.

ANDREW OLENDZKI: As a skillful means, that might be very effective, but containment as an image seems too limiting. For a householder trying to get by in the day-to-day world, there are ways in which the experience of dissatisfaction can be contained—through stress reduction and wiser choices, for example. But what's radical and inspiring about the Buddha's message is that the fundamental mechanisms in our mind and body that construct suffering can in fact be dismantled. The roots can be pulled up from the lowest levels, such that the suffering is no longer constructed at all.

ZENKEI BLANCHE HARTMAN: What I like about the containment image is that we can talk about the fire of passion and not needing to put it out, because fire is useful. If it can be contained and controlled, if you put it in the oven, you can cook with it. But you want to protect it, to keep the wind of greed, hate, and delusion from blowing it out of all proportion. At the same time, you don't want the embers to go dead. You want to employ them for a useful purpose.

Doesn't that sidestep the notion of extinguishing?

GAYLON FERGUSON: Can't we have both? Yes, there is pulling up by the root and extinguishing, but in the *Lankāvatāra Sutra* it says, "Skillful farmers don't throw away their manure. They use it." They spread it on the field of *bodhi*. So the containment is the sense that the basic energy could be used for waking up.

If you're not stopping the fire, what are you stopping?

ANDREW OLENDZKI: I think it is the fire that you're stopping. The three unwholesome roots of greed, hatred, and delusion—these three fires are blazing across the whole field of experience. Awakening and nirvana has to do with extinguishing the fires. But we have to be careful not to be too hard on ourselves. Just because the Buddha says it's possible for these fires to go out, it doesn't mean we should expect it to happen by Tuesday.

More to the point, he's saying this fire is burning in almost every moment of your experience. You are craving, and therefore you are suffering. Just come to know it, understand it, befriend it. You're not encouraging it to continue *per se*, but rather you're being at home with it. It's not so much about an ideal state where this just doesn't happen, although that is a placeholder at the end of the path; it's more about what is happening every moment.

Notice that. Look at it. Learn from it. Understand it. Experiment with how you can hold yourself differently in any given situation to diminish its effect. It's really a matter of how to play with fire, rather than how to extinguish it. But when you play with it long enough and skillfully enough, it goes out.

GAYLON FERGUSON: It's very helpful not to beat yourself up if you're not getting to it. If we are contemplating our experience and inquiring into our experience, we will notice it, just as the historical Buddha did when he remembered a time sitting under a tree at the plowing festival, when he had a moment of cessation, stopping.

ZENKEI BLANCHE HARTMAN: That's true. Most students, most of us, have had some taste of that.

GAYLON FERGUSON: People can recall a glimpse. I'm not saying they've had full or final cessation, but they can recall a moment of not struggling.

ZENKEI BLANCHE HARTMAN: And because they've had some taste of it, they turn to practice and they can breathe freely in the world. They have a taste of dropping the boundary that separates me from other. They can feel that expansive inclusiveness, the interconnectedness of everything with everything. We have experiences like that, but we don't know what they are or what to call them.

The Third Noble Truth has sometimes been called the "the goal." Does that make sense?

ZENKEI BLANCHE HARTMAN: The idea of goal kind of jangles me when I remember how strongly Suzuki Roshi said, "No gaining idea, no goal-seeking mind." Practice is about fully opening ourselves and accepting what is, as it is, in all its stuffness.

GAYLON FERGUSON: According to the teachings of Dōgen, that's not a goal but rather our original state, right?

ZENKEI BLANCHE HARTMAN: To have some gaining idea or goal means that as you are right now is not OK.

ANDREW OLENDZKI: I would add that since we construct our reality every single moment, and the five aggregates arise again with or without the influence of craving and ignorance, there are multiple moments throughout the day in which you could experience cessation. It could be the cessation of one of the defilements, one of the obstacles. For example, you could be sitting in meditation and your foot starts hurting. You see the physical sensation mounting along with your resistance to it, and your concern around it becomes more and more proliferated. At a certain point, you can recontextualize what's happening, let go of the resistance to it, and settle in to what's actually happening. In that moment, the whole complex of resistance to that sensation ceases, and in the next moment something new is created. Perhaps we overdramatize the idea of what this whole awakening experience is. Well, maybe not the Zen tradition.

Like with everything else in the Buddhist tradition, this notion is useful as a verb and harmful as a noun. Teaching people how to have things cease is very useful. It's very dynamic and alive. Getting fixated on the notion of cessation as a noun, either occurring or not occurring or being attained or not attained, is heading in the wrong direction.

But cessation is essentially nirvana, which is a state, or at least a noun?

ANDREW OLENDZKI: Actually, it's more often used as an adjective in the Pali canon, applied to a person who has become quenched. The fires have been quenched, extinguished; they're cool. They've become cool.

All we're saying is that nirvana is what the Buddha attained under the Bodhi Tree, and that there's incremental progress toward it. But I don't see it as a state in the sense that, you know, I slipped into nirvana for an hour or two. There are also gradations—stream-enterer, nonreturner, and so forth.

GAYLON FERGUSON: Dzongsar Khyentse talks about the classic four marks of view in his book *Why You Are Not a Buddhist*, and the fourth one is "nirvana is peace." He emphasizes that nirvana is beyond conception.

ZENKEI BLANCHE HARTMAN: I would call it the inconceivable.

GAYLON FERGUSON: Yes. It's certainly not our concept of happiness.

ZENKEI BLANCHE HARTMAN: My actual experience is that after a number of years of practice, I'm a hell of a lot happier than I was before I started practicing. That's undeniable. My teacher named me Zenkei, which means total joy, and at the time I asked myself what the heck he named me that for. Now I really appreciate it, because there is a lot of joy in my life.

Isn't the ego's search for happiness the very root of suffering?

GAYLON FERGUSON: I'm sure we all agree that seeking happiness is the cause of a lot of suffering. That's classic Buddhadharma. The very struggle to always be in any particular state is what the Second Noble Truth is about. Yet it makes sense to start where people are and lead them to something deeper. Then we can open into a wider sense of what happiness is. Happiness isn't just the limited positive states we strive for, but rather there is a larger openness that includes sorrow and joy. That would be true happiness.

The conventional understanding of happiness is materialistic, but people come to realize that a good life actually might be a life based on compassion and serving others. And indeed, longtime practitioners often do say there is more happiness in their lives.

ANDREW OLENDZKI: Our word "happiness" is probably too limited. With "suffering," we were saying that there's physical pain and then there's the resistance to that, which is a greater existential meaning of *dukkha*. Maybe the same could be said for pleasure. There's physical pleasure and mental pleasure, but the Buddha was saying that it's possible to cultivate a mind that's larger and more balanced in the face of either pleasure or displeasure. It's a matter of getting to a wider mind that can embrace both and still experience profound well-being. Well-being is not necessarily the same as happiness. Happiness is just a matter of stringing together pleasant moments.

Compared to happiness, isn't the truth of suffering an off-putting place to begin presenting the Dharma?

ZENKEI BLANCHE HARTMAN: Not necessarily. Acknowledging suffering can set up a connection among us, the sense that we're all in this boat together.

GAYLON FERGUSON: In a consumerist culture, you wouldn't usually deliver a product by beginning with unhappiness. But of course the teachings of Buddhism do go against the stream that there is pleasure and then greater pleasure and then greater pleasure after that.

ANDREW OLENDZKI: In my experience, it's not a very good place to start. Trying to convince Americans of the truth of suffering is no small challenge. So many people are insulated from it, or have thought their way around it, that it's an uphill struggle.

GAYLON FERGUSON: Not all teachings begin with the truth of suffering. In the buddha nature teachings, one begins with nonstruggle, basic sanity, as the basis. Then one might proceed to discovering how we've covered over our fundamental nature, open spacious awareness, through habits of karma and kleśa. We have become constricted and we struggle. The Buddha taught a variety of skillful means for different beings, and the Four Noble Truths we are familiar with is one such skillful means. In the *Flower Garland Sutra*, a slightly different version of the Four Noble Truths is presented, from the buddha nature viewpoint.

ANDREW OLENDZKI: In the classical teachings, the Four Noble Truths is not so much the beginning point as the ending point. It summarizes the essential insights that the Buddha had that brought about his awakening. I find it more effective to mention the truth of suffering halfway through the curriculum rather than on the first day. At that point, we understood enough to know how much we're kidding ourselves and constructing an illusionary life. We can see that underneath the illusions we create is the tangible experience of discomfort.

The goal of Buddhism is sometimes described as the lessening of suffering. Is that a sufficient description of cessation?

ZENKEI BLANCHE HARTMAN: It seems that complete cessation is to prevent the arising, rather than do something about it after it's arisen.

But surely we want to lessen suffering.

ANDREW OLENDZKI: Classically, we're invited to do both. With unwholesome states that have already arisen, we work toward understanding what's causing them, and abandoning them. That lessens suffering in the sense that we're able to catch it earlier. In the case of those unwholesome states that have not arisen, we're supposed to do various practices to help guard against them, to prevent them from arising.

GAYLON FERGUSON: Buddhism involves the lessening of suffering, but it's not only about the lessening of suffering. That's the distinction.

ZENKEI BLANCHE HARTMAN: With respect to the lessening of suffering, I'm interested in not just working on our own states of mind. What about hunger in the world? What about homelessness? What about war? What about the massive social suffering we see in the world? Does cessation in Buddhism have anything to say about that?

ANDREW OLENDZKI: Once again, I think it works at both levels. Yes, by all means, go out and alleviate suffering wherever you see it by whatever means are available. At the same time, gain a deeper understanding that any suffering in the world is caused by greed, hatred, and delusion. Ultimately, one can best influence others by setting an example oneself.

GAYLON FERGUSON: It also helps to make a distinction between something therapeutic and something radical, something that goes to the root. The therapeutic model is about offering temporary relief. The Four Noble Truths are a radical diagnosis. They are about going to the root of and then preventing the causes of war, domestic abuse, and so forth.

ANDREW OLENDZKI: I'm an optimist. I think we can do it. I think we can perfect human nature. I think we can clear up all of the violence in the world. But we're going to do it primarily by transforming the hearts and minds of human beings. We do have to go out and heal the sick and feed the hungry, but, ultimately, what's going to be more transformative is changing the attitudes and attachments and aversions of individuals running the societies in which the abuse and violence is happening. Given the interdependence of self and other, that has to happen in concert with changes within ourselves. A simple analogy from the early texts is that a person who's embedded in quicksand can't help somebody else in quicksand. You've got to step out and get on solid ground in order to pull someone else out.

13

Rebirth and Free Will:
How Buddhists Understand Karma

VEN. AJAHN AMARO

ROBIN KORNMAN

ZOKETSU NORMAN FISCHER

First, would each of you like to describe your understanding of karma and its importance in the Buddhist path?

VEN. AJAHN AMARO: The basic approach in the Theravāda is that karma is based on intention. There's a frequently quoted passage where the Buddha says, "Intention is karma." Having will, we create karma through body, speech, and mind. The intention is what creates the potency behind the action. So it's the things we intend and then act upon that are the key creators of karma. Those actions arising from our intentions in the past, we then experience as fruit in the present moment.

Often people think of karma in a fatalistic way or deterministic way. They'll say, "It's my karma," by which they mean it had to happen that way. That view is antithetical to the Buddhist teachings. The effects of past actions can cause a particular tendency, but the ripening of karma is never fixed. Over and over again in the Pali canon, the Buddha tries to counteract the view that life is created according to an inescapable, determined pattern. Karma preconditions our present experience, but what we do with that is entirely based on the choices we make—and the degree of wisdom or good-heartedness, or greed, hatred, and delusion, we bring to our experience in the present moment.

ROBIN KORNMAN: Karma has nothing to do with fate, predestination, providence, or destiny. There's a tendency to hold to a religious belief of one's destiny. Karma has nothing at all to do with that kind of thinking. Quite the contrary, karma means that the world could be operating in a terribly impersonal way, not in a way that gives your life meaning through destiny.

If you didn't have a teaching on karma, you wouldn't be a Buddhist, no matter how much you believed in the Buddha otherwise, because without karma we would become nihilists ethically. Karma is what tells us what's good and bad; nothing is inherently good or inherently bad, but some things lead naturally to states of suffering and some things lead naturally away from suffering, and that's how you define good or bad karma.

ZOKETSU NORMAN FISCHER: Each of us, given our tradition and personalities and the students we encounter, will emphasize different points with respect to karma. Here's how I often put it. Because of our intentions and actions of the past, we find ourselves in a given situation in every moment. A great deal of that is due to our personal deeds and thoughts in this lifetime. Some of it is due to a given condition that predates this life. For example, I didn't create myself. In any moment, then, I've got a determined situation in which I am fully responsible to act.

So you could say there's some determinism in karma, and also some responsibility. We cultivate the past so that we can be clear and responsible in our actions going forward. The slogan I often use with people is, "The situation you're in is not your fault, but it's absolutely your responsibility to take care of it going forward." And then they ask, "What do you mean it's not my fault? If I did actions in the past that led me to this place, how can you say it's not my fault?" I respond that the person who did those things in the past is no longer here. However, the person in this present moment has a huge responsibility to take volitional action from this moment forward. The Buddha taught a path of action and responsibility in a very realistic way.

Does a person who has a profound understanding of karma perceive himself or herself as having choice, free will, in the simplest understanding of that phrase?

ZOKETSU NORMAN FISCHER: Every moment is a choice.

ROBIN KORNMAN: Yes, I agree. And yet, as my teacher used to say, if you see the situation clearly, you are faced with the choicelessness of one path. I don't think he was talking about free will. He was just saying that most situations are choiceless, when you realize what your alternatives are.

ZOKETSU NORMAN FISCHER: You could say every moment is a moment of choice, and if you really see clearly, there's only one choice to make.

VEN. AJAHN AMARO: And that one choiceless choice changes millisecond by millisecond.

It's interesting that both free will and determinism depend on the idea of a "me" that either has a predetermined future or a "me" that is exercising free will. But when there is enlightened mind, it doesn't really sound like free will, because it's ever so slightly dictated by the completely open heart responding to the way things are, moment by moment.

ZOKETSU NORMAN FISCHER: Judeo-Christian thought presupposes concepts and problems and issues that simply dissolve from the Buddhist point of view. Free will versus determinism—from a Buddhist point of view there is no such issue.

ROBIN KORNMAN: Nevertheless, perhaps we can find points of connection. The simplest teaching on karma I know is dependent origination (*pratītyasamutpāda*), as expressed in the chain of the nidānas. There are gaps in the chain, when the next act is not determined, which is what makes enlightenment possible.

VEN. AJAHN AMARO: In the Theravāda, they particularly point to the gap between feeling and craving.

ZOKETSU NORMAN FISCHER: The choice gap.

VEN. AJAHN AMARO: The difference between "I like" and "I want."

ZOKETSU NORMAN FISCHER: Karma is the crucial teaching in Buddhism, because there is cause and effect rather than determinism. It presents the possibility that we can transform our life and the lives around us. The Buddha taught that we're all empowered to do that.

You mean karma is not bad news. [laughter]

VEN. AJAHN AMARO: No, it's very good news.

An ethical system that doesn't have an ongoing person at its core is shocking to many people. Such shock has caused some people within Buddhism to simply sidestep the issue and say, "Well, I don't really know about or believe in karma and rebirth. I'm just trying to be a good person and follow the Buddha's path." As teachers of Buddhism, how do you address that conundrum? How do you teach an ethical system that doesn't require a person?

VEN. AJAHN AMARO: This is not a new issue. It's been going on since the time of the Buddha. It does seem counterintuitive. If the body, feelings, perceptions, consciousness, and so forth are not self, who is it that receives the results of the karma made by this nonself? It requires a wisdom approach—a meditative, contemplative approach—to see how that might work.

If you consider the teachings on nonself, there is a subtle presumption that there is a doer. The meditator examines every perception, every thought, every memory, and every action and intention, but when the meditator looks for the doer, the agent, it can't be found, which is the very point of the process of meditation. In that experience, they can see the selflessness within a thought or sensation.

And yet there is choice. There seems to be a decision-making agent, someone who's choosing between helpful courses of actions and deleterious courses of action. But when we use the same analytical method as we used in looking at sensations, and so forth, to look at this act of choosing, there does not seem to be a central agent; it's a concatenation of circumstances.

ROBIN KORNMAN: But Buddhism is a religion, and all of us here are often in the position of being pastoral counselors, trying to convince people to do things as if we believe they existed. In some sense, you have to ignore the emptiness of the self to preach the religion.

VEN. AJAHN AMARO: I agree. You have a name, I have a name, we all have names. In the normal conventions of personal use, there is individuality. I'm responsible for my actions in the eyes of the law. But if we are talking about the deep tissue philosophical structures and the heart of karma and nonself, we end up talking in a different way.

ROBIN KORNMAN: When I talk to a student I find it helpful to assume, if not actually say, "You feel like you exist and I feel like I exist. From the point of view of existence, you have a buddha nature you haven't discovered and I have a buddha nature I may be beginning to discover." Then we can move ahead and talk about a vaster ethical system than simply avoiding the negative results of our previous karma.

ZOKETSU NORMAN FISCHER: From the standpoint of the Zen tradition, and also in my own experience working with people, I like to point out that we all have an experience of subjectivity. Otherwise, we wouldn't be so interested in "the self." There's an experience people have of being a subject somehow. The problem is not that this experience needs to be denied but rather that we're mistaken about the nature of the experience. Rather than understanding that the experience of subjectivity is an ever-changing, ongoing flow of experiences, we take this flow of experience to be a graspable person who must look good and be happy and on and on.

So karma makes sense in terms of the ongoing, ever-evolving, ever-changing, ever-disappearing and reappearing subject, because downstream that subject experiences events that were caused upstream by actions of the subjects of the past. The problem arises when I think that there is a graspable subject here and a graspable object there. But in fact, even if I understand the true essence of my self, I still want to pay attention to karma, because there will still be effects in the future—although the effects come to bear not on a permanent graspable self but on the ever-changing, ongoing stream of self.

It's a tricky kind of language, and we have to be careful to draw it out for students, because most people take the no-self language to be a denial of the experience of subjectivity. And such a denial is absurd.

The idea of not having an agent, a doer, runs counter to philosophies that celebrate will as what makes life worth living.

ZOKETSU NORMAN FISCHER: In the Buddhist worldview, there is no equivalent to this celebration of will. It is a totally different view of life. Rather than the assertion of my will as fulfilling my destiny, as the reason for my existence, the Buddhist view has more of a sense of a sharing, a cooperative and creative discovery of experience moment after moment in concert with everything. That's our destiny and that's our joy. The whole idea of will implies a separate individual asserting his or her will. That asserting of will escalates to asserting my will against the will of others, so if I want my will to have its satisfaction, I will have to do battle with the wills of others. In Buddhism, that whole construct is just called ignorance.

VEN. AJAHN AMARO: I think there is a gulf of difference separating will and the notion of resolution, such as you would find in the Theravāda system of the ten perfections (*pāramī*) of the bodhisattva. One of them is resolution or determination (*adhiṭṭhāna*). You cannot become a fully enlightened buddha without perfecting the capacity to be determined, to be resolute.

The latter view is what we call vow, which can lead to the end of karma. The Buddha says that the action of perfecting wisdom brings about the cessation of karma. There's wholesome karma, unwholesome karma, and then there's the karma that leads to the cessation of karma. That is the pinnacle of spiritual practice.

ROBIN KORNMAN: When you completely stop believing in ego, karma no longer has the slightest effect. It ceases to function and you are free of karma.

VEN. AJAHN AMARO: Enlightened people are subject to no law whatsoever. The heart is totally freed and unfettered, completely unbound. All they are is an inclination guided by infinite wisdom and infinite kindness, so their actions in the world are immensely powerful but not guided by ego's concerns. Hence, they have powerful presence and an enormous capacity to manipulate the world, but the self does not motivate that so-called manipulation. It merely responds to people's needs and the needs of the situations put before them. They are guided by wisdom and compassion and not by any kind of reactive ego concern.

It seems easy for people to accept the principle of karma on a small scale, but it is much harder for people to accept the notion of karma working over lifetimes. What is the mechanism through which this happens?

ROBIN KORNMAN: In the Mahāyāna, we talk about the storehouse of consciousness (ālaya), which stores the seeds of our actions that will bear fruit later on.

But that simply posits a place where seeds are stored. It still begs the question, how does the actual mechanism of karma work?

VEN. AJAHN AMARO: Today, Buddhadharma exists within a very skeptical materialist society. It seems important to me, then, to be faithful to the simple teachings. For example, the definition of mundane right view is recognizing the workings of karma—that there are past lives, there are future lives, and that they are the results of good and bad actions.

Even though many of the canonical teachings and classical commentaries stress seeing the rebirth process stretching over lifetimes, more often than not the Buddha talks about the rebirth process in moment-to-moment terms. Acting on an angry impulse, one is reborn into regret and so forth. And of course, the whole process cascades. Its workings are responsible for the day-to-day conditioning of human beings, for how society works, and how the whole world is structured.

ROBIN KORNMAN: Yes, in that sense, we can speak of societal and national karma.

VEN. AJAHN AMARO: Yes, and on a very deep level, the tendencies of different species, and the very fact of being born as a human being in a particular time and place, arise from certain causes and carry their own constellation of effects and imprints of memory.

ZOKETSU NORMAN FISCHER: In trying to understand karma in a very deep way, I find the need to go beyond the doctrinal or philosophical. The understanding has to come from the deep experience of ongoing meditation practice. The short-range karma can become very clear, but long experience on the meditation cushion can allow you to realize that this moment contains dimensions that you will never be able to entirely grasp with your five aggregates and six consciousnesses.

The bigger questions of the karma of past lives or the karma that gives rise to whole world systems, and all the various doctrinal elaborations, are efforts to explain in logical ways an experiential and intuitive feeling about the inexorable working of karma that arises from deep practice. It is not really possible to account conventionally for such an understanding. Your explanations will be found wanting.

VEN. AJAHN AMARO: When I think and talk about the workings of karma on a large scale, I liken it to the first law of thermodynamics: the sum total of all energy in the universe is constant. With respect to karma, I think of it as the law of the conservation of consciousness. All causes must have their effects, and those effects will ripple through the whole system. What is reborn from one life to another, one day to another, one moment to another, are heaps of habits and insights.

How are they carried? An action in one place can bear fruit in a far-off place. The rebirth process is like that. The kind of movement of energy across space and time is what we experience as the rebirth process. So even if we can't understand conceptually exactly how karma works, we can attend to the whole system. As Norman was saying, there's an intuitive sense that deepens with meditation over time and that gives a sense of where things are going, what things are important, what shape they have.

So while we can see that larger scope through the insight that arises in meditation practice, there's no rational argument that explains how cause and effect work on a large scale.

VEN. AJAHN AMARO: In the Theravāda canon, there is what are called the Four Imponderables, and one of them is the workings of karma. The Buddha said that if you tried to figure it out intellectually, your head would explode. The thinking mind doesn't have enough dimensions to encompass the reality of it.

ZOKETSU NORMAN FISCHER: I am reminded of a kōan concerning karma that is central to Zen practitioners. There's an old man attending abbot Pai Chang's lectures. Pai Chang asks him who he is, and he answers, "I'm really a fox, and I've been reborn as a fox for five hundred lifetimes, because in a previous life when I was the abbot of this very temple, someone asked me, 'Is the enlightened person free from karma or not?' I told them the enlightened person is free from karma, and because of that I've been reborn for five hundred lives as a fox. Can you please help me?" Pai-chang replies, "The enlightened person does not obscure karma," and this answer enlightens the old man. He's later freed from the body of a fox, and the fox body is given an honorable burial.

The crux of the kōan is, what does it mean to not obscure karma? The enlightened person is free from karma—and we know what that means— but there's more to it than that. The deep answer is not to be found doctrinally but rather on the cushion. This kōan describes the Zen understanding of karma. One can say a lot about this kōan, but the important point is that the situation is not quite so simple or convenient, from the Zen point of view, as saying that the enlightened person is free from karma. The way to clarify that is not by doctrine but by intuition on the cushion.

VEN. AJAHN AMARO: I don't think the teaching on karma necessarily needs to be sophisticated or refined. In the Southern Buddhist countries, karma is taught on a very simple and straightforward basis. That approach is as much a part of bringing the understanding of karma and its result into the Western culture as are detailed explanations of *paṭiccasamuppāda*, because essentially the simple teaching in the form of a simile expresses the same thing. The Buddha's teaching is: if you sow the seeds, you reap the fruit. It's an aphorism that two- and three-year-olds learn in Thailand and Sri Lanka. It becomes a basic format for existing within the world.

Such simple directives are a recurrent theme introduced all the way along through one's education.

ROBIN KORNMAN: In the Tibetan traditions we have great practitioners who are also great metaphysicians, following the Indian tradition of people like Candrakīrti and Nāgārjuna. Teachers like Mipham the Great and Jamgön Kongtrül say that our karma is subtle and very difficult to study, and then they go ahead and study it in great detail. They say that there is no teaching of the Buddha that can't be demonstrated through inference. They are inspired to figure things out for the culture, for the civilization, philosophizing out the details of the functions—what karma is and what it does. There is an approach that says that it is worthwhile to present comprehensive systems of thought that can have civilizing effects throughout the world and, in so doing, can actually bring about whole Buddhist civilizations.

14

Training the Mind and Heart:
The Lojong System

KEN MCLEOD

B. ALAN WALLACE

JUDY LIEF

What does the word *lojong* mean?

KEN MCLEOD: Although lojong (*blo sbyong*) is often translated as "mind training," the meaning of the term in Tibetan is closer to "refining" rather than training. Lojong is counterintuitive in the sense that it's opposed to our ordinary way of relating to the world. It is intended to create friction between our habitual patterns and the experience of the present moment. This friction generates heat to burn up our habituated patterns.

B. ALAN WALLACE: Lojong is largely a matter of reframing our perspective on the phenomena that arise before us. We perceive them from a fresh perspective. Rather than taking the usual tack of trying to transform our external circumstances, we shift and refine our way of viewing, experiencing, and engaging with reality.

JUDY LIEF: Lojong takes us through a three-step process. First we move from our habit of putting our own interests above everything else to the provocative thought of putting others' interests somewhere on our horizon.

Then we move to putting others ahead of ourselves. Finally, we transcend that altogether. It's not simply replacing a this-that orientation with a that-this orientation. It's going beyond this and that altogether.

The real issue is egolessness. Ego of self and ego of other are equally limited views of reality. Ego of self is the sense of self-fixation and fascination, clinging to a notion of who we are as something solid that can be separated out from other aspects of reality. Ego of other, or ego of phenomena, is taking what we perceive, all of our perceptions, experiences, moods, and thoughts, and solidifying them into "other." We estrange ourselves from the basic fabric of reality when we let our mind have a bias in either direction. Lojong is designed to remove that estrangement.

B. ALAN WALLACE: Lojong runs right in the face of the inclinations that have kept us in samsara for a long time. In general, we are driven by self-grasping, so our natural inclination is certainly not to take in the negativity of the world and give away everything good in our lives. Quite the contrary.

When people are first introduced to lojong, they often have a hard time with the notion that self-interest isn't really the ground of life.

B. ALAN WALLACE: It is said that the Dharmakāya is the perfection of the Buddha's self-interest (*rang don*), while the sambhoghakāya and nirmāṇakāya are the perfection of the Buddha's other-interest (*gzhan don*). It is not the case, then, that the Buddhadharma entails turning your back on your own aspirations to be free of suffering and achieve enlightenment. That would be a weird distortion of the Buddhist teachings. Rather, we're counteracting the self-centeredness that prioritizes one's well-being over that of everyone else, especially where one's interests seem to be in conflict with others. But our own aspirations are part and parcel of the Buddhadharma all the way to enlightenment.

JUDY LIEF: One of the reasons that mind training is such a marvelous body of teachings is that it can work for people at all levels of familiarity with Buddhadharma. A danger can arise, though, if you don't have some understanding of emptiness. Then the lojong sayings can be perverted into moral credos, and *tonglen* (*gtong len*) can become a kind of martyrdom. It is important to understand that the flow of energy is not being held any-where by anyone. Rather, one is working with an energetic reversal that goes beyond our usual sense of virtue, of who's good and who's bad.

Once we overcome that misapprehension, we find that the practice is very earthy, practical, and relevant. One can work with every one of the slogans in many different ways, and at many different levels of understanding.

Do you need a teacher to guide your practice of lojong?

B. ALAN WALLACE: If you can find a qualified teacher of lojong, there's no question that's best, as it is for learning virtually any other skill. But if there are no teachers around, you can pick up a good text on mind training and follow that as carefully as you can.

Whether you have a teacher or not, I feel one important element is required. Just as Vajrayāna has its root system deeply embedded in the Mahāyāna, so does the Mahāyāna tradition have its root system deeply embedded in the early teachings of the Buddha. Mind training is not an introductory teaching, or at the very least, it would be a very steep step to be making at the outset. For the lojong teachings to make much sense, they need to rest on the fundamental framework of the Four Noble Truths and the basic constituents of the practice: ethics, meditation, and wisdom.

JUDY LIEF: I never present lojong without presenting at least some preliminary ground of mindfulness and awareness. You need to let the mind settle and rest with uncertainty—get down to the bare bones. It helps to have a sense of the logic of the Sutrayāna, and without a basic meditation practice, lojong can become just a way to be goody-goody.

KEN MCLEOD: What I've found is that lojong, and particularly tonglen, taking and sending, is for many people an immediate way to get in touch with compassion. So I'm not sure that it can't be used as an introduction. If it is presented as a natural expression of innate compassion, people can connect with it quite easily and quite deeply. Lojong can take you right to the heart of the intention to be awake, *bodhicitta*. It can allow you to be completely awake to all aspects of your experience in order to correct your basic imbalances. The practice of sending and taking has that kind of power.

B. ALAN WALLACE: Putting tonglen into a secular context can be helpful, but lojong is more than the practice of tonglen. I don't see how one could properly work with the meaning of bodhicitta—the achievement of enlightenment for the sake of all sentient beings—without having a sense of who the Buddha is, what the Four Noble Truths are, and so forth. These are not isolated meditative practices. They come to us as very theory-laden, textured, multifaceted disciplines of practice. I don't see how they really make any sense without the whole package.

JUDY LIEF: I've certainly presented tonglen as a very practical thing to do, separated out from the context of lojong. For example, it's very helpful as an applied practice in working with health care professionals, who are dealing with death and dying on a regular basis. They don't need much background, and it opens up an incredibly awakened, tender experience for people. It's very useful, but I agree that it isn't the same as doing the full lojong practice.

The ultimate bodhicitta slogans at the beginning of the seven-point mind training can be quite challenging, such as investigating the nature of unborn awareness.

KEN MCLEOD: Dealing with ultimate bodhicitta is where things get interesting. Frequently when you say things like, "Regard everything as a dream" and "Be a child of illusion," there's usually at least one person in the room who resists this strongly. That person is usually expressing the fears of everybody in the group. They fear openness, the lack of reference points, particularly social reference points and connections. Taking the perspective of ultimate bodhicitta, trusting in an awareness, which is no thing, can be very intimidating.

B. ALAN WALLACE: If you do start to get it, it challenges your very sense of personal identity, which you have been cherishing as the most precious thing in the universe. Suddenly that is being challenged right at the very core.

JUDY LIEF: That's when the lojong practice starts to bite. This is the heart of the practice that underlies the more relative benefits of cultivating kindness. However, if you simply lapse into philosophical musing about the nature of reality and not paying attention to what is going on day by day, the relative slogans can offer their own bite, lest you become pretentious about your view of reality while treating everyone around you like dirt.

I find that if you memorize the slogans and study them on a regular basis, they just pop up at the most embarrassing times. When you've really blown it and you've lost your mind and you're completely freaked out, a slogan pops up in a provocative way. In that way they are almost effortless (annoyingly so). They pop up whether you like it or not. And when they arise for me, it's not as if I have unraveled all the sources of my multitude of neuroses, but somehow the neuroses at least get pricked a little bit. The slogans are almost like mosquitoes buzzing around your ears, frustrating your neurotic patterns.

KEN MCLEOD: A very old metaphor is that compassion and emptiness wisdom are like the two wings of a bird—without both, the bird goes nowhere. One has to keep in mind that the aim here isn't really to make the world a better place; the aim is to know one's own experience completely. What arises out of that, from a Buddhist point of view, is universal good. But to know one's own experience completely is to know its nature, which is emptiness. To relate to it as it is, is compassion. The two are inextricably bound together.

The relative bodhicitta sayings provide an interesting interplay between wisdom and compassion. Perhaps we could unpack a couple of the relative bodhicitta slogans. One of the most provocative and important is "Drive all blames into one."

KEN MCLEOD: That "one" is the tendency to attach to a sense of self, which in Buddhism is understood as the source of all suffering. Suffering is our reaction to experience., and that is always based on a sense of self. We drive all blame into that tendency to attach to a sense of self, because that's where our suffering comes from. When we react based on preserving self, we create suffering for others, so the suffering of others comes from attachment to a sense of self, too.

JUDY LIEF: This is one of those slogans that is easily misunderstood. It is in some ways more difficult for women, because it can be understood in a superficial sense that is belittling to one's self relative to others, which is merely a cultural pattern.

Like most of the slogans, this one can work at many levels. It can work at the profound level of dissolving ego, that which separates us from the fabric of reality, but it can also simply counteract our tendency to always seek some reason outside of ourselves for why things go wrong. Dropping that habit can provide tremendous relief.

B. ALAN WALLACE: The import of this is not looking at the disasters in the world and saying they're all my fault. Rather, it says that since each sentient being is the center of their own universe, the suffering they experience stems from their attachment to the self. But it is not saying that everything is blamed on one's own self. That would just be flat-out silly.

JUDY LIEF: One thing that's interesting about this slogan is the sense that there is no other reality; there is nothing from which we are totally separate. Taking the blame onto oneself is not structurally all that different from the bodhisattva vow to save all sentient beings. If you can take all blames onto yourself, then you can actually generate compassion for all beings. It's the same sense of no separation.

Since Buddhist practice clearly has goals, what is the meaning of "Abandon all hope of results"?

JUDY LIEF: This encapsulates the dilemma we see throughout all the Buddhist teachings. One moment you are told, "Practice hard, hold your discipline, and maintain strong posture," and the next moment you are told, "Relax and just let things hang loose." You are told, "Try to be enlightened, but don't be attached to gaining anything." It's Buddhist humor.

If you have ever had to do something hard, you find that the gearing up begins to get in the way. But when you are actually fully engaged in something, you do abandon all hope of results, because you just do what you are doing. The hope seems intimately connected with fears of goofing up and not achieving results. All that gets in the way, so why not abandon it?

This slogan makes it abundantly clear how we always cook up hopes of results before we have hardly done anything at all. Over and over again, our hope for results immediately transforms into fantasies of having achieved the results. This slogan puts a mirror to that. It is a tool for our mindfulness that lets us know how, in the slightest little thing we do, we start fixating on the goal and miss out on what is actually going on moment to moment.

B. ALAN WALLACE: From an ultimate perspective, there is nothing to be transformed, nothing to be thrown off, and nothing to be acquired. The essential nature of awareness is primordially pure and all that needs to be done is to unveil it and to be perfectly present with it. On the other hand, we have thousands of skillful means and teachings about transforming ourselves, and we can apply criteria to determine whether we are getting any result, such as the saying "All Dharma is included in one purpose." That purpose is to free ourselves of self-grasping, and we are asked to investigate to what degree that is happening. On a relative level, then, we are on the path of developing toward enlightenment. On the ultimate level, it is all simply a matter of being present with the perfection that is already there.

At the end of Dilgo Khyentse Rinpoche's commentary on the *Seven-Point Mind Training*, he says that when you come to the very end of the path, you lose even the preference for nirvana over samsara. You relinquish even the desire to achieve enlightenment. But you don't want to lose that too soon. Otherwise, you end up mucking about in samsara, like we all have been for countless lifetimes.

JUDY LIEF: It's also important to be careful not to view any slogan purely in isolation, as if it were an eternal truth. The slogans work as a system and they balance one another. If you become too generous, so to speak, perhaps you need to sharpen up. If you are too sharp, perhaps you need to soften. If you take the slogans personally and you let them be mirrors, they expose the obstacles, shortfalls, pretenses, and mistaken views of all sorts.

People often wonder when they practice sending and taking whether they are really helping others or simply cultivating their own bodhicitta. If you do sending and taking for a person who is ill, do you actually have an effect on their health?

B. Alan Wallace: It can happen, but one doesn't bank on that. The primary reason for engaging in tonglen practice is to overcome your own tendencies for prioritizing your own well-being over that of others. Nevertheless, one hears many anecdotes about people being able to affect others with whom they have a strong karmic connection.

Ken McLeod: To look at doing tonglen as actually having an effect on others is right in the area of hoping for results. Regarding the anecdotes one hears about something magical happening, it is very difficult to attribute a given result to a given cause, so I do not encourage people to approach things that way. This is a practice that refines your attitude to the world and not something you use to heal people. Jamgön Kongtrül is very clear about that in his commentary.

Judy Lief: I think the practice of tonglen does help to connect you with another person sometimes, especially in the context of health and healing. Simply being present with another person while doing tonglen has an immediate effect on the connectedness of self and other. Beyond that, though, I definitely agree that one shouldn't view oneself as the great tonglen healer.

Ken McLeod: The essence of compassion is being present with suffering, and what comes out of that presence no one can predict. Very wonderful things may happen, but approaching this with the intention of getting a certain result contradicts the spirit of the lojong teachings.

15

Do Buddhists Pray?
Asking for Help in a Nontheistic Religion

**MARK UNNO ▪ REVEREND SHOHAKU OKUMURA
BHANTE SEELAWIMALA ▪ SARAH HARDING**

Perhaps we could begin our discussion of the role of prayer in Buddhism by considering the Pure Land tradition, which is renowned for supplicating or invoking what it calls "other-power."

MARK UNNO: One of the primary practices of the Pure Land tradition is intoning the name of Amida Buddha. In the Shin school, we say *Namu Amida Butsu*, which roughly translates as "I take refuge in Amida Buddha," or "I entrust myself to Amida Buddha."

Saying this name is understood as an act of taking refuge, or entrusting. This concept of entrusting, known in Japanese as *shinjin*, is widely regarded as a key to the Shin religious experience. Shinjin is often rendered in English as "true entrusting." Understanding true entrusting can be helpful for understanding the nature of supplication or devotion in this tradition.

On the one hand, shinjin means trusting oneself to the Buddha Amida, through saying the name. On the other hand, true entrusting is an expression of the practitioner's truest, deepest nature. For that reason, one of the primary teachers in the Shin tradition, Shinran, taught that true entrusting is also none other than one's own buddha nature. The force of true entrusting is the nature of Amida Buddha itself, something beyond the merely human, and it is one's true nature.

Aside from representing one's true nature, does Amida Buddha offer assistance to the practitioner?

MARK UNNO: On the philosophical level, what it really offers is the vow to bring all beings to liberation or enlightenment. If one wants to address what actually happens in individuals' lives, one will find that followers of the tradition supplicate for a variety of goals that may or may not be addressed by the deeper philosophical understanding I described.

There are people, for example, who will invoke the name Namu Amida Butsu in the hope of fulfilling all the usual human hopes and desires, such as health, wealth, and in premodern times, successful crops. Just as one might find in any tradition, not all followers have necessarily attained the philosophical understanding of devotion to Amida Buddha. People may supplicate for the fulfillment of various needs, and the Shin tradition does not deny these needs. Every human being has desires. Whether we express them in an explicit form of practice or not, at some level we are hoping—and in a sense praying—that we and others, especially those who are close to us, are healthy, that we can pay our bills, and so forth. The Shin tradition does not deny this. In fact, it addresses this quite specifically.

The story of Amida Buddha, and the story of the Pure Land, is a story of a world in which all levels of suffering are addressed. On the one hand, there are ordinary human needs and they are included in the specific vows of Amida Buddha. But ultimately, all these conditions can only truly come to fruition by conforming to the vow to liberate all beings.

It is better to illustrate this than to explain it philosophically. Consider a community of people who want to create a wonderful place to live and they all share this same desire. They will achieve all their ends—including financial stability, education, medical needs—only if there is the right spirit of cooperation, of interdependence, of mutual awareness. So even though many people wish for the fulfillment of ordinary desires, ultimately we can only achieve them with the right spirit.

Reverend Okumura, are there practices of prayer, devotion, or supplication in Zen?

REVEREND SHOHAKU OKUMURA: People sometimes think of Zen as

a "self-power" (*jiriki*) practice. I think, however, we must be very careful about the meaning of "other-power" (*tariki*) and "self-power." As Dōgen Zenji said, "To study the Buddha way is to study the self." But he also said, "To study the self is to forget the self." Dōgen called our practice of meditation *shikantaza*, which means "just sitting." This "just sitting" is actually the way we study the self, but this is also the way we forget the self. When we sit, we sit on the ground that is beyond the dichotomy of self and other. In that sense, our sitting practice is a prayer to give up the self and to put our entire being on the ground of interdependent origination.

In that sense, this is a prayer. It does not mean that the self prays to the other for some benefit, but rather we place our entire being on the basis of interdependent origination. That is an essential meaning of prayer in Buddhism.

MARK UNNO: This way of thinking is very resonant with the sense of "other-power" in the Shin tradition. The "self-power" is considered illusory because it is based on the ego, which doesn't exist as an entity. "Other-power" in that sense means other than ego. One's true nature is the nature of Amida Buddha, which is none other than the universe itself. When one speaks of one's own true nature, that nature is not separate from other natures.

Dōgen goes on to say, "When you forget the self, you are enlightened by the ten thousand dharmas." Are the ten thousand dharmas the same as the other-power?

REVEREND SHOHAKU OKUMURA: It is the power beyond self and other. In Pure Land Buddhism, it is called "other-power." In Zen, we call it something like "Ten Direction World." In that sense, the self and the other are not opposed to each other.

Bhante Seelawimala, what is the Theravāda tradition's view of supplication and prayer generally?

BHANTE SEELAWIMALA: In the Theravāda tradition, we are very reluctant to use the word "prayer" when we speak English. We don't even think of it as a Buddhist word. I never say, "I'll pray for you" or "I'll think of you in my prayers."

The main reason is that in the Theravāda tradition, we don't have bodhisattvas or other deities we pray to, as in the Mahāyāna tradition. We don't get into the discussion of self-power or other-power. We don't use the notion of "power" in the same way to begin with. We believe our minds are weak in certain areas of our thinking. The ordinary mind is not working to its fullest capacity, but we can correct its drawbacks by proper mental exercises, by following the step-by-step guidance of the Buddha. Gradually, the mind starts to work properly and see things clearly. As a result we can overcome our suffering, frustration, and fear.

If we understand that we are ignorant of how things work, we see what causes the ignorance. That help came from the Buddha, to be sure. We appreciate the Buddha for that and we appreciate the Dhamma, which is the knowledge given by the Buddha. We appreciate other people who use the knowledge and thereby improve their conditions. That is called Sangha. We respect Buddha, Dhamma, and Sangha as our model and our support system, but the actual work is done by ourselves. We don't have the notion of praying to someone or asking for help from someone.

In the Vajrayāna tradition, there is strong emphasis on blessings and connection to the lineage of buddhas, bodhisattvas, and teachers, who have the power to assist practitioners on the path. What is the Vajrayāna view of prayer and seeking the assistance of outside beings?

SARAH HARDING: Vajrayāna is famous for having quite possibly more deities than any other religion on earth. I'm a little reluctant, though, to make this dichotomy between self-power and other-power. Making the distinction between self and other is what is problematic in the first place. The one thing that seems to run through all traditions of Buddhism is that the question of something either existing or not existing—something being either inside or outside—is in itself the problem. All the different ways of looking at that are just different language to get at the same thing.

Vajrayāna accepts all of the views that have been mentioned already, and includes for instance, supplication to Amida Buddha. It also accepts formless meditation, looking directly at just what is. In Vajrayāna, all the traditions are seen as skillful means. In fact, if there is one thing that Vajrayāna defines itself as, it is as a vehicle of skillful means.

As Master Dōgen says, if you try to find the self, you find everything. Vajrayāna allows there to be vast and myriad ways of approaching the interconnectedness, while all the time accepting that you're not going to find it to be either other-power or self-power.

So if there is no self and other, why are there practices of supplication at all? Why is that a skillful means?

SARAH HARDING: It is skillful means for the very reason that we are conditioned to a certain dualistic way of thinking. When you are praying to Amida, ultimately that may be buddha nature. That is not to say, though, that one view takes superiority over the other—that this is the absolute truth, whereas the other is relative truth, or one is definitive whereas the other is interpretive. All these means are a way to get past that kind of dichotomizing. In the meantime, they provide effective language, effective mind sets, which work for different kinds of people.

MARK UNNO: The language of self-power and other-power in the Shin tradition—and the practices associated with that language—arose precisely to dissolve, transcend, or liberate the practitioner from these implicit dualistic assumptions in daily human life, which are themselves the source of suffering.

The language was not formulated in order to establish self-power and other-power as entities, but to do precisely the opposite. The language is there to address the fact that, either explicitly or implicitly, people live their lives as if they are separate beings. As Ms. Harding said, this language is an expression of skillful means. In the Shin tradition, Shinran himself addresses Amida Buddha as the Buddha of Skillful Means.

Bhante, all of our panelists are discussing prayer in a very nondual way. Is there anything in the Theravāda tradition comparable to this particular approach?

BHANTE SEELAWIMALA: If any practice that leads to ultimate purity, or unlimited perfection, is defined as a prayer, then Buddhism is a prayer.

Because that is what Buddhism is: it is a practice that leads to an end. What is the goal, the end result of the practices? In that sense, perhaps we could say it is prayer.

SARAH HARDING: There is another way of seeing prayer. It can be seen as aspiration, as setting your mind in a certain direction. Whether you have a particular other being or other-power in mind is not necessarily the main thrust of it; the main point is that you are putting your mind in that direction.

For instance, if you send a Christmas card that says, "May there be peace on earth," you are not necessarily asking someone to bestow it; you are simply making that aspiration.

BHANTE SEELAWIMALA: I agree with that. That is very clear from our tradition also. We constantly remind ourselves what our goal should be. That comes in many different ways, in many kinds of language.

MARK UNNO: When one makes that aspiration, which can be considered as the working of bodhicitta—the aspiration for enlightenment—one is tapping into the path. The path may be understood as the bringing of all beings to enlightenment, so in that sense, even if there is a specific object, it embraces the whole world in an awareness of this larger path.

In his book *Secret of the Vajra World*, Reginald Ray talked about the importance of "unseen beings" in Vajrayāna Buddhism. He says that while ultimately the buddhas, bodhisattvas, and enlightened teachers are not distinct from our own true nature, this is also true of all beings in the universe. Therefore, these cosmic or unseen beings have at least as much relative existence as the other beings we relate to. So are the beings or forces we may relate to through prayer or supplication any less real than you or I?

SARAH HARDING: To attribute degrees of existence to beings based on whether they are seen or not seen is, I would think, a product of scientific thinking. I wouldn't want to try to do that. At the same time I wouldn't want to either refute or prove the existence of any such beings. How could you eliminate all forms of energy and force just because you don't see them?

In that sense, I agree that maybe ultimately they are our own nature, but that wouldn't be reducing them in any way. Our tendency to reduce something by saying, "Oh, it's only in the mind" is a mistaken approach. It is not only the mind; it is everything. It would be foolish to single out what you see with your eye sense and not to relate to the whole universe of energy.

MARK UNNO: Recently I had an opportunity to speak to a Shin Buddhist congregation, and they asked me to address the children first. I started by asking them, "Where is Amida Buddha?" The first child said, "Everywhere." And then I asked, "Where is everywhere?" The second child said, "Here." I asked, "Where is here?" The third child said, "In your heart." And I asked, "Where is my heart?" The fourth child said, "In my heart," and pointed to his heart.

Of course, in the Shin tradition an awareness in the heart, however profound, remains insufficient. Practice requires the full manifestation of body-mind-heart, in which Amida Buddha as formless compassion becomes manifest through the embodied act of saying the name.

In the Vajrayāna tradition, there are many supplications recited as part of the daily liturgy. When you are doing these supplications, who are you addressing?

SARAH HARDING: Anybody who will listen! If you come from a tradition, there are the ancestors of the tradition. If they have had an effect on you through their teachings, you couldn't say that they do not exist now. You are the accumulation of all of their wisdom, because they have passed it on through the teachings.

You acknowledge that presence just because it's there. You don't have to think that they are alive as people somewhere. This is talking about wisdom that you acknowledge, just as you acknowledge the Buddha's wisdom. Again, however, I don't want to reducing it by saying "Oh, it's only in my mind." You acknowledge all of the wisdom that has come from the various ancestors and that may exist currently in a variety of ways. That is who you are supplicating—whomever will listen.

In the Japanese tradition, there is a strong sense of reverence for the patri-

archs and ancestors. In Zen, what is the relationship between the current practitioners and the ancestors?

REVEREND SHOHAKU OKUMURA: In one sense, those people are models of our practice. They are the predecessors who practiced the way we are following. To study and practice, we follow the same motives they followed. People who practiced this way in such difficult situations, because of their bodhisattva vows, also serve as a kind of encouragement for us. We remind ourselves that our Dharma teaching and practice has been transmitted from Śākyamuni Buddha to us through those people. We also express our gratitude; because of their practice and teaching, we can continue to practice.

BHANTE SEELAWIMALA: Supplication or prayer is not a necessary part of the process of mental exercise as taught in the Theravāda tradition. We don't regard the Buddha as universal spirit, or self as universal self, or personal self. We don't discuss things in those terms. We don't have any power beyond Dhamma. Dhamma means things as they really are, the power of cause and effect, real knowledge of how things are, *dhammatā*. That genuine knowledge—knowing what causes what—can be used to improve our condition.

MARK UNNO: In the Shin tradition, we actually don't use the word "prayer." That term has a specifically hopeful association, which may not be helpful to the understanding of Shin or other Buddhist traditions. At the same time, the common understanding of prayer is often not even an accurate representation of what prayer is properly understood to be in the Christian tradition. It is a reduction, a popularized notion that doesn't carry deeper significance. It could be helpful for us to appreciate that Buddhism has a contribution to make to the ongoing meaning of the term "prayer," since meanings are always changing.

BHANTE SEELAWIMALA: This might be a good opportunity for us to define what prayer is from the Buddhist perspective. As people have been saying, in this culture when you hear the word "prayer," it has a different connotation than what we have been talking about.

It seems we have not been using the word "prayer" to denote a relationship between a supplicant and a higher being but a process of opening or surrendering.

BHANTE SEELAWIMALA: If you have some word that represents a non-being, that also might be helpful. Can it be something other than a being? Like a power, an other-power, a power in general, what we call dhammatā?

MARK UNNO: What is known as "other-power" in Shin Buddhism is an expression of the Dharmakāya and dharmatā. They are very similar.

SARAH HARDING: Ultimately, everyone would agree with that. Since we are getting into terminology, I would like to add that there are two words in Tibetan that relate to this area. One is mönlam (*smon lam*), which is the "aspiration" that we were talking about, directing the mind. There is another term, solwa dep (*gsol ba 'debs*), which means "supplication," something very much like prayer in the Christian tradition. This is the skillful means of acknowledging that we live in a world of relationship, that a human being is a relating being. Beyond aspiring, it can be very effective in our practice to use the tendency we have to be relational. Prayer is an expression of that tendency.

16

Dropping Body and Mind:
Understanding Dōgen

BONNIE MYOTAI TREACE, SENSEI ▪ TAIGEN DAN LEIGHTON
ZOKETSU NORMAN FISCHER ▪ STEVEN HEINE

First, why is Dōgen such a pivotal figure in the history of Zen?

BONNIE MYOTAI TREACE, SENSEI: Beyond Dōgen's significance as the key figure in the establishment of the Sōtō school, I think he is tremendously helpful to practitioners because he was a very good student. He combines radical thought with the poignancy of a spiritual disciple's journey. Dōgen speaks right to the heart of the matter. He has the poet's vastness and the practitioner's commitment to particulars.

Dōgen challenged not just conventional thought but conventional activity. He asked us to look into the real nature of expression—the mystery of birth, death, and time. He asked us to take up these issues in a genuine way and to question every word.

TAIGEN DAN LEIGHTON: Dōgen is uniquely important to American practitioners because he introduced the Zen mode of Buddhism to Japan. Likewise, we are now in the early stages of introducing Buddhism to our culture, so there are a lot of lessons we can take from how he faced this challenge.

Dōgen's practice is counterintuitive to how a lot of Buddhists think, whereby meditation and practice are seen as a means to future enlightenment and the achievement of a goal. Part of what makes him a little difficult for Americans is our consumer orientation. He presents something complete as it is. Practice and realization are one thing. Practice is the expression of realization. His writing is difficult because he is not trying to present a doctrine or philosophy but rather talking to practitioners in a very playful way.

ZOKETSU NORMAN FISCHER: Dōgen really did set the tone for Japanese Zen. He inspired the whole flavor of Zen we are familiar with. It's the feeling of entering into the present moment profoundly, the feeling that produces the tea ceremony and flower arranging. It's the sacredness and power that comes with just being present. This sacredness is the underlying feeling of Dōgen's writing and it sets the tone for the Japanese approach to Buddhism.

In another vein, Dōgen's philosophies and intellectual contributions are stunningly contemporary, especially his philosophy of language, which has been much discussed and written about in various arenas of postmodern thought. When the Japanese were looking for an indigenous, profound philosophy that could stack up against Western philosophy, they hit on Dōgen as a thinker equal in sophistication to Western thinkers of a much later time.

TAIGEN DAN LEIGHTON: The *Shōbōgenzō* essays are very philosophical—that's why modern philosophers have been very impressed with Dōgen—yet these long essays make it a little more difficult for people to feel the person of Dōgen. Even though the shorter talks in the *Eihei Kōroku* were given to monks in a more formal style, paradoxically they reveal Dōgen's personality more.

Dōgen is commonly thought to have emphasized monasticism, and he did work hard to train a group of monastic disciples. Yet I think Dōgen is very relevant in America, where most people doing Zen are practicing in the context of their everyday lives of work and relationship. Paradoxically, Dōgen's monastic writings, like *Instructions to the Cook*, give an orientation to applying awareness and presence to everyday activity. These monastic writings are relevant to the way that Americans are practicing precisely because they deal with the mundane details of day-to-day living.

ZOKETSU NORMAN FISCHER: The *Shōbōgenzō* is written in informal

Japanese and is much more difficult and formal. The *Eihei Kōroku* is written in a formal Chinese and yet is much more informal and easier to understand. For one thing, there is a language game that Dōgen plays in *Shōbōgenzō*. If you read it for ten or twenty years, you begin to get a feeling for it. It's a kind of intellectual yoga. In many cases, Dōgen is dealing with the nature of language and thought and how to bring language and thought in line with Buddhist practice. Reading *Shōbōgenzō* itself becomes a practice of mental yoga that involves trying to harmonize with Dōgen's way of expression. Once you get used to it, it isn't nearly as impenetrable as it seems when you are outside of his style.

BONNIE MYOTAI TREACE, SENSEI: To encounter Dōgen is to be stopped in the course of your events, to lift the needle from the record. When you have the willingness to be stopped in the middle of the flow of language or to have your attention brought to a seemingly mundane activity, you are encountering Dōgen. The way that Dōgen seems to work on us may be particularly pertinent in our culture, where people seem so insistent on charging along. Whatever level of formal practice you are engaged in, if you are willing to let attention be a way to encounter the matter at hand, you shift away from the usual spirit of acquisition, of getting it, of gaining access.

That is the first step: a willingness to allow genuine attention to be there. When that is in place, then you have trust, as opposed to the kind of arrogance that discards what is not immediately revealed. We shift for a minute from instant soup Dharma to the deep flavors of a long-cooking soup. Then if you apply the real heat—the zazen, the study with a teacher, and the liturgy that maintains your allegiance to mystery—you have rich possibilities that can work within or outside a formal training structure. Part of what we miss when we allude to Dōgen's difficulty is that when we spend time in the kind of attention he demands we become inspired, encouraged, and involved in a way that is impossible to describe.

ZOKETSU NORMAN FISCHER: One of Dōgen's chief purposes is to show you that the conventional, ordinary, taken-for-granted way of thinking and looking at the world is actually the cause of your being bound and suffering and confused. So he demonstrates it rather than saying that to you in the conventional way. His language is the undoing of language. That's what makes it hard to understand on a conventional level. When you do have the experience of going along with him in unmaking language and exposing your conceptualization, it is soaring, wonderful, and inspiring.

What is the central characteristic of Dōgen's zazen?

TAIGEN DAN LEIGHTON: Zazen is not a practice for future realization in Dōgen, as we noted. For Dōgen it is a celebration, a ceremony. I think it has to do with his roots in Tendai, the Vajrayāna of Japan, which he practiced before going to China. Zazen, for Dōgen, is a way of expressing something deep, of enacting it. It is expressing the possibility of just being present with the reality appearing in our thoughts and feelings, as well as in sounds, sensations, and posture.

BONNIE MYOTAI TREACE, SENSEI: Perhaps the central characteristic of Dōgen's zazen is that there is no central characteristic.

ZOKETSU NORMAN FISCHER: I don't know of anybody who writes about and speaks about zazen in such an inspiring way as Dōgen does. His understanding of zazen is crucial.

We thought it would be interesting to choose several short selections from Dōgen for you to comment on, to illustrate how one works with Dōgen's expression of the Dharma. We could begin with these passages from the Gabyō fascicle in *Shōbōgenzō*:

> An ancient buddha said, "The painting of a rice cake does not satisfy hunger." This statement has been studied by ancient buddhas and present buddhas. Nevertheless, it has become the mere chatter of seekers in grass-roof huts and under trees. . . . If you say a painting is not real, then the myriad things are not real. If the myriad things are not real, then Buddhadharma is not real. As Buddhadharma is real, a painted rice cake is real.

TAIGEN DAN LEIGHTON: He's taking a traditional saying from a kōan, going back to the idea that Zen is not expressed in words and letters and that the sutras are only a painting of a rice cake. What Dōgen does in this section is a typical example of his undercutting false dichotomies and dualistic thinking. He ends up by saying that only a painted rice cake can satisfy hunger.

In so doing, he is stylizing the whole thing. He's talking about truly understanding what our hunger is and what our satisfaction is and that, in fact, everything is painted. Even our idea of painting is yet another painting. He is undercutting the way we think of satisfying and satisfaction. This relates to the First Noble Truth, and the nature of our hunger and dissatisfaction, how we create suffering by separating ourselves from the world and by reifying false dichotomies.

There is no remedy for satisfying hunger other than a painted rice cake. Without painted hunger, you never become a true person. It is necessary to take on something that looks artificial—the forms and the structure of Zen—in order to see true reality, because there is no understanding other than painted satisfaction.

STEVEN HEINE: The pattern is to create a conceptual reversal. Dōgen starts with the original expression "painted rice cakes do not satisfy hunger," and leads us to the conclusion that only painted rice cakes satisfy hunger. I think we could safely guess that if the original expression had been "painted rice cakes do satisfy hunger," he would have turned it the other way round.

BONNIE MYOTAI TREACE, SENSEI: He lifts the burden from what is a word and what is silence and asks, what is it that satisfies hunger? It beckons us to just say hello, to meet eye to eye. Even if it's just passing a bag of groceries from cashier to customer, there is a living realization at that moment, and the bottomless hunger and the immeasurable offering meet right there, right here.

Is Dōgen like Nāgārjuna, the founder of the Madhyamaka school, in the sense that there is no ideology to look for but only a process of working on your mind?

STEVEN HEINE: Dōgen's bottom line is remarkably similar to Nāgārjuna's, in terms of deconstructing misconceptions and not leading to a fixed conclusion but open-endedly divulging the array of possibilities.

ZOKETSU NORMAN FISCHER: I agree. But on the other hand, the writings of Nāgārjuna that are usually cited are wholly philosophical. Dōgen wonderfully combines philosophical perspectives, mind yoga, and very specific details about how to practice.

He is also leading a community.

TAIGEN DAN LEIGHTON: That's very important. In all of Dōgen's writings, whether they were written or given as a talk, he was talking to particular people. It's easy to abstract Dōgen's writings as if he were a philosopher presenting doctrine, but he is always talking directly to someone. He is a spiritual teacher, not a philosopher, even though what he left us could be seen as profound philosophy.

STEVEN HEINE: Dōgen was developing this multiperspective outlook in his teaching so that it would address different audiences but not compromise its ability to be heard by many other possible receivers of the message. This was an important feature of the monastery system he was trying to develop.

Let's consider a passage from one of the *Shōbōgenzō* fascicles that many people find quite difficult, Uji, or "Existence-Time":

> **Time is already just Existence, and all Existence is Time. The sixteen-foot golden body is Time itself. Because it is Time, it has the resplendent brightness of Time. We should learn it as the twelve hours of the day.**

TAIGEN DAN LEIGHTON: Uji relates to traditional Buddhist ideas about time. When I talk about this, I always refer to the ten times of the Huayan school: the past, present, and future of the past; the past, present, and future of the present and of the future; and all nine of those together. Dōgen's point is that time is our being, our presence, our experience. It's not some external container. Time also moves in many different directions; it's multidimensional. It's not, as he says, yesterday to today to tomorrow. It's moving in many different ways. We start to understand, for example, how talking about the past changes the meaning of the past right now and in the future.

The story we tell about the past makes the meaning of the past different, depending on what story we choose to tell.

He says we should question our idea of time. We don't get rid of the idea of nine o'clock, ten o'clock, eleven o'clock, but we can get rid of the idea of time as an external container. There is not an absolute, ultimate envelope of time that we are in.

ZOKETSU NORMAN FISCHER: Recently I was studying Uji once again and at the same time I was studying a book by Abraham Joshua Heschel called *The Sabbath*. It turns out that the Sabbath is all about time. Heschel's philosophy of time divides time and space. He says space is the material world and time is inherently sacred. That's also Dōgen's take-home message. He's saying that we think of time as some objective physical container in which we are moving, but, in fact, time is a flow of being. It's a flow of our being not limited to our small, physical, locatable selves; rather, it is our immense buddha-selves. When we recognize time as that, our experience of being, our experience of time, becomes quite different. Heschel's idea of time is not the same as Dōgen's idea of time, but I think it does help to understand and appreciate what Dōgen is saying. He's making an argument for the sacredness, the nonobjectivity of time, and the inseparability of time from ourselves.

STEVEN HEINE: You can compare Dōgen's view of time with modern physics. You can compare it with Jewish mysticism or other forms of philosophy or theology. You can illuminate it from a number of different directions. For example, philosophers from Aristotle to Heidegger have had ideas that have similarities. However, Dōgen is not particularly systematic in his approach to time. We wish we could sit him down and say, "OK, give it to us straight." But the message overall seems to be about the internalizing time. You are in control of time; you are the master of the moment. Break down the barriers of practice and realization, the barrier between means and ends. Time is being, being is time, and it's within us.

BONNIE MYOTAI TREACE, SENSEI: "The resplendent brightness of time" is a good phrase to let wash over you. This is Dōgen's great shout. Knowing without knowing is resplendent. You trust that shaking of the eardrums.

When one of these arrives from Dōgen, it settles in my heart and I feel like someone's hand is on my shoulder. It leaves my intellect and becomes a sense of pressure on the skin, a touch.

ZOKETSU NORMAN FISCHER: This teaching is also quite practical. The other day I was working with a group of business people on time management. Everybody was so freaked out, doing all these things at once and feeling oppressed by time. So I talked to them about Uji. I'm working on this myself, because I also run around. So I remind myself, "Wait a minute. Time is not this objective, outer phenomenon whereby I have to do this many things in this amount of time. Time is my life, time is being." As soon as I realize that, I don't need to feel time pressure. The businesspeople understood this.

Let's consider a famous line from *Genjōkōan*: "To study the self is to forget the self."

TAIGEN DAN LEIGHTON: Many students, when they hear this, want to jump right to forgetting the self. The point of it is we need to keep studying the self. That is forgetting the self. As the Dalai Lama has said, nonself in Buddhism doesn't mean getting rid of the ego. Just keep watching the experience of the self as it is; the forgetting happens all on its own.

STEVEN HEINE: In Chuang Tzu and philosophical Taoism generally, they use "forgetting" in the positive sense as letting go. It's not absentmindedness but a sense of casting off distractions. In the same passage, Dōgen refers to the casting off or dropping away of body-mind (*shinjin datsuraku*). What is emphasized here is the positive sense of moving beyond the distractions, limitations, and the conventionality that binds us and causes us to struggle. Forgetting the self happens naturally in the process of study because we move beyond it each time we study it a little bit more.

ZOKETSU NORMAN FISCHER: These two phrases are identities. If someone asks, "What is studying the self?" it is forgetting the self. If someone asks, "What is forgetting the self?" it is studying the self.

The other two sides in this famous section are also identities. If you really study the self, you are confirmed by all dharmas. If you are really confirmed by all dharmas, you have understood the nature of the self. If you are talking about ego, that means you understand the context and the point of the ego-self rather than being tied up in knots by it. You understand its purpose and its function and how to work with it. So, as Taigen was saying, the object here is not to kill the ego but to see it as it actually is. It should function in a healthy and beautiful way in the context of the entire universe, rather than being a matter of "I am just stuck on me."

TAIGEN DAN LEIGHTON: Forgetting the self is "dropping body and mind." Dōgen uses that phrase much more than he uses, for example, just sitting. All through the *Eihei Kōroku*, he uses this phrase as a seeming synonym for zazen.

This whole paragraph in *Genjōkōan* is a description of what our practice is. Dropping body and mind is an ongoing thing. It's not that it happens once and you're finished with it. Practically speaking, we see that even after studying Dōgen for thirty years there's no end to studying the self and there is no end to dropping body and mind. In each moment, we are faced with new situations, a new moment of being-time. Once again, we have to bring this whole process of studying the self, forgetting the self, dropping body and mind, into our experience right now.

BONNIE MYOTAI TREACE, SENSEI: It has to slap you in the face a little bit. We hear the words and we tend to receive them as if we were receiving a commandment, rather than an implicit question about the nature of who we are. What is it to remember the self? Is that not studying? What is it that's not studying? What is it to be enlightened? What are you talking about? The slap is the quality of catching you when you think you know the significance.

We could conclude by considering Dōgen's statement from the Kattō chapter of Shōbōgenzō, "My life has been one continuous mistake."

BONNIE MYOTAI TREACE, SENSEI: We should appreciate how freeing that is. There is no escaping the mistake.

TAGIEN DAN LEIGHTON: It's extremely important in practice to make mistakes. We can never learn anything if we don't make mistakes. It has a lot to do with beginner's mind, or not knowing. To accept the limitations of this moment of being-time means that we know we are making a mistake right now. Yet we have to be willing to do that to actually practice.

We can say that we learn from our mistakes, but the attitude of just being open to the reality of the mistake in front of me and witnessing mistake upon mistake and being willing to meet, engage, assess, and celebrate the mistake is the ongoing practice. This is the Buddha going beyond Buddha that Dōgen speaks of. It's a very dynamic, enlarged process.

BONNIE MYOTAI TREACE, SENSEI: It asks us to look at how to make mistakes perfectly. When we are aware of causing pain or causing confusion and that's palpable, it hurts. To be able to face that and not let that break our life and our practice is one of the highest mountains. And it is born in that very deep valley that we usually like to avoid.

ZOKETSU NORMAN FISCHER: In our practice, the process goes on forever. "Continuous" implies that. We don't come to the place where we say, "Now I've got it. I've got the whole thing down. It's perfection." The sense of an ever more subtle, ever more refined understanding and development without end is what this saying implies. It always unfolds in front of you. I wouldn't want any other way of practice.

17

Healthy Ego vs. Nonego:
Can Psychology Help Buddhist Practitioners?

JACK KORNFIELD

HARVEY ARONSON

JUDY LIEF

Do you think Buddhism is a complete path to liberation, requiring no practices outside of itself, or will practitioners need the techniques of psychology as well?

JACK KORNFIELD: Of course Buddhism is a complete path to liberation that requires no practice outside of itself. It offers an enormous number of practices and skillful means, all of which are rooted in the fundamental understanding of liberation, emptiness, and compassion. That being said, it would be too facile to say that since Buddhism is complete, we can just forget psychology and therapy.

Even though Buddhism is a complete path, students do not always have access to the complete teachings in an environment where they can spend a great deal of time with a teacher. Also, there are many different kinds of teachers and they specialize, so one teacher alone may not be offering the complete package, which is understandable and fine.

So yes, Buddhism is complete and it's wonderful. But there are also a variety of very helpful, skillful means coming from the field of psychology that complement what someone can get from a given teacher and a given practice. The majority of our Buddhist communities in the West have used these. There's tremendous benefit that comes from the tools of psychotherapy because they can allow a person to be present as a witness. They also have good technologies for going into the body and working with the content of experience, something that particular teachers or techniques might not offer.

HARVEY ARONSON: I like to look at this whole issue from a cross-cultural perspective. In traditional Tibetan Buddhism, for example, there was a lot of cultural stability. There was an extended family system with extensive contact between child and parent. Buddhism worked extraordinarily well in that context, and in terms of spiritual life, it did what it needed to do. But when we try to transplant the traditional Tibetan approaches to spiritual life into the West—which is dramatically different in terms of values, language, child rearing, ideals, expectations, and so forth—we almost certainly run into difficulties. There are a host of problems that individuals have that Buddhism was never designed to address, including the whole spectrum of mental illness, from anxiety to depression to psychosis, and to the nuts and bolts of couples' issues.

When Buddhism came to the West, we injected it into our culture under the rubric of mental health, and that was to some extent an arbitrary injection. It could have come in under religion or philosophy, but there was a lot of interest in Buddhism in the mental health world. As a result, some of us probably carried a misguided expectation that Buddhism would offer everything to everyone. I've heard Buddhist teachers say, "Take care of meditation and it will take care of you," with the implication that it will cure everything by itself. But I have seen students of these teachers suffering from psychosis, and the teachers didn't know what to do with it.

Buddhism is a system that is full of techniques and wisdom. It is a path that leads successfully to liberation—that is clear. But it is also clear that there are people practicing these paths who have medical, emotional, and mental health issues that few, if any, Buddhist teachers can address.

JUDY LIEF: Buddhism is a complete path to liberation and it existed as such long before psychotherapy developed. Yet I know many practitioners who have without a doubt benefited from the skillful methodology of various forms of psychology and counseling. I would say, though, that the entry of Buddhism into our society using psychological metaphors so strongly may have led some people to think of Buddhism as a kind of magic pill, as a way to go beyond problems that we might not have wanted to face personally or as a society.

The goals of psychology and the goals of Buddhadharma have often been confused as well. In the bargain, Buddhadharma can turn into a means for becoming a remodeled, better person—a new and improved version of yourself—able to cope with difficulties of all kinds. This is a very different approach from looking directly at who you are, as you are, and mining the wisdom within that. There is a radical difference of view there. Buddhism has a very strong trust and belief in some quality of basic goodness, no matter what your moment-to-moment traumas and states of mind are or what your personal history might be.

The confusion between Buddhism and psychology also goes the other way. I've seen students ask Buddhist teachers questions that seem to me appropriate to talk to a psychologist about, with the expectation that Buddhist teachers should know everything. For example, a person will sometimes ask a monastic teacher detailed questions about how to deal with relationships or parenting.

JACK KORNFIELD: Or how to raise their children.

JUDY LIEF: Yes. Why on earth would you ask a monk how to raise children? That comes once again from the misguided idea that Buddhism is designed as a problem-solving methodology. Overall, Buddhism comes from the ground of understanding the qualities of your basic nature. So one does not need to somehow reject oneself in the hope of constructing the better self we envision.

JACK KORNFIELD: The liberation that's offered at the core of the Buddhadharma is indeed beyond the self. The realization of selflessness and of emptiness is not found in very much of psychology. There are a few transpersonal and perhaps even spiritual perspectives that come into that terrain, but for the most part it is based more on what Judy called the remodeling of the self.

Psychology has focused on healthier functioning, but there's a possibility of liberation and freedom offered by Dharma practice that is far beyond what is encompassed in the vision of human capacity in psychology. It's as if we could take psychology's DSM—the voluminous listing of all the diseases and mental illnesses—and reverse it and create a DSM that showed all the possible positive capabilities of love, compassion, inner luminousness, and freedom that Buddhist practice causes a human being to realize. Those are far beyond what is normally a part of the discourse of psychotherapy.

JUDY LIEF: That's a great idea, Jack. I think you should produce that reverse DSM.

So you all seem to agree that while there is nothing lacking in Buddhism *per se*, people in certain circumstances may need something more?

JUDY LIEF: The very notion that Buddhism is supposed to do everything for everyone can create a tremendous sense of failure for people. That can make it hard for them to realize that they do need some help, and I know people who feel they must have failed as practitioners. They keep asking themselves why their practice hasn't worked and why they still need help. That's an unfortunate way of viewing the Dharma or, for that matter, of viewing themselves or therapy.

HARVEY ARONSON: Frankly, I don't think it's so important to emphasize the idea of a complete path. I'm willing to be agnostic about that. I think we can simply say that there are practitioners in certain circumstances who, for whatever reasons, do not have important needs met.

At the same time, I would say that there is a very powerful assimilation of Buddhism in the West to a certain kind of pragmatism, hedonism, and peak performance. That trend represents an almost unconscious slipping away from the traditional motivations, vision, and orientation of Buddhism, which is liberation and compassion. The worldly orientation that uses Buddhism to facilitate wellness and performance—to optimize our life as a material, hedonic experience—can have benefits, but it's a far cry from what the vision really offers and from what I think inspired our involvement with Buddhism.

JUDY LIEF: I think of dealing with stress, physical pain, and illness as applied Buddhism, in the sense of applied science, as opposed to the deep exploration of pure science. It's helpful, but it's not the core.

JACK KORNFIELD: Yet within the Buddhist tradition, there's a lot of applied science: right speech, right action, right livelihood, Buddhist personality theory, teachings on community relations and many other forms of wisdom. It's important not to establish a hierarchy that says that emptiness and liberation are the great thing that Buddhism teaches and that the applied methodologies are lower class. The absolute and the relative are different dimensions of our experience, and the Dharma approaches both of them through a wide variety of skillful means, through form and emptiness, two different aspects of the Dharma.

HARVEY ARONSON: The applied science part of Buddhism is extraordinarily important, but when that is emphasized in a way that divorces it from the view, and from the extraordinary teachings on compassion, we end up with something that loses contact with what I think is uniquely a contribution of Buddhism to the culture of humanity. At that point, the true beauty of Buddhism is not communicated.

JUDY LIEF: One could lose the genuine acting out of Buddhism in everyday life, or one could lose the view. Either would be half-baked Buddhism.

If we agree that psychological approaches can complement the applied aspect of Buddhism, what are those approaches uniquely good at?

JACK KORNFIELD: A teacher who's very good at training people in the highest states of samādhi came to me looking for help, because half the students who came to him couldn't do the practices he was teaching. They were suffering from depression, anxiety, and trauma, and he wasn't trained in how to work with people encountering such extreme states.

Dharma can of course be applied to such situations, but so can some of the skillful means of psychotherapy that follow Dharma principles. Psychological approaches are particularly helpful for the trauma and historical injury that a lot of people in our culture carry. These approaches can be very helpful for people who are practicing meditation and then find the history of suffering we carry in our culture starting to arise as they sit. Without help, someone can get caught in, or lost in, that trauma for a long time.

Are there aspects of Buddhist tradition and practice that we may be leaving out or overlooking that would accomplish some of what psychotherapies do?

HARVEY ARONSON: This is a complicated issue. It's not so easy to put something into operation when you don't have the supporting system. Even if we have three hundred people meditating in a hall together, they're really three hundred atoms who don't usually feel very connected. The people meditating in the hills of Tibet would feel very connected to the village at the bottom of the hill because of the whole context within which they were working. That provided an embedded Dharma, an implicit Dharma world, that's very hard for us to duplicate in the West.

JACK KORNFIELD: Of course that culture has a shadow side, which is a kind of complacency. In this atomized culture, our shadow is a kind of individualistic materialism.

What about practices that are intended to activate compassion, such as lojong? Can we make use of these in some cases where others might use therapy?

HARVEY ARONSON: There are all sorts of practices for absorbing other people's suffering into one's own, being aware of one's own kleśas, and absorbing others' kleśa activity into one's own being, especially the darker emotions of envy, hate, and anger. But most people do not have the capacity to recognize that under their own anger lies sorrow, pain, disappointment, and trauma. Not seeing this and not knowing this intimately, they act out. Without professional assistance, many people are not able to make that turn away from acting out their fear, sorrow, loss, and unhappiness. They act it out in anger, and shaming and blaming behavior, and it takes a lot of supportive guidance to help people go from that dysfunctional process to a much more functional way of being.

JACK KORNFIELD: When you're sitting in meditation, or doing compassion practice, often you're more or less on your own, even if you are sitting with other people. Many traumas and injuries, such as those that stem from abuse and from childhood, don't show themselves very clearly until you are back in relationship. You can sit in meditation and not even have the stuff come up, or you can be practicing and when the stuff comes up, you get so triggered by it you are overwhelmed.

A therapist, or a skilled Dharma teacher who knows how to work with these kinds of difficulties, can create an ongoing relationship with that student, so that their sufferings can be held in a field of wisdom rather than a field of identification and belief. Meditation alone in many cases doesn't reveal to people what's really going on with them.

HARVEY ARONSON: Also, when the meditation starts to threaten your sense of self, you may get more reactive rather than less reactive. There may be a heightening of vulnerability. You may react more strongly and angrily to things because you're trying hard to reconstitute the self that is under pressure and slowly dissolving.

JUDY LIEF: That's supposed to happen. A certain amount of irritability and hitting those walls in practice is a good thing. But when people hold on to a false sense of how together they are, it gets in the way of working simply and honestly with their experience. When they're practicing, they are seemingly together—until they get into any kind of relationship or visit their family. Then suddenly they realize that all of this unworked-with material is still there. People's view of Buddhist practice can stray into repression—a repressed, romantic view of Buddhadharma, which can spread and be fostered in a community of practitioners. In many of our communities, any expression of anger or criticism is suppressed. There's an attachment to a kind of niceness and false gentleness that leads to very passive-aggressive group situations.

JACK KORNFIELD: There is a fear of conflict in a lot of Buddhist communities, since we are not really skilled or trained at how to work with this stuff when it comes up. As long as you keep your mouth and your eyes shut, it will be fine. But as soon as it actually comes out, it scares everybody. They don't know what to do, and they haven't had the modeling from teachers for how to work with it in an active way.

HARVEY ARONSON: The closer the relationship, the more older imprints will become activated. So couples and families are hotbeds for this sort of thing. As the people in a couple or a family practice meditation, they may see things that they will react to very strongly. These are points that require close attention, and most Dharma teachers are not in a position to offer the specialized guidance it takes to work with families and couples.

How do you know whether it's better for a meditator who is having psychological difficulties to seek psychotherapy or to do more or different Buddhist practices?

HARVEY ARONSON: When people come to our Buddhist center, they're not explicitly looking for therapy. But since I am a therapist, I pay attention when things seem to move outside a certain range. Once you get to know people and see how they're practicing, you notice if something is going into the range where their turmoil is affecting their functioning in life. If they're reporting that their appetite is off or their interest in life is waning or they're not sleeping well or their anxiety is extreme, I certainly think that's worth attention. If we've been working together for a while, and there hasn't really been any movement in those particular areas, or they are getting worse, I feel very comfortable suggesting that somebody seek therapy.

Is there a difference going to a therapist who is also a Buddhist practitioner?

JACK KORNFIELD: Any good therapist will have to have some appreciation of the principles of mindfulness, compassion, forgiveness, and non-identification that are central to the Dharma, or their therapy won't be very helpful. They don't have to be Buddhist or know Buddhism so much as be skilled in what they do and supportive of the spiritual path of that person. They have to be respectful of the student's spiritual practice and understand that it offers dimensions not offered in the therapy.

JUDY LIEF: Just because you're a Buddhist and a therapist doesn't mean you're a good Buddhist therapist. [laughter] I'd rather have someone go to a good therapist no matter what their tradition is. There's a kind of fundamentalism in the notion that you have to go to a Buddhist therapist, which automatically means they'll understand you and be good.

Nonetheless, the question of when to advise someone to seek therapy is sensitive. I have definitely done so, when I felt someone was a little off kilter. But I find it very important to counsel someone when they are going to therapy not to identify with their problem and use it to define themselves. It's vital to see the problem without covering it up, but it's just as important not to grasp on to it as a solid identity: victim, addict, depressed, anxious, phobic. I would try to lighten the identity but not diminish or dismiss the problem.

Some people say, well, Buddhism didn't work for me but therapy did.

JACK KORNFIELD: You can't say Buddhism "didn't work." A particular practice with a particular teacher may not have been helpful to that person—that's all that you can say. It's fundamentalist to say Buddhism does this or is that, or works this way or that. That is a very limited way of seeing the multiplicity of Buddhism. At Spirit Rock, many of our Buddhist teachers are also trained as psychiatrists, psychologists, or psychotherapists, and they draw on those skills when they're needed. The point is to listen to what frees the heart. If you are stuck, you need to find whatever skillful means you can to help free the heart. That's really what Buddhism teaches. The freeing of the heart may come in the framework of a Buddhist center or a Buddhist practice, or it may come from a skillful therapist.

JUDY LIEF: Working or not working is beside the point. The Buddhist path is a way of life that has its ups and downs like anything else. Sometimes it seems to be working splendidly and other times you wonder why you're doing it. Appreciating things not working is one of the best parts of the path.

You've talked about how psychotherapeutic work can offer something to Buddhist practitioners. What does Buddhism offer to psychology?

JACK KORNFIELD: We could say that the psychologies—plural—tend to be oriented toward the healing of a certain level of mental distress and coming into a healthy sense of functioning. In some ways, Buddhist practice almost assumes some healthy functioning. It hasn't been the Buddhist focus to try to take people from mental illness to a level of healthy functioning. Buddhism has a vision of what is actually possible for a human being that goes way beyond healthy functioning, and that vision is something we can offer not only to psychology but also to the West at large. That is huge.

HARVEY ARONSON: I wonder really whether mainstream psychology would ever attend to those vast teachings, which are an addition to the vision of what is humanly possible. They are Buddhism's great contribution to world culture.

On a nuts-and-bolts level, though, the thing that has contributed most to the practice of psychotherapy is mindfulness. At this point, you could find mindfulness taught in books on just about every mental-disorder syndrome. There's lots of research work also going on into the effects of mindfulness, which is helping to change how many people view human potential.

JUDY LIEF: Beyond mindfulness, one of the things that Buddhism offers is the acceptance of a wider range of possible human experiences as valid expressions of who you are and how to live. Things are becoming narrowed to a few acceptable ways of being human, and therefore the number of treatable conditions lying outside of that is becoming larger and larger.

HARVEY ARONSON: Buddhism encourages us to appreciate the value of working with the mind directly. At a certain point during a patient's treatment, I might hear from an insurance company that if the patient doesn't get on medication, they're not going to support further therapy. I'm not opposed to it when it's appropriate, but it's clearly being overdone.

JACK KORNFIELD: The idea that we just give someone a pill so he or she can go back to being a productive worker runs completely counter to the vision of who we are as human beings—a vision that lies at the heart of Dharma. Medication can be helpful at times, but Buddhism offers a vast view that isn't evident in most of what passes for mental health care at this point.

JUDY LIEF: In some ways it goes right back to the First Noble Truth. If we accept a certain amount of discomfort and pain as part of being a human, then instead of just trying to free ourselves of hassles, we take a much richer view of what it means to be human.

Is it realistic to think that this broader view of what it means to be human can actually make inroads into mainstream psychology?

JACK KORNFIELD: Scientific research in neurobiology will continue to show a much richer view of human possibility and affirm the power of meditation and other forms of practice and training. That said, we live in such a materialistic world that there's a missing piece that goes beyond ordinary well-being. It's remembering our incarnation and what we are here for and who we really are, connecting back to our buddha nature and the possibility of liberation. This is a big stretch for our culture.

JUDY LIEF: If there is a meeting point between psychological understandings of mind and the Buddhist view, I think it has do with the nature of consciousness. Buddhism has been looking directly at the nature of consciousness for thousands of years. The fact that science is taking an interest is an exciting development.

JACK KORNFIELD: This whole discussion of the scientific approach and its relationship to Buddhism is not an either/or proposition. There are important things to learn from psychotherapy and science that complement and support deep Dharma principles. That's the dance we're involved in. We have to become comfortable with paradox.

It's actually through our suffering, our conflicts, and our trauma that we understand what real emptiness is. We can find the necessary healing in our lives and use the skillful means of interpersonal relations—close relations with teachers, therapy at times—and ground them in the great vision of Dharma. That's being a mature Dharma student. Anything else would be a one-sided, fundamentalist view, rather than the view of someone who is thoroughly dedicated to the liberation of their own heart.

18

The Tantric Experiment:
Bringing Vajrayāna to the West

ANNE CAROLYN KLEIN

LARRY MERMELSTEIN

DZOGCHEN PONLOP RINPOCHE

Tantra is by its very nature exotic and esoteric, so it can cause puzzlement or even disdain. How do you think tantra, Vajrayāna, is perceived in the West today?

ANNE CAROLYN KLEIN: In academia, there's a lot of interest in tantra. There's interest in assimilating it into other themes in religious studies. Because of its investigation of mind states, it becomes associated with different kinds of psychology. It is also associated with "the transgressive," the encouragement to transgress certain societal norms.

But while scholars like to talk about tantra as transgressive, in my view that misses how tantra actually functions for its practitioners. It doesn't take into account the long history of how tantric ideas and practices have been assimilated very gradually and very thoughtfully—first in India, but particularly in Tibet—into an organized, graded path that leads to the realization that is central to all of Buddhism. Vajrayāna is not predicated purely upon being radical and iconoclastic.

LARRY MERMELSTEIN: The understanding of tantra among Buddhist practitioners, translators, and scholars has changed radically in the last thirty years or so. It's gone from being viewed as extremely bizarre to being everything from reasonable, albeit still strange and provocative, to having a kind of Hollywood allure. We now have dozens of genuine representatives of this tradition on Western soil. Compared with the early days, we have many more human exemplars of what it means to practice in this tradition, and the reality tends to replace the fantasy. People are therefore coming to understand tantra much better.

DZOGCHEN PONLOP RINPOCHE: In the West, there is a growing understanding of the tantric path. At the same time, I still see a lot of misunderstanding among practitioners of different Buddhist traditions. I interact with members of the Theravādin School, Chinese Mahāyāna, Zen, and so forth. There still seems to be a lot of misunderstanding of what each of us is doing and the theoretical grounding, if you will, that each path rests on. Perhaps there's a lack of trust. It would be good if we could make our path more theoretically approachable, so that the theory it operates on would be better understood.

What do you mean by more theoretically approachable?

DZOGCHEN PONLOP RINPOCHE: The precise details of Vajrayāna practices are not something we can share publicly. They involve details that require a lot of context and initiation. However, we can share the basic theory of Vajrayāna: the principles of *prajñā* and *upāya*; the view of *śūnyatā* and how that leads to the idea of *sampannakrama* (completion stage); the view of compassion and loving-kindness; and the understanding of luminous mind. We can also discuss the wide range of skillful means, such as deity meditation and mantra recitation. We can make Vajrayāna practices and view more approachable, so people can understand the theoretical basis of what tantric practitioners are doing. That will clarify a lot of confusion, including the way in which tantra is not transgressive, as Anne was saying, and the way in which it is.

What is being transgressed, then?

DZOGCHEN PONLOP RINPOCHE: Ego. If there's no true sharing, about the Vajrayāna tradition with those outside of it, many people will only come to understand it from one individual or another. Some are very skilled practitioners and some are pretty crazy practitioners. Some can represent the tradition very well and some can actually generate more misunderstanding.

ANNE CAROLYN KLEIN: I agree that some kind of larger-scale sharing is very important. Tantra seems at times to be talked about as if it's another category, completely outside the main thrust of Buddhism. One of the harder things for practitioners of other Buddhist traditions to understand about tantra is that its goals are completely in line with Buddhism's central goals of wisdom and compassion. That needs to be explained and understood, because that's what will help make tantra more comprehensible to those practicing other Buddhist traditions, and perhaps to the world at large.

What about the fact that tantra is often talked about by its practitioners as being more advanced than other forms of Buddhism? Doesn't that automatically put someone from another tradition on the defensive?

LARRY MERMELSTEIN: That's an interesting and tricky area. There can be a superiority complex that radiates from Vajrayāna practitioners. My teacher Chögyam Trungpa Rinpoche once stayed with a few professor friends of mine. One of them, who had spent a lot of time in Burma, said to Rinpoche, "I know you're from the Vajrayāna tradition of Tibet and I know in Burma they practice Theravāda, but I have to say you're completely like the people I knew in the monastery I lived next door to." Trungpa Rinpoche himself recounted many times his experience of meeting a Burmese monk during his first days in India after he had escaped from Tibet. They compared notes about meditation practice and they both found themselves asking each other, "When did you travel to my country to study?"

In Vajrayāna, we are taught the three-yāna view: Hīnayāna, Mahāyāna, Vajrayāna, which are properly understood as stages on the path. But these categories can be misunderstood as referring to particular groups of people. For example, when we talk in the Vajrayāna context about Hīnayāna, we're not talking about Theravādins. For Theravādin practitioners, I suspect there's a huge amount of what we might identify as Mahāyāna and Vajrayāna in their manifestation and their practice life.

ANNE CAROLYN KLEIN: I heartily agree with that. One thing that would help is for us to talk about our various practices for cultivating equanimity, compassion, and love. Every Buddhist tradition has these. What are our various practices for cultivating mindfulness? There's a lot of potential for fruitful convergence. There are many wonderful techniques in the Theravāda tradition that would certainly be of value to Vajrayāna practitioners, and the dialogue would be good for the vibrancy of the Vajrayāna tradition.

Rinpoche mentioned that there are details in Vajrayāna that are not shared, that are secret. How do you explain why secretness is used? It can be misunderstood as the basis for a cult.

DZOGCHEN PONLOP RINPOCHE: For people to have an understanding of tantra will take some time. The details of what Vajrayāna means and how it works will come across in time as we begin to share more and see more teachers. It would be difficult to clarify everything in a short period of time. Many great Vajrayāna masters traveled to America, such as His Holiness the Sixteenth Karmapa, His Holiness Dilgo Khyentse Rinpoche, the venerable Kalu Rinpoche, His Holiness Dudjom Rinpoche. The very venerable Trungpa Rinpoche took North America as his seat and set a very good ground. Nevertheless, we can see how acculturating people to tantra is necessarily a long process.

Practicing tantra requires a strong community context and careful training. How are we doing in creating Vajrayāna communities in a society that's very different from the one in which Vajrayāna flourished for a thousand years?

ANNE CAROLYN KLEIN: People become attracted to Vajrayāna largely because of its teachers—because of their charisma, and their palpable compassion. The sparkling presentations of the great teachers are like beacons drawing people to them. Once the honeymoon has passed, there's a process, which is not always so easy, of actually understanding and benefiting from the practices.

One of the first obstacles is that ritual is not prevalent in many parts of the modern West. So a core challenge for many people is to be able to work with ritual—to be able to experience it as way to realization, rather than experiencing it as a superficial traditional requirement. Often people see ritual as a bunch of rules and forms. The obsessive mind kicks in and it becomes a pursuit: How do you do this? How do you do that? Certainly one tries to do things correctly, but when that dominates, the quality of the ritual as a means of teaching can fade away.

LARRY MERMELSTEIN: This has been a difficulty for many people. I'd say we're doing the best we can, and one of the things we can benefit from is translator–practitioners to support that process. In time, many if not most people find a good relationship with ritual, but we should always be attuned to helping them along.

ANNE CAROLYN KLEIN: Another challenge is that steps have to be taken to include the body in practice. It's possible to be reciting a mantra and imagining you are a deity but your body is completely checked out and not resonating with what's going on. It's all in the head. A certain amount of training is necessary to help people be in their body. What we usually translate as "visualization" is something that is much broader than that word implies. It does a great disservice to what one is actually doing.

The word "visualization" is very eye-sense oriented.

ANNE CAROLYN KLEIN: It's also very subject–object oriented. Our notion of visualization conjures up something like watching a movie. In the traditional cultures in which tantra arose, you never saw anything that wasn't alive in front of you. Seeing has a certain richness and aliveness and freshness in that kind of culture.

So embodying a deity is not just done with the eyes; it's done with the whole organism. We can also forget the power of the mantra itself to evoke the deity and her world, and the extent to which one needs to get out of the way and allow it to do that. Too often we stand in the way, and worry and obsess. It becomes a real interference with practice.

LARRY MERMELSTEIN: Making the ritual practice relevant and workable requires training, which is one of the jobs that our translation group takes on, in addition to simply translating. We try to help people engage with the texts and the methods in a way that allows that engagement to become a natural extension of their prior Buddhist practice, rather than a bunch of new bells and whistles.

ANNE CAROLYN KLEIN: It's also very important to bring general Dharma understanding to the practice, so that you really understand absolute and relative truth and how the practice of tantra shows you their union. That does not come automatically, so at the very least some basic Madhyamaka helps a lot.

DZOGCHEN PONLOP RINPOCHE: I work with a lot of students in America, and I agree that there need to be progressive stages of training in the view of meditation, bringing it to one's experience, and then manifesting that in one's action. I would say, though, that the students generally are doing pretty well. Of course, the path is a path. There is a quotation from Maitreya's teaching that the path at the beginning is mostly impure with lots of mistakes; in the middle, the path is half and half; toward the end, it is more pure and perfect. That's what everybody goes through, even in one sitting session. We start out very challenged, in the middle we calm down a little bit, and toward the end when we have to leave for work, we actually start to enjoy it.

LARRY MERMELSTEIN: We are part of a very big experiment of bringing an infusion of incredible wisdom from Tibet to the West. We have rapid communications across the globe, but the rate of transmission of the Dharma has a kind of natural rate. We're proceeding slowly, from some aerial perspective. Or perhaps we're moving quite quickly. Only future generations will be able to judge how we've done. It's hard for us to see since we are in the middle of the experiment. Overall, though, the students seem to be finding the teachings very useful and relevant and are connecting with them slowly but surely.

It seems easy to want to be a sort of cognitive superstar in working with these practices, rather than engaging them with our whole body and mind.

ANNE CAROLYN KLEIN: As Rinpoche said, a path is a path. And part of the path for many of us may be transcending the cognitive superstar syndrome. Because we're so used to cognitive learning, we feel that if we can just get it intellectually, we'll have it. On one of the very first visits that His Holiness the Dalai Lama made to the West, he said that if you've been practicing for about five years and instead of getting angry ten times a day you only get angry seven or eight times a day, you should understand that you've made progress.

That's a very compassionate teaching. It helps people to understand the extent of the path—what a big job it is even to reduce your anger by 20 percent. Too often we idealize things. We suddenly feel we've changed radically and then are devastated when we see the old habits creep in again, as of course they will. The path is a path. It unfolds and it's important to savor and appreciate that what may seem like a small thing is actually quite an important achievement.

DZOGCHEN PONLOP RINPOCHE: Patience is very important, especially in this time when instant gratification is expected. People think they must achieve something right away, and that becomes an obstacle. It is true that the Vajrayāna teaches about sudden awakening, but all of those teachings are based on the idea that our mind is primordially awake, already awake. So we discover that. That's very different from instant gratification.

ANNE CAROLYN KLEIN: I am reminded of something I just read from Longchenpa: the fact of primordial buddha nature does not contradict the fact that there's much to purify.

LARRY MERMELSTEIN: Trungpa Rinpoche said, "I have achieved the *bhūmi* of patience due to the kindness of my students."

DZOGCHEN PONLOP RINPOCHE: Wonderful!

ANNE CAROLYN KLEIN: Another of the challenges is that we're householders, by and large. There are constraints on the amount of time we have to practice. Will a few short, intense retreats ever add up to what people were able to do in Tibet? That's a huge question.

LARRY MERMELSTEIN: I firmly believe that tantric practice is workable in the world we live in. If the Vajrayāna actually began with King Indrabhuti supplicating the Buddha for teachings that would work for him as a king, who was not willing or able to give up his worldliness and responsibilities, that means the Vajrayāna teachings are ultimately meant for householders.

Our world is moving a lot faster than it probably was back in those days and so, yes, the stresses and complexities seem to be much greater than centuries ago. But so what? The very choicelessness of it is good for us. We have to do everything we can to incorporate the teachings on a continual basis in our lives, knowing full well that many of us may not have time for intense long retreat. The teachings are geared to being applicable in our lives, as they are. It's extremely workable. Thousands of people are currently engaged in that experiment. Many of us do experience the frustration of wanting it to be better, but that is the essence of path.

DZOGCHEN PONLOP RINPOCHE: The Buddha's response to King Indrabhuti's request clearly indicates that the tantric path is meant primarily for lay practitioners. In many of the *mahāsiddha* stories, their families also thoroughly engage in a Vajrayāna practice. Tantric practitioners manifest in many walks of life: as a carpenter, bartender, or farmer like Marpa. Of course we can be monastic yogis, but in many ways these methods are more suitable for lay yogis and yoginis.

ANNE CAROLYN KLEIN: Even if we feel that tantra is a workable path for householder yogis and yoginis, we still need to work with time management. It helps if we can constantly reflect on what is meaningful in life, and how precious time is. Almost any amount of practice is going to be beneficial. It's not all or nothing. There's a black-and-white thinking that can intrude. If I can't be the next Milarepa, why bother? It's always worthwhile to do what is possible and we need to get over the superstar, overachiever syndrome.

19

Dzogchen: The Great Perfection

YONGEY MINGYUR RINPOCHE

MARCIA SCHMIDT

RON GARRY

What is Dzogchen and what is unique about it?

YONGEY MINGYUR RINPOCHE: Generally speaking, the Vajrayāna includes all three of the yānas, or vehicles—Hīnayāna, Mahāyāna, and Vajrayāna. These subdivide further, so there are nine yānas in all.

In Dzogchen practice, you must begin with all the usual preliminaries—taking refuge, generating bodhicitta, and so forth. Then the main project of Dzogchen is to look directly at the nature of mind, *rigpa*. Rigpa is not our ordinary, everyday mind. It is not conceptual mind. It is the mind that is beyond concept, the mind that is free from subject and object.

Since rigpa, the natural state of awareness, is our innate nature, not the result of a process, there are many ways to enter the Dzogchen path. In fact, Dzogchen is the essence of all the paths and all the practices. It is called "the Great Perfection" because everything is there. It is the condensed meaning of all the paths and the essence of everything, samsara and nirvana both.

MARCIA SCHMIDT: As the pinnacle of the nine yānas, Dzogchen is a part of the total path, and you cannot extract any element of it and isolate it. It requires working directly with a master qualified in the Dzogchen tradition.

It is through the kindness of one's teacher, and through the kindness of all the lineage gurus, that one is able to enter the Dzogchen path.

Even though Dzogchen is sometimes referred to as a path of simplicity and doing nothing, that describes just the isolated moment of remaining in a nonconceptual awareness. We all would love to think that we can practice Dzogchen and be able to remain for long periods of time in the nature of mind. But for some reason we can't.

So it is not a path for someone without diligence. There's actually quite a lot to do to really be a Dzogchen practitioner. The complete path includes: purifying the obscurations—those things that prevent our mind from being in the natural state; gathering the accumulations, or merit—the many necessary positive circumstances that allow us to practice intensively; and working closely with a qualified teacher.

YONGEY MINGYUR RINPOCHE: It is important to emphasize the role of the teacher. Do-it-yourself Dzogchen is impossible. You need the lineage, and since everything is interdependent, you also need many other causes and conditions. We must rely on this power of interdependence, not simply our own power.

However, when you practice Dzogchen, you do not get the rigpa from someone else, or from somewhere else. It exists within all sentient beings; it's already present within us. We are buddha, but we are obscured by bad karma, by the negative causes and conditions that give us the illusion of subject and object, that cause us to experience impure body, speech, mind, and an impure world.

How does the teacher help us to experience the nature of mind?

RON GARRY: In my experience, traveling the path always involves working with my various states of mind, and that's why it's so critical to have a wisdom teacher. Quite often I might feel that I'm having an experience of awareness, but more likely my experience is connected with consciousness. It's only through the blessings and the connection with my teacher that I'll be able to come to an experience of awareness, my true nature, beyond consciousness.

Based on this, my focus is more on preliminary practices and the *ngön-*

dro practices of refuge, prostrations, Vajrasattva mantra recitation, mandala offering, and guru yoga. Through those practices, and through faith and devotion in my teacher, I feel I am protected from getting caught up in false states of spiritual experiences, like mistaking dull mind for rigpa.

YONGEY MINGYUR RINPOCHE: The teacher's role is to point out. There are many, many experiences that can be quite similar to or confused with rigpa. For example, the practice of formless or objectless śamatha—resting the mind without an object of meditation—can be similar to Dzogchen practice, to rigpa, but it is not the same. Similarly, one may experience a kind of dullness of mind that has very little conceptualization, which we call the base consciousness (ālaya). Many people think that ālaya is the essence of the mind, but that's not really Dzogchen. So the teacher keeps pointing out the natural mind, so you can see very clearly the difference between conceptual mind and natural mind, between ālaya and rigpa, between objectless śamatha and rigpa.

MARCIA SCHMIDT: My teacher, Tulku Urygen Rinpoche, Mingyur Rinpoche's father, taught that even though the words are the same, the meaning becomes more exalted as you go through the different stages. The vipaśyanā, or clear seeing, practice of the lower vehicles is actually a form of śamatha from the perspective of Dzogchen and Mahāmudrā. It is not the same, but people often think it is the same.

What is the difference between objectless śamatha and rigpa?

YONGEY MINGYUR RINPOCHE: In objectless śamatha, the instruction is not to meditate and not to be distracted, but just to rest. But just resting alone does not become rigpa practice, because you don't have recognition. The main difference between objectless śamatha and natural mind is recognition. You get that recognition from the pointing-out instruction of the teacher, and then you can cultivate it further.

To cultivate the recognition of natural mind, you can hold the gap between first and second thought. But if you wait for the gap, that is a big mistake, because you don't have to wait for natural mind. Rigpa is always present. It is spontaneous presence. People are always thinking that to meditate on rigpa, natural awareness, means you have to extinguish thought and emotions. They think, "I . . . have . . . such . . . openness . . . and . . . spaciousness," but what they have is strong grasping for spaciousness, openness, and rigpa. Their meditation becomes tiny, because they are focusing on having something to practice and something to abandon.

People think like that because they have been told that rigpa is beyond subject and object. Since thoughts and emotions are tied up with subject and object, they think they have to block them to experience rigpa. But rigpa doesn't do anything with thought and emotions; it lets them be there. If you recognize natural clarity, then everything is transformed. Although something might look like an emotion, it is not a real emotion. That's why rigpa is not impermanent. But of course, that's why it's not permanent, either.

RON GARRY: When you learn from a Dzogchen master, it speaks directly to your experience. Everything is a practice. Everything you learn points directly to your own experience—jealousy, envy, anger, and so on—and how to free yourself right on the spot. These teachings deal with the fact that you are a human being.

YONGEY MINGYUR RINPOCHE: The authentic Dzogchen teaching has to be received with proper timing. Some teachings you have to receive first, and some teachings you have to receive later. If you receive the later teachings too early, that is not good for your practice. You will not get the real taste of the teaching. It becomes just an idea to try. If you receive the teachings step by step, then you can really feel the meaning of the teaching. You can get to the heart. The general idea of Dzogchen practice can be shared with everybody, but the real pith instruction is very secret and must be received through the lineage blessing.

What does "lineage blessing" mean?

RON GARRY: Lineage blessing means that Dzogchen is something living and it comes from a real-life teacher who is a living embodiment of that nondualistic awareness. They live it every day.

That is the source of everything. The fancy words are just indications, ways of communicating with us about that living essence. So when Dzogchen words get out into the general public, people start thinking that they have had that realization, and the power gets watered down. It's just Dzogchen words coming from dualistic minds. Then there is no lineage anymore.

The authentic lineage is something intimate and direct for the student. It is about being in the presence of buddha mind. If the teaching isn't coming from there, if it's just on paper or it's being transmitted by someone who is imitating, then even though it may be called Dzogchen, the lineage blessing has been cut at that point. People who are drawn to Dzogchen are drawn to it partly because of its live and very human quality. If we publish everything, it impersonalizes and dehumanizes the tradition. It is not a book on a shelf or a TV program. You need human interaction.

MARCIA SCHMIDT: You do not just receive the teaching from the teacher sitting in front of you at that moment of transmission. It comes from teachers stretching back thousands of years and their disciples, in an unbroken line.

The lineage is stabilized in the practice. Although all of the teachers may not be fully enlightened, they have a lot more realization than us to pass on. Tulku Urgyen used to say that having some recognition of rigpa is like having a candle in your hand, but if you have not stabilized that and you try to pass it on, you will hand the candle over to someone else and end up in darkness yourself.

Many people have heard of Mahāmudrā and Dzogchen. What distinguishes these two Tibetan practice traditions?

YONGEY MINGYUR RINPOCHE: The meaning of the two is not different. They just come from different angles and use different terminology. For example, in Mahāmudrā we talk about ordinary mind and in Dzogchen we talk about natural awareness. Mahāmudrā is more focused on the meditation, from the experiential point of view, and on the minute details of stillness, movement, emptiness, appearance, and so forth.

Dzogchen has more emphasis on the view. You make the distinction between conceptual mind and rigpa at the level of the view, and then you have to practice. The meaning is not different, but there is a different angle and therefore different words and different styles.

MARCIA SCHMIDT: There's a famous quote from Tsele Natsok Rangdröl that says, "Mahāmudrā and Dzogchen, different words, but not meaning. The only difference is Mahāmudrā stresses mindfulness, while Dzogchen relaxes within awareness." For the practitioner, it has to do with the approach you take, and which path we travel will depend on the karmic propensities we have.

The path of Mahāmudrā goes through various stages. The teacher takes the student through them step by step and works within the context of the student's experience to get closer and closer to the recognition of mind nature. Dzogchen starts right from the beginning to introduce the student to natural awareness, rigpa.

All of you have stressed the difficulty of Dzogchen and the need to go through a progression, a path. So is Dzogchen not really a shortcut in the way it is sometimes discussed?

YONGEY MINGYUR RINPOCHE: It's the very best shortcut! It's the number one shortcut.

How can it be both a shortcut and a path with many stages?

YONGEY MINGYUR RINPOCHE: Dzogchen gets right to the heart. It's more direct than any other method. You need preparation and various kinds of support, but the practice itself is direct. Even if you have a shortcut, there still needs to be a road there to travel on. Otherwise, you can't use the shortcut.

MARCIA SCHMIDT: Dzogchen is a shortcut because you're taking the fruition as the path. Your nature can be pointed out and then you can recognize and use that nonconceptual state through all practices, through every stage along the way.

Even though it is revealed, we still have to go through the path. Yes, we're told it's the effortless great perfection, that there is nothing to do and that it's your inherit nature. That's true in the absolute sense. But in the relative sense, we're not necessarily connecting with our absolute nature. We have lots of discursive thoughts; we have very little bodhicitta. So we have to be honest and ask ourselves, what's going to change that? If we do that, we can receive the training and make use of these methods that have a very good track record. Then they will be a shortcut for us. But we can't avoid the path.

Is rigpa exclusive to Dzogchen? Is it possible that a practitioner of another tradition may attain the quality of natural mind, rigpa?

YONGEY MINGYUR RINPOCHE: Rigpa is within us twenty-four hours a day. It doesn't matter who we are—human being, animal, part of a tradition or not. Recognition is the key. If you want to practice rigpa recognition according to Dzogchen, you need all the causes and conditions from Dzogchen. Otherwise, you cannot recognize rigpa according to Dzogchen. If you miss one component—no lineage or no real pith instruction—then there is no Dzogchen, and no recognition of rigpa according to the Dzogchen tradition.

Under what circumstances would a practitioner of other Buddhist traditions benefit from an intensive Dzogchen retreat?

YONGEY MINGYUR RINPOCHE: People who are genuinely practicing in other paths, Theravāda and Zen, for example, have a very good foundation for engaging in Dzogchen practice. Many practices are shared in common. If they decided to take part in Dzogchen practice, that could be helpful for them, because the real Dzogchen is within the mind. In order to engage in Dzogchen practice, you don't have to change your Buddhist path. Your Buddhist path would be brought to Dzogchen.

Sangha:

The Community

20

Dharma for All:
Diversity in American Buddhism

CHARLES PREBISH ▪ PAUL HALLER
MARLENE JONES ▪ GUY MCCLOSKEY

In James Coleman's book *The New Buddhism*, he indicates that the groups he researched appealed only to "a relatively small slice of the public" that was "overwhelmingly white," from the middle to higher reaches of the middle class, and highly educated. How accurate is that description?

CHARLES PREBISH: Coleman is talking about what he calls "New Buddhism," and for him that means almost exclusively "converts." In the context of convert Buddhist communities, he's probably quite accurate. But in the overall Buddhist community in the United States, it's likely that as many at 80 percent are not converts. They're Asian-immigrant Buddhists.

PAUL HALLER: We need to ask to what degree the way Buddhist sanghas present themselves deters people who don't fall into the demographic you just described. In San Francisco, the overall population is quite diverse. Caucasians represent about half the population, and then we have a large Asian-American population, about a 15-percent African-American population, and a significant Hispanic population. At Zen Center, one of the things we're trying to tackle is to what degree we deter people from this part of the demographic from feeling at home, and consequently returning on a frequent basis to our centers.

The point that Chuck makes is important to emphasize at the beginning of this discussion. Those of us who are convert Buddhists think that we are Buddhism in America. In fact, we're a minority of Buddhists in America. That's a very helpful perspective to keep in mind. Relating with the larger Sangha is another important form of diversity.

MARLENE JONES: What Coleman says fits with my experience. As a meditator who began in 1970, I would say that the communities I encountered left out a lot of people and continue to do so. For one thing, centers have been overwhelmingly white. Many of the centers began because people who went to Asia came back and wanted to start sitting groups or retreat environments. They were white men for the most part, and they tended to draw people to the centers who were like themselves.

GUY McCLOSKEY: Coleman's description does not reflect my experience in Soka Gakkai. I've spent the last fourteen years practicing in Chicago. If I look at the people present on a Sunday morning or at some large-scale Soka Gakkai event, the majority are African-American. We've also very substantially increased our Hispanic membership. At our last annual gathering in Chicago, we had about five hundred Spanish-speaking people, which was very progressive for us, because we have not been so strong among Spanish-speaking people.

Why does diversity matter? Why do communities need to reach out beyond those who already come to their doors?

GUY McCLOSKEY: We need to start from the premise that we are interconnected. We all arise from dependent origination. Then we can recognize that if our small ego, the narrow ego contained within our skin, is the extent of our sense of selfhood, that is all we are going to experience.

As we continue to practice, we open up, and our sense of self expands. Ultimately, the Buddhist sense of self is to embrace all living beings. As we progress along the path of Vimalakīrti, who is our example of the accomplished layperson, we can come to recognize that the suffering of anyone, anywhere, is our own. As I deal with suffering, the greatest relief I can find is to share the suffering of others.

MARLENE JONES: I have found the Four Noble Truths to be extremely important in teaching people of color. Suffering is the human condition. I wouldn't say that the suffering in communities of color is greater than anybody else's, but because of racism, because of struggles in surviving every day in our society, the suffering is out front.

I have spent a lot of time focusing on that theme, asking, "How can we turn suffering around to liberate the world? How can we bring healing and liberation to all beings through looking at our experience of suffering, knowing that it's true for all?" Suffering leads you to care and nurturing.

PAUL HALLER: What inspired our outreach initiative was compassion, the motivation to be of service to society at large. Diversity is one of the consequences of serving people. For example, I teach in a drug rehab center. I do that to help people, most of whom happen to be working-class people from minority groups. Inevitably, several of those people want to visit the center, and that has been a learning experience for us. The class difference stood out, so we had to devise strategies so that it wouldn't feel so difficult for these guys.

CHARLES PREBISH: Social engagement can be a means to create an environment that facilitates people of all different backgrounds feeling comfortable. Buddhist communities might well adopt the four brahma-viharas—love, compassion, sympathetic joy, and equanimity—as a basis for a new *Vinaya* for the modern world.

I also think it's helpful to emphasize precepts as practice. Once people are able to affirm a strong ethical pattern for themselves, they can manifest that ethical pattern in society in a strong way.

GUY MCCLOSKEY: Soka Gakkai is now the largest Buddhist movement in Japan, but at the end of World War II it was an organization of the poor, the sick, and the disaffected. The people we could have excluded have come to us in stages. In 1981, I first held someone in my arms while he died of AIDS. We had members at that time who refused to allow people with AIDS into their homes, where our neighborhood discussion meetings were being held. We had to confront that directly.

Nichiren said that the model of Buddhist practice is found in the *Lotus*

Sutra, in the guise of Bodhisattva-Never-Disparaging, who said, "I deeply respect you because you are on the path and you will eventually be a buddha. How can I discriminate against you?" Even though I certainly have discriminated against people at times in my life, I could never justify that from the Buddhist perspective.

PAUL HALLER: Within the Zen tradition, we have the teaching on the merging of difference and unity, the *Sandōkai*. Difference and unity is the heart of diversity. We are all the same. We all come from the same human stock, and suffer under the human condition, and every one of us is also unique. Whether you want to call it form and emptiness, difference and unity, or whatever, this is an essential theme of the Ch'an and Zen approach to practice.

If that is the goal, why are most convert Buddhist groups reaching only a narrow slice of the population?

CHARLES PREBISH: For one thing, the vast majority of convert Buddhists gravitate toward the meditation traditions. That's more of an individualistic approach, whereas in the Asian immigrant communities and in Soka Gakkai, there's a much greater emphasis on making the community a significant part of your religious life. This is appealing to people who are disenfranchised from other parts of the American community.

GUY MCCLOSKEY: The attraction of Nichiren Buddhism is human relationships. They're attracted to someone who has made a noticeable development in their life, and they ask, "What's different about you? What do you do?" Having never had an attraction toward the meditation practices, I don't know what draws people to Zen and other such traditions. I would guess that it starts off on a more intellectual rather than social, emotional level.

CHARLES PREBISH: In my research, the thing that people in Soka Gakkai say repeatedly is that the sangha is nurturing for everyone.

MARLENE JONES: I started the people-of-color retreats and the diversity council because I was uncomfortable with Spirit Rock as it existed then. It attracted people who were like the people who were already there: European-American people, who like being with people who are highly educated, have a lot of money, and who have the resources to sit a long retreat without having any financial burden.

People of color usually can't do long retreats without a scholarship. But even if you have a scholarship, you still need income to take care of your children and family. I have noticed, in fact, that many of the people of color who do come to Spirit Rock tend to be pretty educated. Some have advanced degrees; some are published authors. Many of them are similar to the European-American population here at Spirit Rock.

So there is a strong class barrier as well.

MARLENE JONES: Absolutely. That's something we're now spending some time talking about. We decided a long time ago that to begin with we were going to focus mostly on racial issues, as opposed to class, gender, and sexual orientation issues, just because they were so very prevalent. Now the diversity council has started looking at class issues as well, because they really seem to be popping up. Many people are feeling left out.

We will need to explore this more, just as we have with racial issues. It's a new frontier.

PAUL HALLER: Talking to people who have had difficulty entering the community has helped to drive what we are doing. Our diversity-initiative steering committee pays a lot of attention to what people have to say. One thing we've done as a result is formed a people-of-color sitting group that holds weekly sittings and periodic longer sessions. Their advice and what they report to us helps us formulate what we do.

CHARLES PREBISH: Over the thirty-five years that I've been investigating Buddhism in North America, both as a practitioner and a scholar, I've seen the landscape change dramatically. In the seventies, the groups were almost completely exclusive and continued that way on into the eighties. At that point people studying American Buddhism argued heatedly in the literature about how to classify the many kinds of people who were coming together to practice Buddhism. Maybe some of the distinctions we are talking about between different types of people who practice the Dharma may be starting to dissolve in a way that could be very efficacious for the evolution of a genuinely American Buddhism, one that is inclusive of all types of Buddhism and all types of people practicing Buddhism.

MARLENE JONES: I see integration gradually growing. Originally, many people said that if it were not for a people-of-color retreat, they wouldn't be here. That has started to change. Many of those same people are starting to go to the regular retreats, although not in huge numbers. It also depends on who the teacher is. People are concerned about racism for sure, but more than anything they need cultural inclusion, to feel part of what is represented.

We know that it works if we have teachers of color. It's not that we're teaching the Dharma any differently; it's just about being with people who look like you, talk like you. But other teachers are learning to be more culturally inclusive. If Jack Kornfield is teaching, he draws more people of color. He talks about racism, he deals with cultural issues, he quotes James Baldwin, he integrates cultural information, and people recognize what he's talking about. So he can draw people who are different from him, because he spent so much time learning about various cultures and ways of living in the world. We had a retreat where the goal was to have a mixed representation of people's colors, and it was successful. But it takes a lot of work, and there need to be enough people of color who can trust that the process is going to work for them.

GUY MCCLOSKEY: We have deliberately applied diversity training for our leadership, but at this stage our leadership has come to reflect the demographics of our membership. We don't have to go looking for people of color. White people are getting used to listening to black people, as opposed to the other way around.

Many people find their first experiences in a Buddhist center were far from nurturing. In fact, they were intimidating. Many people find the atmosphere of Zen, for example, austere and uninviting.

PAUL HALLER: Yes. That is often people's experience. There is a kind of an implied austerity in the Zen attention to detail. That is the feedback we get. After all, Zen is traditionally a wisdom tradition. But one thing I have noted is that in many of the Zen communities, the *Metta Sutta*, a Theravā-din text on loving-kindness, has been brought into the standard liturgy. As Zen finds its way in America, I think the active expression of compassion will become a more significant attribute. The traditional Zen notion that "we don't reach out to you; in fact we make it a little bit difficult for you" is something we are working directly with these days. We are regularly asking ourselves, "Are we creating too much of a barrier?"

I would like to add, though, that I am working-class Irish from Belfast. I did get a college degree, that's true, but my family background is working-class. So it doesn't seem to do us much good, either, to stick too tightly to this notion that everybody is upper class and highly educated. There are people from many different backgrounds in the various sanghas I am involved with.

Does it make more sense to put emphasis on integration or should the emphasis be on specific programs to meet the needs of particular groups of people?

MARLENE JONES: All of the above. But the first and most important is program for separate groups, because they draw new people who are not familiar with the Dharma.

When I first came to Spirit Rock in 1991, I felt like I had to leave myself outside. I had to assimilate or I wouldn't fit in. Over and again I watched people of color walk in the door and not come back. Or maybe they would come back once, and then never again. That's when it occurred to me that we needed to create an environment where they could feel safe and welcome, and be able to access the Dharma without facing cultural exclusion—without, in a word, being ignored.

Separate events give people an opportunity to enter comfortably and access the resources of a center like Spirit Rock, which should belong to everyone. Once people have entered, I try to encourage them to integrate into what is already established. So now we are trying to create more environments that are mixed, where there is some confluence.

PAUL HALLER: The strategy accords with our experience. Someone must feel safe enough and connected enough before their participation becomes full. Until that point, they have a guarded and qualified connection. That is just the human condition.

It is not a one-shot deal. It's a process. Maybe fifteen years ago, the notion of being gay or lesbian was a little problematic within our community. Since then, gays and lesbians have been completely integrated and hold all sorts of positions of authority and prestige. That's happened, to a large extent, because the level of safety and acceptance has grown. It's a very small issue for us now.

That would be my hope for people who are marginalized because of race or class. That over the next decade or two—through familiarity, exposure, and growing diversity in our demographics—the boundaries and separations that now require active strategies will no longer be a major concern. We will end up with a similar kind of integration as we have had with gays and lesbians.

What advice would you offer to communities that are just starting to pay attention to diversity?

PAUL HALLER: The first thing I would say is "Don't be afraid." Our whole Dharma tradition is based on the inevitability of change. We can embrace change. Diversity is not a problem to be solved. It offers riches, it offers explorations, and it offers a new way of seeing and feeling the world. My advice would be to embrace diversity, not out of a sense of duty or guilt, but out of a sense of appreciating your life.

MARLENE JONES: I've challenged all-white groups to look at themselves and wonder why there are no people of color in the room, or why people of color show up once and don't come back. During one question-and-answer period, someone asked, "What can we do? How do we recognize the people? How do we talk to them? What do we say when they come in?" I repeated to them what the Dalai Lama says: "Greet people as an old friend."

So my advice is to first get beyond fear, and greet people as if they're part of your sangha, as if they belong. We simply need to see people for who they really are—to see their true self, their buddha nature.

GUY MCCLOSKEY: My advice is to teach everyone basic elements of Buddhist philosophy, including the fact that we are indistinguishable from our environment. We are all related. We need to discover that. Paul talked about a different way of seeing the world. I think that means seeing the world as it actually is.

Also, I would advise expanding the cultural orientation of what we present for the benefit of everyone, no matter what audience we are addressing. That is something that is quite natural. We should feel awkward when we avoid it.

CHARLES PREBISH: Alan Senauke said that passivity means white supremacy. We have to remind ourselves continually not to be passive. One of the *pāramitās* is vigor. We have to take that vigor out into the world with us. Maybe it needs to be tempered by patience, so that we can do the work of bodhisattvas, but we can never be satisfied just sitting on our cushion. We have to take what we learn out into the world and share it.

How do you think the Western Buddhist Sangha will evolve over the long term as it works with issues of race and class and inclusiveness?

MARLENE JONES: There will be more sanghas and centers in urban settings, in the communities where people of color live. Also, hopefully, we'll see much more integration in the traditional white sanghas. I don't know how long that's going to take, but in the last ten or fifteen years I've seen change in that direction. It took us a long time to come up with the money to hire a full-time diversity coordinator, but we've done that and we've started a whole diversity movement as a result of that commitment. Hopefully we'll see a lot more of that kind of work going on.

CHARLES PREBISH: Perhaps we've seduced ourselves to think it will happen faster, because we're Americans and because we have better communication, and we have the Internet, and so forth. But we're still just people. I imagine that I will not see a complete integration during my lifetime, but that it will happen more gradually over time.

PAUL HALLER: I don't agree entirely. We create the future. I hope we will continue to approach it with the commitment we're taking on right now. That's essential. It might be possible, then, that in twenty to thirty years, in just the same way that issues regarding sexual preference or orientation have diminished as divisive issues within groups like ours, issues of ethnicity and race will also diminish. We will have integrated communities.

GUY MCCLOSKEY: We will need to learn more and more from each other about how to translate Buddhism in a way that communicates to Americans generally. I have no doubt that if we apply the values of Buddhism, integrated groups will form. Chicago has been described as the most segregated city in America, and yet we developed many racially diverse groups. When people in those groups get together, they share similar experiences about how to apply the values and the practice of Buddhism to their daily lives. That is what brings them together, and I see that continuing to develop.

I think Buddhism definitely can be a strong force in decreasing racism and discrimination. It has the ability to lead people into the future, as a way of life, as a way of living harmoniously with their environment and all living beings.

21

Who Will Take the Dharma Seat? Choosing and Training Teachers

JACK KORNFIELD ▪ YVONNE RAND
DZOGCHEN PONLOP RINPOCHE
RICHARD SHROBE ▪ VEN. AJAHN AMARO

What are the important qualities for a Buddhist teacher that a successful selection process would identify in a candidate?

JACK KORNFIELD: The qualities a teacher needs include true compassion and connectedness with all beings; emptiness, liberation from the identity with the small sense of self; fullness, an ability to be present and awake; maturity, someone who has a great deal of life experience; and a kind of sensitivity.

And along with all that, a Buddhist teacher needs profound Dharma practice—a deep experience of the teachings of the Buddha in their own heart and mind-stream—and a fundamental virtue and morality that is both beautiful and unshakable.

YVONNE RAND: For someone to be effective as a teacher, they have to be grounded in the culture of their students. They need to embody the clear seeing and wisdom that are possible in the world we actually live in, and not merely in the cultures that have carried Buddhadharma to the West. We need this integration so we don't split or compartmentalize the process of spiritual cultivation from our life as ordinary human beings.

DZOGCHEN PONLOP RINPOCHE: According to the Tibetan Buddhist tradition, it is important to train in the intellectual understanding of Dharma and to achieve meditative realization of emptiness and wisdom. So the main qualities are intellectual understanding of Dharma and the meditative or contemplative realization that manifests as both compassion and wisdom.

RICHARD SHROBE: I think the quality of ordinariness that Yvonne mentioned is very important—integrating Dharma with life in the society in which we're embedded.

VEN. AJAHN AMARO: One of the qualities that I would underscore is morality, *sīla*. Morality refers to a basic kind of trustworthiness and straightforwardness that someone who's going to be a teacher and guide requires. Students need to know that teachers are trustworthy and have a fundamental empathy, so they can depend on them.

This needs to come from a pragmatic rather than an idealistic perspective. Sometimes it's easy to manifest those larger qualities, but from a very idealistic position that doesn't connect with people in a direct or heartfelt way. Along with this empathy, which is grounded in practice, should come profound communication skills. To be able to hear others is extraordinarily important.

YVONNE RAND: Something else that's important for teachers, and that I've appreciated in my own teachers, is the willingness not only to take the teacher's seat but to sit in the student's seat, too.

Through what process have your schools traditionally chosen teachers and spiritual leaders?

VEN. AJAHN AMARO: In the Theravāda world of Thailand, where my experience lies, there are two basic systems—the bureaucratic system and the actual Dharma practice system.

The bureaucratic system deals with who administers the local district or province, and it's generally based on your academic accomplishment, years of practice, and where you were trained. That kind of leadership, then, is transmitted based on quite superficial characteristics. Someone might be a high-ranking monk and head of the province but have very little stature as a spiritual authority or Dharma teacher.

Then there is the forest monastic tradition, which is dominated by people who deliberately try to get away from the bureaucratic hierarchy and who avoid titles and positions. In that realm, spiritual authority and the role of being a teacher is passed on in a very organic way. There's no formal Dharma transmission and the teacher does not officially name a disciple as Dharma heir. It works in a very hands-on, organic way. It's generally based on individuals living with a teacher or in close proximity to a teacher for at least ten years before being put in a position of leadership.

It comes down to which of the students has the capacity to practice, to understand the teachings, and to communicate. Based on that, a teacher will say, "Why don't you go start a monastery someplace," or, "Why don't you go and look after this particular teaching session?" The person is put into a living situation where they can try things out, and the teacher will watch closely to see how it works. If it succeeds, insofar as people are benefiting and the person teaching is thriving, then it's okay to let it keep going. If it collapses in a disaster, then the teacher will draw that person in and try somebody else out.

JACK KORNFIELD: Dharma succession, transmission, is a very mysterious and numinous issue to discuss, because it's about the carrying the lamp of Dharma from one generation to another. In the *Mahāparinibbāna Sutta*, the Buddha, who is about to die, looks around him and says, "My friends, it may be that you'll think that the teacher's instruction has ceased because you no longer have the teacher. Don't think so. Instead, take the teachings, the Dharma that I have taught, and the Vinaya, the way of living and the virtue, and let those be the teacher." So to go along with the Dharma and the Vinaya, a council of elders was set up.

Within our tradition, as Ajahn Amaro described, there are a variety of ways that people become teachers. Some are handpicked by their teachers. Sometimes a leader is chosen from the council of elders by election or by acclaim. Sometimes it's by seniority—people actually don't want the role, but there needs to be an abbot or meditation teacher within a certain community and one of the elders must do it.

Sometimes it's spontaneous, as with great teachers such as Buddhadāsa Bhikkhu or Ajahn Dhammadharo or Pa Auk Sayadaw in Burma. Their vision and understanding was so deep and the impact of their teaching so strong that even though no teacher anointed them, the people proclaimed them a master.

YVONNE RAND: The Sōtō Zen tradition of Japan has some of what Ajahn Amaro described in terms of bureaucratic function. For several centuries, you would go to one of the big training monasteries, characteristically Eiheiji Monastery, for a period of formal practice and training, and upon receiving Dharma transmission you would be able to inherit your father's temple. It was something very functional and ordinary. I think of Dharma transmission in the Sōtō Zen school in Japan as almost like what you have to do to join a union. But in the United States we got so caught up in the reverence for transmission that we assigned it a meaning it hadn't had in Japan for quite a while.

DZOGCHEN PONLOP RINPOCHE: In Tibetan Buddhism, spiritual authority is generally conferred on a candidate in one of two ways. The first kind of spiritual authority is based on the achievement of high realization in the meditation practice. The second kind of spiritual authority is based on a candidate's having gone through a necessary course of study and meditation training and achieving strong results. In both cases, the candidate must possess genuine qualities of a Dharma practitioner, such as loving-kindness and compassion toward sentient beings, being very patient and tolerant in nature, and having a good understanding of the culture and society.

Lastly, we also have the *tulku* system, which is a way of recognizing an incarnate lama. Once a young child is recognized as being the reincarnation of a previous great master, that child also goes through extensive study and training in meditation. Therefore, tulku recognition is connected to the first qualification, because it is believed that tulkus have some kind of realization. And then they also have the other qualification, because they go through this training.

VEN. AJAHN AMARO: I would add a point that the Dalai Lama made at one of the conferences he had with Western teachers in Dharamsala a few years ago. We were having a similar discussion about authorization and he made the point that essentially the authorization is given by the student. Because if nobody shows up, what does your certificate mean? You can have all the titles and authorization in the world, but if nobody shows up—if no one's listening and no one pays attention—then it has no meaning. The point is whether people want to study with you, whether people feel your teachings affect them in a beneficial way.

In the Theravāda homelands, things get pulled apart by the weather—tropical heat, monsoon rains, moisture and mold. Things don't last as long as they do in rocky Tibet. Monasteries fall apart very quickly and easily, so someone might have been a great teacher in a particular place but once the teacher dies there's no compulsion to keep the monastery together if none of the students understood the teachings well enough to succeed him.

As a result, monasteries literally fall apart and vanish. There's no sense that a place has to be held together just because it was there last year or twenty years ago. When you have a living situation where the teaching is being transmitted effectively, there's a sense that it can work for a while, but eventually it's going to fall apart. And when it's time for it to fall apart, then it can fall apart. It's not held together out of devotion to some kind of historical momentum.

YVONNE RAND: That kind of forced impermanence could work against a hazard we face, which is building very beautiful places for practice but losing sight of the fact that this path is about being rather than having. In what Ajahn Amaro describes, the physical environment is a great blessing with respect to that particular danger.

JACK KORNFIELD: In one of the Buddha's teachings, he says that as long as followers of the way cultivate their own personal mindfulness, as long as followers of the way have unstained virtue and develop compassion, equanimity, and dedication to the path, so long will the dispensation of the Buddha prosper and not decline.

In the lineage of Thai, Burmese, and Sri Lankan practitioners, there is a collective trust in this, and I feel it myself. Although a particular temple may die out, we trust that people's dedication is such that the Dharma will spring up anew in another province or another cave or another mountain. And so we hear that there's a new group of people practicing very sincerely over here, and there's a wonderful teacher who's spent years in that mountain or cave over there. I expect that this is true of Tibetan Buddhism as well. Is that so, Rinpoche?

DZOGCHEN PONLOP RINPOCHE: Exactly. Many of the monasteries became institutionalized later on. In the beginning, as you can see from the stories like those of Milarepa, the yogis wandered in caves and mountains. There is no big monastery or institution called "Milarepa's Monastery." It's very much like the great masters of Zen or of Theravāda. I think that's something we all share in the Buddhist world.

Let's turn now to what's currently happening in the West. Are communities here rethinking the way teachers are selected?

JACK KORNFIELD: In the Asian lineages, there are very strong monastic traditions. One challenge in the West is how this transmission of Dharma can happen when most of the practitioners—and even a generation of teachers—are laypeople with families and financial responsibilities and so forth. These are people without the long training, support, and protection afforded by a monastery.

Then I have a couple of other questions to raise. In transmission you find a mixture of archetype and history. In Zen, for example, you put your name at the end of a long beautiful scroll that has the name of every teacher who received transmission from the time of the Buddha, up to your teacher and yourself: beautiful rice paper with a hundred names on it. But it's not necessarily literal—if you study Buddhist history you see that some of those people didn't live in the same century, so they couldn't have known one another. But they might have received transmission in a more archetypal way.

So while there is that luminous, archetypical quality of transmission, how do we also understand it in the most human way? Maybe there's a monastic community and the teacher has died. Or a group of students has sprung up in New York and they don't have a teacher. How do they get a teacher in a country that's not a Buddhist country?

Then there's the question of isolation. In our tradition in Asia, a charismatic teacher will often live in a monastic setting. By contrast, we have found that being a solo teacher in America is very isolating. Certain Zen masters and Tibetan lamas I have talked to have also found it very isolating to be the only teacher. So our community has tried to have several teachers share the responsibility of carrying the Dharma, rather than focusing on just one person. There can be so many expectations laid on that poor person. It helps to create a community of elders who can carry the teachings.

YVONNE RAND: Americans these days seem to be hierarchy-averse. Maybe not across the board, but there's a strong quest for the central place of egalitarianism in our culture to be reflected in our spiritual practice—focusing on horizontal relationships as opposed to vertical, hierarchical relationships. There are problems that have collected around hierarchy and power and authority, and one of the challenges for those of us who are sitting in the teaching seat is to not throw out the baby with the bath water.

What happens when the teacher no longer wears robes? What are the hazards of some practitioners in the meditation hall wearing a version of the Buddha's robe while other people don't? Are we focused on looking good or being "somebody," when that's in exact opposition to what Dharma practice and training is about? It is extremely important to address how we understand power and authority and how they relate to American practitioners before getting into the whole question of transmission.

How do your communities now choose teachers and leaders, and how does that differ from the way that it was done traditionally?

VEN. AJAHN AMARO: The way we do things in our monastery is remarkably consistent with the way it's done in Asia. Our community came to the West in the mid-seventies and we were prepared to change things. But it's striking how little we have needed to make adaptations, particularly in the area of training people for the monastic life or bestowing authority on people.

The hierarchy in our community is very rigid in certain areas yet extremely flexible in others. It's very important to relate to your role in the hierarchy as you would to wearing a piece of clothing, that is, to be able to put it on and take it off when appropriate. If you think you have a rank as an absolute reality, then you've really gone too far. To be a monastic for many years and high up in status in some way, and yet also able to step down from that and be on the level of simple friendship with all other beings, is crucial for the health of the whole system.

We also have an advantage in that there is no sign of accomplishment, no insignia you acquire. You don't get a purple robe if you become an abbot or a stream-enterer. Your dress is indistinguishable from that of the other nuns and monks. There's a simplicity to that.

Personally, I lead something of a double life. Spirit Rock has a community of about twenty teachers, of which I am one, and I also have my life at the monastery. I've found a great deal of benefit from mixing in both worlds—the nonhierarchical Spirit Rock lay teacher way of functioning and the hierarchical monastic world. Letting both those worlds inform each other has been a very helpful aspect of being in the West.

JACK KORNFIELD: Every five years in our community, teachers across the country will consult with one another and talk about who in this last period of practice seems to have matured, whose realization is the most evident, who has the kind of compassionate good heart and other qualities that would make them a good teacher. Then we come to a consensus on several candidates to add to our pool of teachers. If they choose to respond to our invitation, they undertake a training period, usually five years. They engage in extensive practice, train in teaching skills, and study important texts and histories of the tradition. Then they are gradually mentored to become part of a collective of teachers.

We have found that a certain degree of hierarchy is really needed. There has to be spiritual leadership in a community—it can't just be everybody getting together and voting on what they would like the Dharma to be for them. But we've found it helpful for the leadership to be collective, so that no single person is the abbot or the leader. So there's the equivalent of a council of elders, such as you would have at a Theravādin monastery.

This is an amalgam of some aspects of what one would find in Thailand and Burma. It is altered, however, by the more collective approach. Rather than having a single abbot or one clear meditation master, there is a handful of people—a half-dozen, or in a large center perhaps a dozen or more—who collectively hold the teaching responsibility and share decision-making.

That's been very healthy for us. It's also been much less isolating and healthier for the students, because they hear several different expressions of Dharma. Yet there's also a willingness among the teachers to hold the necessary leadership in terms of study, training, virtue, and all the requisite aspects of being a teacher.

RICHARD SHROBE: In the Kwan Um School we have a somewhat similar collective system. The student has one person who is considered their guiding teacher. If after years of practice together the guiding teacher considers the student ready to take on teaching responsibilities, that student is sent around to four other teachers, who have to agree that this person is in fact a good candidate to take on teaching responsibility. It can't be just at the whim of one person. A teacher can see something in a student, having been with him or her for a long time, but the students may be missing things that other teachers might see from a different vantage point.

In our transmission ceremonies, which are public, Seung Sahn always used to say, "The Sangha is giving the transmission." As Ajahn Amaro mentioned earlier, you can appoint someone a teacher but if students don't gravitate to that person and don't find affinity with him or her, then that person is not teaching. Teaching is a functional responsibility; it's a process. The title itself is meaningless. The same goes with hierarchy; it should be functional. Anything that goes beyond functionality is in danger of becoming rigid.

DZOGCHEN PONLOP RINPOCHE: It is hard to group all Tibetan Buddhist lineages into one system, but I think that all lineages of Tibetan Buddhism in the West are trying to train Western students in exactly the same way as Tibetans have been trained traditionally. I don't think there's much difference in terms of the quality of the Dharma training that they receive. At the same time, of course, the format of the training, and the time required for it, has been modified for Western culture and modern culture throughout the world.

How would a person be chosen to succeed a teacher such as you?

DZOGCHEN PONLOP RINPOCHE: It would require a few steps. First, the candidate must receive all the necessary training and transmissions. Second, they must also have all these qualities of personality—compassion and so on—that we discussed earlier. Third, there must be a selection by me and other sangha members, together. I do not see it as a process of me alone choosing a successor.

YVONNE RAND: Rinpoche, my sense is that if a student has completed three-year retreat, they take the view that they are now a teacher. Is that the traditional view?

DZOGCHEN PONLOP RINPOCHE: It's a little bit tricky. Traditionally speaking, the three-year retreat is not necessarily teacher training; it is for personal development. Some of the students who attend the three-year retreat are later chosen to teach meditation, but not everyone who's done three-year retreat in Tibet or India would be chosen to be teachers.

JACK KORNFIELD: Do you think that Westerners can function as vajra masters in the same way that Tibetan gurus of previous generations have, or will Westerners need to continue to take Tibetans as their root teachers?

DZOGCHEN PONLOP RINPOCHE: We have to go back to understanding what devotion means. We need to look not at the cultural aspect of devotion but rather at the pure practice element of devotion. We have a saying in the Mahāmudrā and the Dzogchen lineages: "Devotion is the path." That does not mean that we have to have 100 percent trust right from the beginning. This trust does not necessarily mean trust toward an external master either. The ultimate master is within oneself—basically one's own nature of mind, which is reflected externally as the great, enlightened masters such as Padmasambhāva or Śākyamuni Buddha.

Yes, I feel there have to be some changes made here, but that change is cultural. It doesn't change anything with regard to the basic principle of devotion. One of the fundamental problems here in the West, in my humble opinion, is that we misunderstand devotion.

Most of the important Western teachers today were empowered by Asian teachers. Does the current generation of Western teachers have sufficient spiritual authority to empower the next generation of Westerner teachers?

VEN. AJAHN AMARO: I was first invited to teach by Ajahn Sumedho, who is from Seattle. I studied for a few years with Ajahn Chah, but most of my training since 1979 has been in the West. I've been trained almost entirely by Ajahn Sumedho. So I'm already one link down the chain.

JACK KORNFIELD: There's no question that I feel much less realized than the great masters with whom I've studied. I think I've become a very good teacher for people in certain circumstances. But if I think of my own masters, like Ajahn Chah and Mahasi Sayadaw, they were considered among the greatest masters of this past century in our tradition.

So part of me thinks that we're in trouble, because when I look at their generation and then look at those who are teaching now, it feels like they had something incredible that isn't being carried forward quite so clearly and strongly. So if I'm supposed to pass this along to another generation, even more is going to get lost.

Maybe it always feels this way. I've talked about this with masters such as Ajahn Chah and some very senior Tibetan lamas, and they would get kind of wistful and their eyes would moisten and they would say, "You should have met my teacher."

On the other hand, I believe that what's carried in this transmission isn't so personal. It is really the spirit of awakening, it is bodhicitta, it is the true nature of mind—and that can never be diminished. Some may be able to point at it more skillfully, and some may be able to embody or carry it more fully, but it can't really be diminished. It's not so much our job to be great teachers, but to carry these teachings that have been given to us as a gift and keep them alive as best we can until another generation can carry them.

RICHARD SHROBE: It's also true that the student sometimes surpasses the teacher. In most of these lineages, there have been times when things went into decline and yet some very exceptional student appeared and revived the tradition. It's important to recognize that our role is to simply do what we can do.

In Vajrayāna sanghas it does seem that many people find it difficult to accept a non-Tibetan as a tantric master.

DZOGCHEN PONLOP RINPOCHE: There are already a number of non-Tibetan ācaryas, those who become teachers by training and study. I feel it will be very important for each Vajrayāna tradition to very clearly define their authority, their role in the Sangha, and to empower them accordingly. At the same time, I also feel that some non-Tibetans must become Vajrayāna lineage holders. There are many Vajrayāna masters who are working on bringing lineage to the West through developing non-Tibetan lineage holders, and in my humble opinion this has to happen. At some point, the Western tradition has to be completely independent from any other culture. At the same time, we have to be careful that the quality is not lost in rushing to have a full transmission of the teachings to Westerners.

How assured do you feel that these methods will create a durable lineage of Buddhist teachers in the West who bring to their role the qualities that you described in the beginning?

YVONNE RAND: One of the strengths of what's happening here in the West is a breakdown of sectarianism. There are many Western teachers who are not only trained in their own home path but who study with teachers from other schools and lineages. There's strength in that. Studying with several great Vajrayāna teachers and practicing within the Theravāda tradition have given me an enthusiasm and wholeheartedness about my home path of Zen.

We can feel our way along and discover what will be effective here in the West and what we have to drop. What I hear over and over again is that we can drop what is essentially culture and return to the essence of the teachings. But it's going to take us a long time to figure out what's effective and what isn't, because the circumstances we are in now are so challenging. I would say that we can't answer the question of what's going to serve best the flowering of the Buddhadharma in the West for quite a long time. If we can rest with a bigger time frame, it may help with the impatience that seems to attend the transmission process.

JACK KORNFIELD: The preservation of Dharma isn't so much about transmission and teachers as it is about sincerity and dedication to practice. If people in this generation and future generations study Dharma thoroughly, if they practice sīla, samādhi, wisdom, loving-kindness, and compassion in a very dedicated way, Dharma will flower here and appropriate teachers will arise. More than merely focusing on the empowerment of teachers, we need to focus on living a life of practice.

RICHARD SHROBE: The sincerity of the student is what's primary. There is a reason many Asian teachers came to this country in the first place. They came because there was a certain openness and sincerity toward practice among American students. That still exists today and in all likelihood will exist into the future.

VEN. AJAHN AMARO: In the Mahāyāna, as I understand it, there's a very strong sense of ancestry. In a way, you are your Dharma ancestors and you have no existence except as part of a line of ancestors. So if you die without issue—without passing on the transmission—this is a kind of disaster.

It could be beneficial to loosen up the tight view around that and consider, "Maybe it'll die down here but it'll probably shoot up over there." When the big tree falls down in the forest, it creates space for all kinds of smaller shrubs to grow where there was no light before, because the big tree created a lot of shade. The sharing of each others' teachings and practices and the fresh soil and environment for Dharma are tremendously important. The lineages as we know them might carry on and they might not. But if there's a sincerity in the students, a genuine quality of practice, and commitment to the training and teaching, then the Dharma will flourish.

DZOGCHEN PONLOP RINPOCHE: Having been in America for a while, I can say that the American Buddhist practitioners are sincere and genuine. They have a wonderful quality of compassion and great talent and open-heartedness. So I don't see any problems for continuing any form of Buddhist lineage in this country and in this culture.

When Buddhist practitioners mature, they have the full wisdom and compassion to participate in any Sangha decisions, including those concerning the continuation of any lineages. I hope to see that develop and happen in this country. May the Buddhadharma flourish.

22

The Practice of Śīla:
Ethics and Morality in Modern Buddhism

LAMA PALDEN DROLMA

ANDREW OLENDZKI

ZOKETSU NORMAN FISCHER

Buddhism's three trainings—śīla, samādhi, and prajñā—are often translated as morality, meditation, and wisdom. Let's start by defining morality in a Buddhist context.

LAMA PALDEN DROLMA: Thrangu Rinpoche explained śīla as meaning "cool." He likened it to a cool breeze in a hot country. It brings relief and happiness, since it cools the fire of desire that's burning us up. Since our runaway desire isn't ultimately going to fulfill us, the contentment with what is and with what we have brings a breath of fresh air.

Paying attention to ethics brings us more in alignment with our true nature. It provides the conditions for awakening by aligning us more with our inherent buddha nature. Acting in an ethical way, having conduct that is beneficial to oneself and others, creates the karma and the conditions that help us awaken.

ANDREW OLENDZKI: Actually, I prefer to define sīla as "integrity," since the terms morality and virtue both have some baggage in our culture. "Integrity" carries more the sense of being something organic that expresses the quality of your mind. "Morality" is coming from outside; "virtue" is something you aspire to, and "ethics" is a big umbrella society puts over you. One of the core insights of Buddhism on this whole matter is that śīla, how you act, is an expression of your understanding.

ZOKETSU NORMAN FISCHER: Ethics and morality are so fraught in our culture because they are generally treated as absolute rules ordained by the divine: You must behave in these ways and if you don't you'll burn in hell for it. Ethics in Buddhism is more about discovering how to live in accord with who we really are, as Palden so beautifully expressed.

I think it's wise for Andrew to choose the word "integrity." It's in the territory but it doesn't bring with it all the fire and brimstone that "ethics" and "morality" do in our culture. Instead of ethics as a set of rules imposed from the outside, śīla is understood as how a buddha would conduct herself or himself spontaneously.

LAMA PALDEN DROLMA: It's a sense of alignment with deeper principles of truth and reality and with our fundamental nature, which is basic goodness. In the traditions that most of us grew up in, there is usually the sense that there is some problem at the core of who we are.

Buddhism's flowering in the West coincided with a flight from rules and convention. How has our relationship to śīla evolved over the years?

ZOKETSU NORMAN FISCHER: In the beginning of the Zen movement here, people were not that interested in śīla. They were interested in meditation experience and awakening. In the 1970s, morality was looked upon as conventional social wisdom, and everybody was trying to escape from that because it was restrictive.

That was very true for the first fifteen or twenty years but then there were spectacular ethical scandals alongside an overall maturing of the people who were in the movement. Now I would say there is a strong emphasis on precepts and ethical conduct.

Since precepts mostly have to do with how we conduct ourselves in relation to each other, Sangha and śīla go together. In our Everyday Zen groups, taking the precepts, studying them, and bringing them into the heart—not just as a set of rules to live by, but as a set of deep reflections—has become a tremendously important part of what we do. It is as important—or more important—than the emphasis on awakening.

ANDREW OLENDZKI: The vipassanā experience is very similar. There was a great infatuation with the meditative experience early on, although the retreats did always begin (and still do) with a formal taking of the precepts. In similar fashion, though, there has been an evolution as students have matured.

Sīla, samādhi, and paññā are interrelated and any one of them can lead naturally to the other two. Even if we come to practice out of an interest in peak experiences, we begin to see more clearly the stuff arising in our minds and we can't help but attend more carefully to its ethical content. As our understanding of paññā deepens and we begin to better understand the impermanent and selfless nature of it all, an increase in integrity will naturally result.

LAMA PALDEN DROLMA: In Vajrayāna in the West, I think there was always more emphasis on conduct and on the bodhisattva attitude and vow, and just fundamental basic conduct. There have been exceptions, but overall there's been a less dramatic change than what Norman and Andrew have described. Śīla has been there all along as a vital component, sometimes more in the background, sometimes more in the foreground.

How do we relate to the traditional rules and vows that guided our forebears in the Buddhist traditions?

ZOKETSU NORMAN FISCHER: We need rules and precepts, but what we're emphasizing here is the spirit behind those rules. If the spirit behind the rules is to align yourself with your true nature, then the rules are understood in a very different way. It's a very different matter when you have rules held as guidelines for awakened conduct, where awakening, kindness, and cooperative living are the watchwords. You don't have fixed principles so much, so you don't debate over when does life start and end. Those debates are less important than finding out what is the kindest thing here, what will bring the most benefit to everybody.

ANDREW OLENDZKI: Rules in the context of sīla also afford refuge. The laws of cause and effect mean that the harm you do is not only going to hurt the people around you but come back and hurt you. Even if you feel disinclined to obey them, having a set of rules gives you a kind of protection from yourself, as well as a protection for everyone else. It's a gift of harmlessness that you give the people around you. Seeing sīla as a refuge and a gift takes some of the edginess out of the "you must obey the rules or else" point of view.

LAMA PALDEN DROLMA: The core of Buddhist ethics is the motivation to not cause harm to any living being and to be of benefit to others.

ANDREW OLENDZKI: The Buddha emphasized intention as the driving force of karma. What you do is less important than the intention behind how you do it. That universal guideline is not bound to cultural vicissitudes. There's a certain timeless quality around working from intention rather than on the basis of a specific set of actions.

LAMA PALDEN DROLMA: The understanding of interconnectedness at the heart of the Dharma offered a huge breakthrough in human consciousness—a transcendence of the principle of preserving one's tribe, which was the source of so many ethical codes. Today our interconnectedness is more relevant than ever. The highest alignment within our hearts is to understand our interconnectedness and appreciate that we really want to protect and enhance the life of every sentient being.

ZOKETSU NORMAN FISCHER: That is what our morality is based on in the biggest context, but there's also a narrow context. In a training situation, practitioners often practice according to a rule. That rule can be very specific and strict, particularly in monastic contexts. If you're following the traditional Vinaya as a Theravāda monk, you take a vow to live by these rules as an integral part of your commitment to being trained. In that sense, Vinaya rules are instrumental. Not eating after noon is not a universal moral rule of kindness. It's a rule you undertake for the benefit for your training.

There's still a place for those rules, and I feel great admiration for those who have adopted them, particularly Western monastics who are taking a great cultural leap. They're preserving something very ancient for a beneficial purpose. At the same time, there's a Buddhist morality that doesn't depend on following the 250 rules. In Zen, we have sixteen bodhisattva precepts, which are in a way the opposite of Vinaya. They're very broad and they're understood in Zen as kōans—not so much specific rules as deep reflections about our conduct. So we have two poles in our practice of śīla: very specific training rules and a much wider sense of ethical principles.

ANDREW OLENDZKI: The Theravāda tradition has always employed a two-part system: very strict rules for monks and nuns as an integral part of their training and very broad precepts for laypeople. The good part of that broadness is that it leaves you a lot of personal responsibility for how you're going to define the precepts. But that is often frustrating for people. Some just want to be told what is right and wrong, so they don't have to figure out whether walking on grass violates the first precept not to kill because there are bound to be bugs in there.

But that's the First Noble Truth: we live in a flawed system. Everybody is kind of left to their own devices in figuring out where to draw the lines. For some Buddhists vegetarianism is an important expression of not killing, but most Buddhists are not vegetarians, and neither was the Buddha. On almost any matter we can think of there's a personal engagement of one's own understanding about right conduct. There is also some natural growth and evolution in how to apply guidelines as one's understanding deepens.

LAMA PALDEN DROLMA: There are core rules in the Vinaya that deeply reflect and reinforce the principles we've been talking about, and ancillary rules that have more to do with relating to the mores in a particular cultural context. The ancillary rules are more situational. It's important to make a distinction between the core integrities and those that we may change according to circumstances of time and place.

Of all the rules, the prohibitions regarding sexual misconduct cause the most confusion, since sexual mores seem so culturally based.

ANDREW OLENDZKI: Once again, it's easier for the monks and nuns—celibacy is nonnegotiable, end of story. But for laypeople, there's a sliding scale.

In the ancient world this precept basically forbade premarital or extra-marital sex. How you apply that today is different, because so many of the cultural definitions are malleable. However, if we're engaging in a sexual act in a way that inflicts real pain or humiliation or is exploitative, we can be pretty sure we're on the unwholesome side of the continuum. But if we're doing a sexual act with an attitude of generosity and loving-kindness, we'll probably be in more wholesome areas of behavior. It's not exactly what you do with whom so much as the quality of mind with which you're approaching what you're doing.

ZOKETSU NORMAN FISCHER: Sexuality is very powerful. It's a heavy karmic act, more than you might think in any given moment of passion. At the time of the sexual revolution we had the idea that sex was just a thing you did, and that if you got over your hang-ups, it was really no big deal. It turns out that it's not so simple to get over your hang-ups and that sexual activity is powerful—it has a powerful karmic effect.

LAMA PALDEN DROLMA: Different Vajrayāna teachers have interpreted "sexual misconduct" differently. Some on the very strict side believe that you're only supposed to have one partner for life. My own teacher, Kalu Rinpoche, interpreted it for us much more in the spirit of what Andrew was talking about. The cornerstone is that our actions be based on a loving, compassionate heart and that any repercussions that arise from one's sexual activities are supposed to be looked into deeply.

As an exercise, I would like to pick a śīla guideline from each of the traditions and ask you to comment. We can start with an example from the Sixteen Bodhisattva Precepts of the Zen tradition: "I vow not to misuse intoxicants but to keep the mind clear."

ZOKETSU NORMAN FISCHER: Intoxication means going beyond an aware and clear state of mind. I tell students that it doesn't mean you can never drink alcohol, because it is possible to have a glass of wine with dinner and not become intoxicated. Some counter that one sip of wine has one sip of intoxication in it. Nevertheless, we would all recognize a kind of line you cross when you become a little tipsy. I say have a glass of wine or a social drink, but if someone said they would like to use marijuana or take cocaine or ecstasy I would suggest they not take that precept. I don't want to give someone a precept that they will not follow, since those substances are always intoxicating. You don't smoke marijuana without getting intoxicated.

Overall, the trouble with intoxication is that it can cause you to break other precepts. In my view, when you feel yourself coming close to intoxication you stop the drinking at that moment. Also, if you find you're drinking frequently, you need to examine that. We try to talk over how we're doing with our precept practice over time with fellow students and teachers. The precepts work best when there's an ongoing sense of reflection.

LAMA PALDEN DROLMA: In Vajrayāna there's the monastic tradition and the yogic tradition. The yogic tradition is much more flexible in terms of intoxicants. Trungpa Rinpoche famously demonstrated a yogic way of life. In the yogic context, the consciousness of the individual and the individual's deep integrity is harder to ascertain. Since it is not possible to judge whether the actions of an accomplished yogi emerge from a deep and uncompromising compassion, despite their external appearance, self-honesty is critical. Otherwise, people may delude themselves about their true progress on the path and believe their behavior is yogic when it's really just harmful.

To continue the exercise, I'd like to ask Andrew to comment on the first precept, not killing, which some people regard as a no-brainer.

ANDREW OLENDZKI: Again, the first precept is talking to quality of intention rather than the action performed. In Buddhist psychology, action is merely the active mode of the passive side, which is intention arising from disposition. The mind is constantly manifesting some emotional state. It could be a state of anger; it could be a state of loving-kindness—anything in the spectrum of the emotional manifestations of being human.

As I understand the first precept, it's largely saying that some of those emotions are harmful to ourselves and others—especially the ones that are rooted in hatefulness, cruelty, or wanting to do harm to others. Whenever harmfulness arises—whether in a very strong form of hatefulness or in a very weak form of mild annoyance or judgmentalism—we should simply notice that. In the noticing, we see whether we can abandon it and let go of the hold it has on us.

The more we do that, at ever more subtle levels, we are purifying our mind. And as a result, our actions will be purified. So we're not working to transform behavior as much as we're working to transform the emotional quality of mind that we have while we're behaving.

Part of the practice of śīla is that you commit to certain guidelines that can help you in the moment to not overreact, even though the deeper practice is to get to the bottom of it.

ANDREW OLENDZKI: Exactly. Buddhist psychology sees our emotional responses happening on three levels. The first is latent or unconscious; we can't see it. The second is what's arising in direct awareness. This is what we access in meditation. The third is what they call a surging stage, where it's out of control. We get carried away, whatever the emotion is. Much of the time emotion moves from latent to surging without any awareness.

So meditation is working on the second level, learning to see ever more carefully what's arising and falling away. Wisdom is working on transforming those latent dispositions so they're not as powerful, while śīla has a lot to do with managing what's already in or threatening to be in the surging state. If we control it in its grossest sense, that allows us to proceed gradually to controlling things in more and more subtle ways.

It seems like advanced teachers in all the traditions have demonstrated examples of breaking the rules. Ajahn Chah's outer conduct caught some people off-guard, and there are certainly plenty of Zen and Vajrayāna stories of teachers acting in bizarre, outrageous ways. What does this rule breaking say about how Buddhism approaches the rules? They apply until they don't?

LAMA PALDEN DROLMA: This brings up a common question about the relativism of Buddhist ethics, since in the cases of teacher behavior it boils down to an assessment of their genuine level of realization. There's no blanket rule about external behavior. Certain behavior might be based on teaching nonconceptuality or cutting through fixed beliefs and ideas about reality.

ANDREW OLENDZKI: I would distinguish things that are unusual from things that are harmful. If you're making the disciple carry bundles of rocks into one pile and then another, and he doesn't see the point of it, I could see that as being a higher wisdom that the teacher sees but the student doesn't. But if the rule breaking is somehow gratifying to the rule breaker, in some direct way, I'm frankly much more suspicious.

ZOKETSU NORMAN FISCHER: Some might say that the higher the degree of enlightenment, the more flexibility one has to use rule breaking as teaching. But I would say the opposite. The more you are serving as an example to the community, the more it behooves you to practice stronger ethical conduct as an example.

From a bodhisattva path perspective, there is the possibility of breaking rules, not to flout convention and teach people, but for purposes of compassion. Breaking a training rule to be kind to someone is permissible when the clear motivation for it is kindness. What becomes more problematic is when rule breaking is destructive. That does happen. In fact, it seems to always happen that someone who thinks they are awake does something thinking, "I know it'll cause a fuss but it'll be good for everybody." That is almost always self-deceptive. Nobody is awakened enough to be hurting people "for their own good."

LAMA PALDEN DROLMA: There is an example often quoted in Vajrayāna about breaking the most fundamental precept—not to kill another human being—in order to do benefit. In the ninth century, King Langdarma was systemically stamping out and destroying Dharma in Tibet to the point of near elimination. At that point, a monk named Palkyi Dorje took on the karma of killing the king. He's seen as a hero because when the greatest good for the greatest number of people supersedes one of the precepts, it would be self-centered to not break a rule. But one must be willing to bear the difficult karma that may ensue if one does break a precept.

ANDREW OLENDZKI: I don't disagree with you, but I do worry about the slippery slope that that sets up. If we start thinking it's all about doing the greatest good for the greatest number of people, it becomes a kind of utilitarianism. There are stories about people in Southeast Asia who executed their wounded friends so the enemy would not torture them. Those are magnificent examples of courage and fortitude, but there's no sense that the law of karma has been altered. If for a greater good someone is willing to spend incarnations in hell to pay for it, that can be a noble sacrifice. But it's very different from saying that killing is therefore right in some cases.

LAMA PALDEN DROLMA: That's a key point. Śīla is not about rules given by a divine authority who also can grant dispensation. It's about deeply understanding the laws of cause and effect.

ANDREW OLENDZKI: These are descriptive laws of nature, not prescriptive laws of a higher authority. Something is unwholesome or unhealthy by definition if it leads to suffering for self or others, and leads away from seeing things clearly. It's by definition wholesome or healthy if it does the opposite. Śīla describes the quality of the event and its effect, rather than saying what you should or should not do.

23

Words and Essence:
The Challenges of Translation

FRANCISCA CHO ▪ ELIZABETH CALLAHAN
VEN. BHIKKHU BODHI ▪ LARRY MERMELSTEIN

Whether it's a sutra, a work of poetry, a meditation manual, or a philosophical commentary, inevitably something is lost to the reader in translation. How do you minimize that?

FRANCISCA CHO: Translation is a huge concern in my academic discipline, comparative religious studies, but in teaching undergraduates about religion, I have learned to become more relaxed about what is getting lost. I accept the fact that translations are creations in their own right and the main role of a translation is to be accessible and understandable to the English reader in the modern context. There's a tendency for academics and translators to be very concerned about what's not said, but I have become convinced over the years that it is not so important as reaching the reader in their own context.

ELIZABETH CALLAHAN: The challenge for me is to join together the strong need to provide something that makes sense to the reader with the need to maintain the integrity of the original. Every translator is always striking this balance. For a more general audience, the primary concern may be readability and allowing readers to derive the meaning more immediately. If it's a technical topic and your audience has more background, then you can show them the bones of it more. In the end, of course, the whole point is to have them derive meaning from it, so it's not a good idea to let meaning get lost in a tangle of jargon that only scholars and people who know the original languages can understand.

VEN. BHIKKHU BODHI: As I study the texts in the original language, I make extensive notes and organize them according to an outline system I have devised. In so doing, I see the extensive underground current of connections between terms and ideas. It's very precise and systematic in the original language, but when one renders it into English or some other contemporary language, no matter how consistent one might try to make one's translation, that underground current of connections, resonances of terms, and overlapping and interconnected meanings largely gets lost.

LARRY MERMELSTEIN: While some things may be lost in translation, there is something that is gained as well. With the very high degree of literacy in the English-speaking world, we have the possibility of many more people understanding something of the teachings. Up until recent times in Tibet, no more than a fifth or a quarter of the population was literate. With greater literacy there is a huge capability for greater access to the literature.

Since Buddhism is so often talking about very subtle experiences, is one translating the experience or the word? Do you consider the experience the English word will evoke in the reader, or do you primarily look for words that accurately reflect the source language?

ELIZABETH CALLAHAN: I think translators are always balancing the two concerns. Tibetans have terms that I call "experiential words." They are words or phrases that are only used to describe meditation experiences. Although they are derived from actual words, they are onomatopoeic in character. When I translated *The Ocean of Definitive Meaning*, I encountered quite a number of these. In each case, I chose a word in English that I felt carried the same flavor of expression. Then I included the Tibetan in parentheses after each occurrence and devoted one glossary to these terms.

An example of this kind of term is the Tibetan word *hrig ge*. I translated it as "sharp." The glossary entry says, "A nonconceptual, unobscured state where one sees one's own nature. Khenpo Tsultrim Gyamtso Rinpoche demonstrated this by staring straight ahead with wide-open eyes." The entry also includes a quote from Dzogchen Ponlop Rinpoche, who said, "It is nonthought, like a gap experience. It is demonstrated by staring. It is like when one sees something scary and one's eyes become wide-open." Then it includes the Great Tibetan-Chinese Dictionary gloss as "vibrant clarity." Finally, it mentions that the term is also translated as "dazzling," "glaring," and "wakeful."

LARRY MERMELSTEIN: In our formative years in working with Chögyam Trungpa Rinpoche, we spent quite a lot of time trying to imagine how a reader might understand a particular term's translation, and this perspective was very important to us. While sometimes an excellent choice might emerge from our consultation with the dictionary, the OED being our chief reference, if this was likely to remain obscure to our intended audience, we would often feel the need to look further.

VEN. BHIKKHU BODHI: I don't think it is necessary to posit a sharp distinction between translating the word and translating the experience. A balance between the two is the ideal and some synthesis between them is a realistic possibility. But I believe that if the translator is in fact translating, and not using the text as a springboard to creative innovation, he or she must remain faithful to the words of the text.

This means the translator must try to understand those words as accurately as possible, both in the context out of which the text arose, and in relation to the larger corpus of which that text might be a part. Since these texts are dealing, at least part of the time, with inner experiences, when attempting to convey his or her understanding of what those experiences involve—and this inevitably engages the translator to some extent in interpretation—the translator will have to select the renderings in the target language that convey most satisfactorily this experiential dimension.

In my own experience, when I have to translate texts using Pali technical terms, I try to understand the meaning of those words against the broader Indian background of early Buddhism and in relation to the network of interconnected ideas that underlie the suttas themselves. Then I try to find words in English that will convey those meanings most satisfactorily.

Of course, there are inevitably huge gaps between the meanings suggested by the Pali words and the ideas that English counterparts will convey. We must try our best to find a terminology that will capture the intended meanings, but we must also remember that translation cannot be a self-sufficient enterprise. It must also be supplemented by explanation and annotation, which will set the terms in their appropriate context of Buddhist doctrine and practice so that the reader can better appreciate how they are being used.

For example, "concentration" is hardly satisfactory as a rendering for samādhi, but unless we decide to allow this word to go untranslated, any other rendering—"composure," "collectedness," "absorption"—will also be inadequate. The meaning of the term samādhi only begins to come to light when the reader is given an explanation of samādhi: how samādhi functions in the Buddhist meditative path, what its practice entails, how the experience of it is described, and so forth.

One way to let readers connect more directly to the original meaning or experience is to leave some words untranslated. Do any of you do that?

VEN. BHIKKHU BODHI: Not very much. It is a gentler inducement to the reader to continue to read a text in which most of the words are in intelligible English rather than to immediately flood them with a barrage of Pali words. If the reader is persistent and intent on understanding the teachings of the Buddhist texts, then through continued exposure to these terms, they'll get an idea of the deep meaning. To help show interrelationships, I may show the original word in brackets and explain other words it is connected to etymologically. But I try to leave as few words untranslated as possible: *Buddha*, and even that can be rendered as "the enlightened one"; *Dhamma, Sangha, nibbāna;* and occasionally *kamma.*

Why not translate Sangha as "community"?

VEN. BHIKKHU BODHI: I think "community" suggests to a modern reader quite different things than what Sangha would have meant—and does mean—in relation to Buddhism. In the context of the early Buddhist texts, it means either the monastic order or the spiritual community of those who have reached one of the levels of realization. One might think of it just as the social community, which would not convey the idea of a specific spiritual order.

Sometimes an untranslated word can travel through several languages. For example, Professor Cho, one of Manhae's poems is called "Samādhi of Sorrow." Why did you choose not to translate samādhi?

FRANCISCA CHO: I was following Manhae's lead. His poems were written in Korean, but he maintained the use of the Chinese characters, which in this case would offer a phonetic rendition of the Sanskrit term samādhi. Since he wanted to use that term and not translate it into something like "concentration" in the Korean, I decided to use the Romanized equivalent of the Sanskrit term in my own translation.

LARRY MERMELSTEIN: We have a similar situation in translating from Tibetan. The Tibetans did not leave that much untranslated from Sanskrit, but they do use some Sanskrit terms and we almost always mirror that in the same way Francisca was describing. If a Tibetan text uses the Sanskrit word *duḥkha*, we would not translate that into Tibetan or English. We have gone even further, though, in using a lot of Sanskrit technical terms whether they had been translated into Tibetan or not.

If we can find a very good English equivalent, especially if it's one that many other translators have already accepted, we will use it, since we prefer to use as much English as possible. But we do use a lot of Sanskrit terminology. We do that if a term is presenting a central concept and we don't feel we can find a suitable English term that is likely to be picked up on by others in the translation world.

Bodhicitta is a good example. There are lots of translations of that term but I don't know that any of them has yet stood out as so good that everybody bows their heads to it and says, "Yeah, we really want to use that." Also, if we render it in English, we wonder whether the reader will instantly recognize it as a technical term of really great import. Leaving it in Sanskrit can let someone know that it's a very important term and they should learn more about it. Like Bhikkhu Bodhi, we feel that the work we do necessitates a glossary, where every single foreign word is dealt with.

Why not get together and come up with an agreed-upon English rendering of bodhicitta that everybody uses?

LARRY MERMELSTEIN: It could be interesting to have a gathering of translators and try to come up with some standard renderings, but I would not be very hopeful about that. Who would have the authority? In Tibet, of course, you had royal patronage, so there could be a decree that said, "We're going to do it this way." I don't see that being likely in the world today.

ELIZABETH CALLAHAN: It's too early to standardize, I would say. We have just begun doing this and from where I sit it seems to me we are just starting to do good work. If we try to standardize right now we might—even if we could agree—end up settling for terms that we might later find don't work so well. Maybe we could find something better if we kept trying.

All translation work is experimentation. When I understand that, I feel freed up to try a new term, float it out for a while, and if it doesn't work, fine. Sometimes one might use the Sanskrit term for a while to see if that will come to common usage in English. At other times one might try to create a technical term in English that will hold up in the variety of contexts in which the original term was used.

FRANCISCA CHO: Perhaps the long-term goal is, in fact, to use the original Sanskrit, Pali, or Tibetan term and make that current rather than trying to find an English equivalent. These ancient words contain universes of meaning and nuances of history, which are very cumbersome to translate.

What we should be moving toward is a general cultural literacy in Buddhist thought and ideas so that people can use at least basic terms, such as *Dharma* and *karma* and so forth, without having to translate. As Bhikkhu Bodhi said, to use "community" for *Sangha* is much too general. It doesn't engage the history and evolution of the Buddhist community that is the Sangha. It's simply more efficient to use the original term. The process of absorbing these terms into the language may take awhile, and it may entail misunderstandings or oversimplified understandings at the beginning. But it seems to me that the goal should be to get to the point where we can use these Buddhist terms as English words.

VEN. BHIKKHU BODHI: That would succeed only with a very limited number of words. If one tries to impose that scheme on a wider range of terms, one risks making Buddhist texts obscure to a large part of the population. There's also a problem with choosing standardized English translations for Buddhist terms, because living languages are constantly changing. When one looks at the standardized renderings of Buddhist technical terms into Tibetan and Chinese, one has to remember that those texts were translated largely by an educated monastic to be read by an educated monastic readership, an elite that would become familiar with these terms in their own languages.

In the Theravāda Buddhist countries, until modern times, the texts were not translated into the vernacular languages. Anybody who wanted to understand them would have to read them in Pali. If one wants to have fixed, standard renderings of Buddhist technical terms into English and to make that rendering valid for centuries, one will be freezing the meaning of these terms, and the terms will not keep pace with the natural changes that take place in the evolution of language. At that point, the meaning of the terms will become obscure to the wider readership and only understood by a limited number of people who specialize in the study of the texts.

LARRY MERMELSTEIN: Our translation committee's allegiance to Sanskrit is exactly for that reason. We hope and expect that more terms will enter English. But I also agree with Bhikkhu Bodhi that it's a pipe dream to think that as many of the words that we currently use in Sanskrit are going to be found in English dictionaries.

FRANCISCA CHO: There already are more there than you might think.

ELIZABETH CALLAHAN: I agree. Sanskrit terms are showing up in English dictionaries these days a lot more than one would expect.

That can be very helpful. When I am casting about for translation equivalents in English, I often come across terms that have a lot of cultural connotations and implications in English that don't exist with the Tibetan or Sanskrit term. However, I might still use an English word, because the value of the meaning it conveys may outweigh the extraneous connotations.

For example, "essence" has two principal meanings in English: the distilled extract of something or what something inherently is. The first of these is a misleading meaning for the Tibetan *ngo bo*. One way out is to translate *ngo bo* as "nature," which is one of those overused translation terms. But I would prefer to use "essence," because sometimes you have to put aside some of the usages in English and focus on one of the other meanings of a particular term. Use it and it starts to take on the Buddhist understanding of the term.

One of the ways I work with this is to use a lot of footnotes or endnotes and glossaries to try to bring out the meanings that these terms have in their original languages so that when people are reading it they can figure out how the word fits in to the overall picture and form other associations with it. It's not so much that we are redefining terms but sometimes we are trying to separate them from their cultural connotations.

LARRY MERMELSTEIN: Sometimes you definitely have to draw the line. We considered and rejected the word "sin" to translate the Tibetan *sdig pa* (*pāpa* in Sanskrit). In many ways, it's an accurate translation, but it is simply too laden. We chose "evil deeds" instead, which is still somewhat laden, but less so.

FRANCISCA CHO: On the other hand, some English words have come to be very widely associated with Buddhism or meditation. Mindfulness is a good example. It works because it didn't have a preexisting standard usage, so people can recognize it immediately as a Buddhist term. Perhaps that's one characteristic that is necessary for a successful English translation to take place.

Does a standard Buddhist vocabulary promote the very solidification that Buddhism is meant to dissolve? Do code words impede understanding?

ELIZABETH CALLAHAN: People can always fixate on terms or symbols, but the Buddhist teachings clearly state that the conventions, which include words and terms, are used as a means for seeing ultimate reality, which transcends such conventions. We use conventions to transcend conventions. People will try to pin things down, especially as beginners, regardless of whether there is a standard vocabulary or not. The translator's job is to convey the right tone of the work. If the teaching is about transcendence, then the words should point people in that direction, but simply using new terms each time will not necessarily accomplish this.

As far as so-called code words go, there is much more value than danger there. Code words, such as the use of *rig pa* (awareness) by students and teachers in the Dzogchen tradition, carry a wealth of import, years of personal experience, and volumes of teachings. Rather than getting in the way, they simplify the matter.

LARRY MERMELSTEIN: It's extremely helpful to develop some amount of standard vocabulary in English, just as is present in Sanskrit and Tibetan. The so-called theistic tendency or the urge to solidify one's reference points is fundamental to human beings, and this is not easy to undermine. Of course, as one's Dharma becomes more jargonized, it decreases in its effectiveness for wide communication, beyond the tribe so to speak. Keeping such tendencies in mind forms part of the general awareness that translators need to bring to their work.

Carl Bielefeldt, a Dōgen translator, talks about providing what he calls "a hypersensitive translation" to try to capture some of the wordplay, poetry, humor, allusions, and the like, subtleties you appreciate in reading a language you know well that are very hard to bring across in translation.

VEN. BHIKKHU BODHI: Translating the play of words is definitely the most difficult aspect of translation. There's lots of word play in the Pali canon. In the early discourses of the Buddha, the Buddha raises the question of how one can be called a *samana*, a true ascetic. He replies himself, saying, "One is a samana because one has pacified, subdued—*samita*—unwholesome states of mind—*manas*."

On the surface, this might look like a straightforward etymological derivation, but it isn't. Rather, it's an example of a pun or what might be called "edifying etymology," a word being playfully derived from another that it resembles to convey a doctrinal point. Similarly, we find the Buddha redefining *brāhmana* as "one who has expelled—*bāhita*—unwholesome states of mind—*manas*."

Rūpa, the first of the five skandhas, is playfully derived from *ruppati*, "to be molested or worn out." The two words have no connection apart from the word play. I have attempted to replicate this in English by translating rūpa as "form" and ruppati as "deformed." Thus we read, "Why, monks, is it called form? It is deformed; therefore, it is called form. Deformed by what? Deformed by cold and heat, by hunger and thirst, by contact with flies, mosquitoes, wind, sun, and serpents. It is deformed, monks, therefore it is called form."

LARRY MERMELSTEIN: Sanskrit has a lot of that same kind of word play, and so does Tibetan to a certain degree. If the word play is doctrinally important or particularly clever, we might try to make a note of it, but most of the time playful language gets lost.

FRANCISCA CHO: It probably isn't possible to preserve word play *per se*, but what one can do is preserve the spirit of the original literature by finding opportunities in the target language. That's an important dimension of translating poetry. You are not translating words; you are transmitting something larger. It allows more leeway in terms of creative translation.

In translating Manhae's work, when I rendered the Korean into English, I ended up with a lot of rhyming words that I could take advantage of. Poetry is different from translating prose and doctrinal materials; poetry offers possibilities to mirror the creativity and play in the source by doing the same thing in the target language.

ELIZABETH CALLAHAN: That's a very good point. As I said before, we are experimenting. We need different kinds of translations. Some people will be able to render more poetic translations and others will do more technical translations. If we could have four or five translations of the major works, I think that would be great.

The translator Red Pine has said that a translation can be better than the original since "the original is dancing by itself. It only becomes complete when there is a translation of it. The nuances become much more evident." He talks about translation as a dialogue with the original.

FRANCISCA CHO: That approach is very much in keeping with the spirit of Dharma tradition and the principle of canonical authority. The whole point of teaching is to speak to the meaning of the Dharma but not to any particular letter, language, or text.

What about the idea of more free-form translations, where the author creates essentially a new work, such as has been widely done with Christian scriptures?

VEN. BHIKKHU BODHI: The idea of giving up translating texts and instead going for fresh creations based on them sounds self-contradictory. It assumes that we can understand the originals well enough to produce free-form creations of them, yet cannot understand them well enough to express their meanings in decent English in a way that rigorously conforms to the original.

Those with creative talent might want to use the text as a source of inspiration for creating new works that provide an outlet for their creative energies. But this should not be taken as a substitute for careful, scrupulous, and accurate translations. Inevitably, these will have their shortcomings, but there will always be a need for them and always an opportunity for more accurate and more eloquent versions.

Some of you translate alone and some of you translate by committee. Can you say something about the pros and cons of working by yourself as opposed to being part of a team?

ELIZABETH CALLAHAN: Most translators would agree that being part of some kind of group process is better than just working alone. We work alone mainly because we don't have the opportunity to work as a group. The middle ground is when you can circulate your work before it is published among other translators for their feedback and checking.

I would say, though, that working alone has probably pushed me to delve into issues much more than I would have if I had had a group to rely on. If I had a group and I was wrestling with something difficult, I could just put it out to the group mind and perhaps we could all come up with something. But if I'm just sitting here by myself with my books, and maybe some Tibetan teachers to discuss it with, I have to keep pushing at the issue until I feel satisfied. That's probably pushed me to be a better translator.

VEN. BHIKKHU BODHI: I've always worked pretty much all by myself, but I think it is preferable for translation to be done with a group. Different people can put their thoughts together and one person can check the translation done by somebody else and make suggestions for revisions. I have had the advantage of sending my translations to other monks who are quite knowledgeable about Pali, and their feedback has led me to make a number of beneficial changes.

LARRY MERMELSTEIN: Most of the members of our committee translate as part of a group, though some of us also translate individually. We all appreciate having colleagues right at hand who are committed to the process.

Even when you have a group like ours that has worked together for many years and has a pretty established vocabulary, the process can still be painfully slow. So the efficiency of the individual translator is far greater than that of a group. Another thing that a group must watch out for is that an individual might have occasional moments of brilliance that the group can destroy, because it wants to be consistent in either terminology or tone. An occasional brilliant moment might be lost with the group mind.

But in my experience, the advantages far outweigh the disadvantages. Besides the tremendous value and protection of the vetting process, there is simply the value of having more minds involved in the process. I wish there were a way to create many more translation groups, but it requires a huge amount of support.

FRANCISCA CHO: Another way of being a community of translators, even when you work largely by yourself, is to look very carefully at previous translations. It may be that you don't like a previous translation, or there are obvious problems with it, but nevertheless you can often find things that you like or things that provoke thought. For me that's formed a dialogue, not with a live person but certainly with living beings from the past.

ELIZABETH CALLAHAN: You can also read what other translators are doing in related texts in the same field. I am working on a text on philosophical tenets and there is a tremendous amount being done in that area right now, mainly by academics. I use that as information and inspiration and see how other people are translating the same words and phrases. Some of it I adopt and some of it I reject and others I just keep in mind. But I always feel that I am working within a larger community that is joined in the experiment.

24

San Francisco Zen Center:
A Case Study in Building American Buddhism

ZENKEI BLANCHE HARTMAN ▪ ZOKETSU NORMAN FISCHER
MYOGEN STEVE STÜCKY ▪ MARY MORGAN

The first issue we'd like to discuss is the tension—one that of course can be very creative—between Buddhist tradition, with its Asian roots, and the values and culture of modern Western society.

ZENKEI BLANCHE HARTMAN: At Zen Center there is a dynamic tension between those two things. There are people who ask why we chant all these things in Japanese since we're not Japanese and we don't even understand the words. Other people say these forms are very important, and we should continue to look at our resistance to doing them in a traditional way. To me, the particular balance is not so important. The important thing is continually looking at it.

ZOKETSU NORMAN FISCHER: Suzuki Roshi, Zen Center's founder, carried this tension within himself. He was very faithful to Sōtō tradition—he wore his robes, he transmitted the rituals very carefully, and when he didn't know the rituals, he brought in Japanese experts to help us. At the same time he wanted Zen Center to be independent of the Japanese Sōtō establishment. He wanted Zen Center to find its own way, and he was very attentive to the needs of Western students. This is why, I think, he turned Zen Center over to an American as his successor. He had Japanese priests who were very good, whom he could have turned to, but he chose an American.

So the tension between the traditional and the modern, the East and the West, was there from the beginning. Zen Center is very conservative, and yet very open and nonconservative at the same time. It's a wonderful creative tension.

MYOGEN STEVE STÜCKY: I was sitting in New York with another Japanese teacher when I heard that Suzuki Roshi had died. This was December of 1971, and I found out that he had named an American as his successor. In 1971 that was a very interesting situation, so I traveled across the country to San Francisco partly to see how this would work—actually making the shift from a Japanese teacher to an American in charge. I read it as a statement of the tremendous confidence that Suzuki Roshi had placed in the sincerity of American practitioners. For me, that was a breath of fresh air, and I stayed at Zen Center partly because he had this confidence in the sincerity of his American students.

There is another creative tension between deep practice and engaging the wider society. At Zen Center, this is reflected in a unique combination of residential monastic training and a diverse lay community.

MARY MORGAN: It's not easy meeting the needs of all these different kinds of practitioners, because there are limited resources. How much energy do we put into our training program for our priests? What about all the people who continue to knock on our door and say we want attention and training from the teachers? This is one of those dynamic tensions that doesn't have an easy resolution. Yet Zen Center continues to respond to all the needs that are presented.

ZOKETSU NORMAN FISCHER: Of American Zen communities, I think Zen Center has the highest number of people who can do monastic residential practice for one month, six months, five years, ten years, thirty years. It's the only place that offers that opportunity to so many people. It seems to me this is a unique situation in Zen—life as practice lived in a practice community. Not just retreat or deep meditation, but everyday life completely surrounded by zazen. I think you can't fully appreciate Zen unless you appreciate that life, and a lot of Zen Center's efforts and problems and joys have to do with trying to maintain that life of practice in the modern world.

MARY MORGAN: To add to Norman's picture, there are families that have raised their children to adulthood at Green Gulch Farm, and there are families living at City Center. We sometimes invite families to come to Tassajara for three-month practice periods. And now Zen Center is exploring the development of a senior living community. The impetus is our commitment to housing our monks who are of a certain age and have worked at Zen Center for at least twenty years. So the residential nature of our practice continues to expand.

Having said that, it's also true that large numbers of people come to City Center and Green Gulch every week to enjoy our public programs. And there are more and more laypeople who want a broader, deeper, richer training program, not just weekly lectures or an occasional class, but an actual training program. So about four years ago Zen Center responded to that need by setting up a yearlong intensive training program for nonresidential students.

ZENKEI BLANCHE HARTMAN: One thing that's interesting is that non-ordained laypeople participate fully in the monastic schedule at Tassajara along with those who have chosen ordination. We go from people who have not taken any vows, to householders who have taken vows as laypeople, to people who have taken ordination as monks. It's interesting that our monastic practice is not just for ordained.

MYOGEN STEVE STÜCKY: The core of Zen Center is dedicated, long-time practitioners, whom you'll find at each of our three centers. Before people become members of the senior staff, we like them to deepen their practice first. Then when they take on responsibility, they are ready and stabilized, with depth and confidence in their practice that they can offer to other people. Residential practice for a core group of people in leadership is really a key to how Zen Center is able to sustain itself and offer what it has to others. Residential practice is the key training component in our system of rotating people through various leadership positions.

ZOKETSU NORMAN FISCHER: Zen Center practice takes in the whole of a person's life. It's not just a place where you access and learn something about Buddhism, and then go back home and figure out what to do with it. Even as a nonresident, your whole life is involved. You have relationships with teachers and Sangha peers. Everything in your life—your economic life, your psychological life, sometimes your romantic life—everything is involved in your practice. It's pretty thorough.

Zen Center has been and remains a leader in gender equality and diversity. What is the history of that effort and what is its focus today?

ZENKEI BLANCHE HARTMAN: Suzuki Roshi came here at a time in American history when women were pushing against the assigned roles that they had had for many years. Suzuki Roshi didn't personally ordain the first woman student he felt was ready to be ordained because he had never ordained a woman before. He sent her to Japan to study with a woman teacher and be ordained there. But not long after that he actually ordained a woman himself. He was not sure he understood how to train women. But I guess the women who were there let him know that they thought he could—and he did.

MYOGEN STEVE STÜCKY: In our morning service liturgy we do the traditional chant of the names of our Chinese and Japanese male Zen ancestors. But people may not realize that Zen Center has also adopted a chant recognizing the women ancestors who have sustained and supported this practice from the time of Śākyamuni Buddha to the present day. We recite a list that begins with some of the nuns named in the *Therīgāthā*, "Verses of the Elder Nuns," and then continues with female Chinese Ch'an and Japanese Zen masters. This started when Blanche and Norman were coabbots in the late 1990s and is completely part of our everyday practice now.

ZOKETSU NORMAN FISCHER: As far as I know, there is no policy on the books that there has to be gender parity in the leadership, but I think there is an informal understanding that we want that, and we feel uncomfortable if there's an imbalance. So I think we're doing really well in terms of gender balance, compared to diversity in general. I think that's a thornier issue. We're working on it, but it's hard to have a diverse population.

MYOGEN STEVE STÜCKY: We try to directly face the issues that come up with all aspects of diversity. We've made specific efforts in our staff trainings to address issues of class and racism. It's something we're paying attention to, but we've not been able to change the balance within Zen Center much beyond the surrounding social structure and context in which we exist. It will take time, but eventually we'll have much more of a diverse population racially, and even with class, which is harder to see and more complex to address.

ZENKEI BLANCHE HARTMAN: It's really a thorny issue, because if we don't have sufficient numbers of diverse members, then each new person of color who comes in the door doesn't see a community they feel that they can fit in to. They don't see themselves here. Making this a welcoming place for anyone who comes through the front door is critically important, and something that we're working on all the time. But it's difficult: until there is enough presence of people of color, and teachers of color, who are fully engaged and visible within the community, it will be very hard for new people of color to find a home here.

MARY MORGAN: We have a diversity committee, and a diversity coordinator creates programs for different communities and educates our residents and leadership about diversity issues. A lot of people don't necessarily think about different people's experience when they walk into Zen Center. People who are in the majority see people like themselves all around and take that for granted. It takes a conscious effort to ask: what would it be like if I didn't see myself here? How would that feel? It's the same with gender parity: it requires a conscious effort all the time. I think if many people in the sangha were not mindful of those issues, we wouldn't have as many women as we currently have in our leadership. All these diversity or inclusion issues require a deep mindfulness to keep them on the front burner.

What is the nature of spiritual authority within the Zen Center community?

ZENKEI BLANCHE HARTMAN: I think the important thing is sincerity of practice. Are people deeply committed to their vow? And the community makes that decision by who they go to for guidance. The people who live with you every day easily see your sincerity and practice.

ZOKETSU NORMAN FISCHER: It's not like there's some big division between administration and the spiritual life. It's all one thing. Everything is part of the practice; everything is part of the spiritual life. So spiritual authority is involved in every aspect of Zen Center life.

MYOGEN STEVE STÜCKY: I think spiritual authority has three primary aspects. First is one's own realization, which comes from deep practice and study of Dharma. Second, it comes from one's teacher, which we formally and publicly recognize through Dharma transmission. And the third source of spiritual authority is the Sangha, as Blanche was saying. The Sangha actually recognizes the faith, dedication, and commitment of a person's practice. The mountain seat ceremony, in which we install an abbot or abbess, is a kind of an empowerment from the Sangha. Without these three, it doesn't feel that someone has a complete basis for the authority that they're teaching from, living from, and acting from.

ZOKETSU NORMAN FISCHER: It's a requirement to be abbot of Zen Center that you are a priest in the lineage with Dharma transmission. Dharma transmission is not a matter of having a certain kind of experience in meditation or lecturing brilliantly on texts. It has to do with really being solid in your practice and bodhisattva vow. Kindness and the wisdom of practice are the main thing.

We don't really have a formal training program. We just live together and practice together and we train in taking different roles, and years go by. Even if it's not explicit, it's an effective kind of training program and we have confidence it will produce good Dharma leaders in the future.

Many of you have lived, practiced, and worked together for decades. I don't imagine anybody can pull the wool over people's eyes to get into a position of authority.

ZENKEI BLANCHE HARTMAN: Yeah, we know each other pretty well.

ZOKETSU NORMAN FISCHER: That's a great point, and it's one of the facts of life of Zen Center that makes it interesting and unique. We do have many people who have practiced together day by day by day, side by side, for decades. And even though the generation of us for whom that's true is slowly fading away, I think there is a new generation who will have the same experience. That's a level of engagement, authority, and Dharma that doesn't appear in any of the official documents but is a major part of what Zen Center is about.

25

Still Work to Be Done:
Women in Western Buddhism

GRACE SCHIRESON ▪ **RITA GROSS**
CHRISTINA FELDMAN ▪ **LAMA PALDEN DROLMA**

When you look at the way things are today for Buddhist women in the West, would you say there's cause for celebration or for dismay?

GRACE SCHIRESON: We do have cause for celebration, but that doesn't mean all our work is done. The fact that things are moving in a positive direction for women doesn't mean there aren't any more problems.

RITA GROSS: There have been a lot of strides for women in the thirty years or so that I've been involved in Buddhism. The important question for me has always been, are there women teachers? There are now a lot more women teaching Buddhism in the West, though in the Tibetan system we're all pretty much teaching under the guidance of a Tibetan and not teaching independently.

There's been a lot of improvement in liturgies in terms of gender-inclusive and gender-neutral language, but it's still not always the case. It's a big stride that people no longer say, "Oh, that's not an issue. We don't need to talk about it." But the younger generation sometimes frightens me. Very recently I was at a retreat and one of the young residents said, "Oh, I don't agree with that at all. That's just genderizing the Dharma. There are no problems."

That's the perpetual issue we face: women make some gains and then people forget how things used to be. It's frightening to think of the up-and-coming generation of meditators rejecting the work of feminists as genderizing the Dharma. To that, I always reply, "We're not genderizing the Dharma. We're ungenderizing it." The Dharma was genderized thousands of years ago when women were first put in a separate class.

CHRISTINA FELDMAN: There have been really great changes since I began teaching in 1975. In the Theravāda tradition at that time there were almost no women teachers and the imprint was still very much a monastic model and lineage. Now we have a wonderful group of senior women teachers and no one is surprised to see them sitting on the stage or standing at the podium. That in itself is quite a turnaround.

With young women, I often find that all they've known is gender equality. Most have never been to Asia, so they haven't seen how hard it is for women practicing there. Their feeling is that the work is done. But there is a long way to go in the Theravāda tradition in terms of gender equality, particularly in the monastic community, and this issue is a hot potato between the lay and monastic communities. Still, I feel heartened by the changes over the last thirty years.

LAMA PALDEN DROLMA: One of the optimistic things in the Vajrayāna tradition that I experienced from the beginning was that the very high masters just threw out some of the old stuff. For example, there were Mahakala rooms at the monastery where women weren't supposed to go. They just said, "Oh no, that's fine, you can come in," and they let us live in the monasteries and study.

But there's quite a difference between the high rinpoches, who have a lot of realization and from the beginning have treated women with respect and equality, and what I think of as the "middle management lamas," who aren't as realized and are more culturally bound, as well as the monks who live in Asian monasteries and haven't had much contact with the West. But even male Western lamas often aren't treated well by Asian monks, so it goes beyond a gender issue into a Western–Asian issue.

However, in general things have come along quite well, and many of the Tibetan teachers have made an effort to ask women to teach. Yet I know a lot of women who are authorized to teach but don't because the situation is intimidating or they haven't had enough practical support.

In the Tibetan tradition, where you have rinpoches and tulkus, it seems harder for women to get a foothold as senior teachers.

LAMA PALDEN DROLMA: I'm not so sure. I've received nothing but support to move forward, but the level of realization is the major factor, and we in the West don't yet have the levels of realization of people such as the late Dilgo Khyentse Rinpoche, or the Karmapa, or the Dalai Lama.

RITA GROSS: Given that 99.9 percent of the people picked as tulkus and trained from an early age are boys, I think it is difficult for women to become senior teachers, and I'm not talking about Westerners, I'm talking about Tibetans.

CHRISTINA FELDMAN: In the Theravāda tradition in the West there hasn't been nearly as much interface between monastics and lay teachers, so lay teachers haven't been shackled by the monastic tradition. Lay teachers and centers have set off on their own journey, so to speak, without needing authorization from the monastic community.

What are the main areas where women are still stuck—where they don't have equal opportunity or support?

LAMA PALDEN DROLMA: None of the gains we've made in the West are necessarily touching monks who've been educated in monasteries in Asia. So that's one area that's kind of stuck. As Christina was saying, Insight Meditation Society, Spirit Rock, and Gaia House have separated themselves to some extent from the old-country tradition and just moved forward on their own. But in the Tibetan tradition, the situation has been much more mixed.

Also, among certain women there's still strong adherence to the patriarchy, in the sense of wanting to be daddy's good girl. Some male teachers who've authorized women really have authorized them to be independent and supported them. But in other cases, women teachers are still expected to be under a male teacher and to behave in certain ways and do it the way daddy wants you to do it. Women need to be educated about the attitudes our male teachers have, and we need to examine how male-identified we are, or how intimidated we are, and we need discernment in terms of who we want to study with or work with.

Sexuality is another area where women have given away their power or men have power tripped them. For there to be equality, women need be educated that they don't have to sleep with a male teacher just because that teacher wants them to. We don't need to give away our power in terms of our sexuality. This is still very much a sore spot for many teachers and students.

GRACE SCHIRESON: The trainings that have been passed on to us have to do with training young men. When young men come into a monastic situation, because of the way their ego defenses work, they need to learn to harmonize and fit in to the community and not to dominate with that sort of raw, intentional energy that young men have. But women, as Palden said, hide behind their ego defenses in different ways. They hide by pleasing others and ingratiating others, and so their training needs to be different. I don't think this has been specifically acknowledged and worked on as much as it can be.

This fits with the whole issue of women's sexuality as pleasers—not taking our position as primary people but coming into our position through ingratiating, pleasing, seducing, or attracting others. This is an ego habit for many women, more so than it is for men. Men take their position differently, and I know in my Zen tradition it works on that kind of samurai spirit. Zen hasn't developed the teachings to help women come forward as women.

This is one of the shadow sides of Western Buddhism's intersection with the Asian tradition. In our own culture, Westerner to Westerner, we might recognize more readily the inappropriateness of certain relationships. But because of the cultural overlay, people can be fooled and not see a sexual relationship between a teacher and student as an ethical breach. They think that somehow it's the roshi's right or entitlement to have these kinds of relationships.

CHRISTINA FELDMAN: In lay Theravāda centers in the United States, and in the centers where I teach, it's always shared trainings of teachers, rather than one person handing on a lineage to another. There's a training program that includes plenty of sustained practice, study, and so on, and that's led by a mix of male and female senior teachers.

There have been a few ethical breaches, which is why the teacher code of ethics is strongly enforced and well known. We publicize it in all our centers. It's on the walls, so it's clear from the outset that a sexual relationship between a teacher and student is a no-go. It doesn't mean there haven't been lapses, but they've been addressed—sometimes very painfully, but they have been addressed.

RITA GROSS: From what I know of Western Buddhism and the Tibetan tradition, there are plenty of male teachers—not necessarily highly authorized teachers, but teachers who have some authorization—who are perfectly eager and willing to sleep with female students.

GRACE SCHIRESON: Still, this is not only a male problem; this is a woman's problem as well. Women need to learn not to be confused by the exotic or foreign or new nature of Buddhist practice, and to understand what their tendencies are. We will not solve this problem if we just focus on the male side of it.

RITA GROSS: I completely agree. Women need to learn how to know what they want and how to take control of their lives.

Another area where we are still stuck, I think, is that when we look at who's teaching in the West, about half of the people teaching at some level of authorization are women. But when you look at the popular teachers or the ones who are frequently leading retreats, especially in the Tibetan tradition and to some extent also in Zen, they are about 80 to 90 percent men. I once did a survey of several issues of the *Shambhala Sun* and *Buddhadharma* in which I counted the ads for retreats, and it came up astonishingly high for male teachers.

In the Tibetan tradition, it's still much more difficult for women than men to be senior-ranked teachers, more so than in the other traditions. It seems to me that one of the key problems is that Vajrayāna is still pretty much controlled by Tibetans. I don't know how to work with that. It's a difficult issue.

GRACE SCHIRESON: Even in the Zen tradition, where women have equal empowerments, there isn't equality in terms of leading large training monasteries and institutions. Women tend to have the smaller places.

In my tradition, the Zen master is associated with the strong, silent type, and we don't have an image of how women inhabit the role of leader. I hear senior women questioning whether any of the women are as excellent as the men, because their image of a leader is the strong, silent male. The other thing that I've heard many women teachers talk about is the lack of support of women by women. I think it's a big issue, and it has been an issue for nuns from the very beginning. Women tend to gravitate to male leadership rather than support other women. The women teachers I've talked to about this say they find this very painful—more painful than men not supporting them.

RITA GROSS: This is one of the areas of gender where we're stuck—women by and large tend to think men are better teachers. There's that lingering inferiority that's so hard to overcome.

LAMA PALDEN DROLMA: I notice as a woman teacher that most men will only go to male teachers. For example in my center, it's completely open and we have some great men who come, but it's 80 percent women.

I recently read several accounts from women who attended the bhikkhunī ordinations in California and their stories were heartening. It seemed that women were very supportive of the women who took bhikkhunī ordination. Christina, do you feel that women are now supporting other women who want to become either bhikkhunīs or senior teachers?

CHRISTINA FELDMAN: In the Theravāda tradition, we've sorely felt the lack of ordained bhikkhunīs. Now that these ordinations are happening, women are greeting them with tremendous support and delight and celebration.

Also, I started teaching women's retreats twenty-five years ago, and a community of women has built up who feel strong in their practice and in their lineage, and who only practice with other women. There's something about having retreats led by women that models a kind of strength and uprightness.

GRACE SCHIRESON: I've also supported women's retreats for a long time, as part of a team of women teachers. When women see other women teach, one of the things they begin to awaken to is that they do prefer men. As a psychologist, I think there's something about daddy's distance—in other words, children grow up taking mother for granted. It's easy to push mom aside and glorify dad. I think women's retreats help to awaken women to this tendency.

Regarding the reinstatement of the bhikkhunī order, I think women are enthusiastic and moved by it, but it remains to be seen whether they will move toward supporting these women teachers, or whether they'll still prefer the traditional male patriarchs.

At what point is it more useful to step outside of existing Buddhist organizations and set up new ones based on leadership styles and models that are more supportive of women?

LAMA PALDEN DROLMA: I've certainly done that—my whole organizational model for Sukhasiddhi is different than the traditional male models. It's a much more inclusive, collaborative, and loving model than some of the more samurai-style models from the past.

CHRISTINA FELDMAN: That has been an important part of the translation of the Dharma into the West—to find a model that addresses issues that have never been addressed in Asia, such as sexuality between teachers and students, and who gets enlightened and who doesn't.

However, monastics are also modeling something very important. They're modeling a kind of renunciation and simplicity and integrity, and it's their responsibility to live up to that. I have reservations about abandoning any kind of interface with monastic communities. We would lose a lot by doing that because there is something very important being modeled there.

The other reservation I have about moving entirely away from cultural models from Asia is that there are a lot of women practitioners there who have never had the good fortune to be exposed to strong women or strong women teaching. They have never been taught that liberation is possible for them. I would find it uncomfortable to say, "You've got to do your own work," and just leave them to their own devices. I feel accountable to a much larger Sangha of women than just Western women.

LAMA PALDEN DROLMA: I completely agree.

GRACE SCHIRESON: We are creating independent models, but at the same time we're acting as a bridge, where we're visible to a great number of people and where women will have the experience of seeing us stand up. When I practiced in Japan in an all-male monastery, I would go to the lectures and 80 to 90 percent of those who came to hear the teacher speak were Japanese women. They were so heartened to see me as a woman practicing with the men, even though that wasn't what they wanted to do.

It's hard for me to stay involved in the larger training centers in the West, which are not usually led by women, because of the different standards and the lack of respect. But I try really hard to stay involved because I think my presence there will make a difference in the long run.

RITA GROSS: Looking at it as a scholar of religion, I'd say the whole Buddhist community needs both people who work within the standard conventional institutions and people who go outside of them.

I've always felt that if you can manage to stay within an institution, and change part of it from the inside, that's very powerful. You really have an impact if you can stay within the institution and, for example, get a whole institution to retranslate its liturgy so that it's more gender-neutral and gender-inclusive.

But there are many people who are not temperamentally able to take the flak of staying in a traditional patriarchal institution. For them, starting new institutions that present other models is also necessary for the overall progress of the Buddhist tradition. It's often the institutions that radical that spur more conventional institutions to actually change from the inside.

How do you talk to young women Buddhists about these issues?

GRACE SCHIRESON: The point I make is that this isn't something we're making up. We're not being grumpy feminists. We want to show them what has happened in the history of Buddhism—the fact that women's names have been erased. We want to show them that there are parts of the scriptures that talk about women hatefully, and that women, because of the eight special rules, have been in a submissive position. It's very important for women to see this, because it's glossed over.

RITA GROSS: It's very important that men see that, too.

GRACE SCHIRESON: And we don't want to see it. We converted to Buddhism because we thought it was a superior practice and religion, and we don't like seeing that it has the same flaws as other religions. We tend to want to idealize it. In Zen, there's this idea that to call out gender is to somehow be attached to form and that we should stay on the emptiness side, the equality side, which is to ignore the Heart Sutra, which says form is emptiness, emptiness is form.

RITA GROSS: Yes, the men who say, "Let's not talk about gender because gender isn't real" don't actually take that seriously at all. They don't apply it to themselves.

GRACE SCHIRESON: No, they don't go to the ladies' room, they go to the men's room.

RITA GROSS: It's so comical and yet so tragic to see people who are very clear intellectually about emptiness but who still cling to gender markers. Somehow they can't imagine gender arrangements being different than they are. It's such a paradox.

CHRISTINA FELDMAN: It's easy for timeless habits of aversion and fear to hide behind such spiritual generalizations. But it doesn't actually address the reality of people's lives. The Buddha taught that we can find liberation within this body, this gender, this form. So when I hear those kinds of statements, to me it doesn't have any real meaning.

Yet it does seem to stop discussions short sometimes.

CHRISTINA FELDMAN: Only if we let it stop discussions short. Women also need to understand that disagreeing is not the same as being defensive; disagreeing can come from an educated place.

The question of ethics in this issue is huge. Gender discrimination is a violation of the ethical guidelines and boundaries. It is doing harm. I think in the Buddhist community, the investigation of what an ethical life looks like has to go beyond the training guidelines. It's where we set in our minds a position that is higher. Gender inequality in Buddhism, or in any religion, is set on really shaky foundations, and I question how ethical they are.

LAMA PALDEN DROLMA: That's why one of the fourteen root tantric vows is not to disparage women, even though that hasn't necessarily stopped it.

GRACE SCHIRESON: This "not disparaging women" is complicated, because there's a "not disparaging women" that means "don't beat them up; as long as they stay in their place, let's not be cruel to them." But as soon as we start to speak up and say this isn't quite right, the "B" word comes up. That can be very hard for women.

I teach women that the most important thing when speaking up on behalf of gender issues is not to come from a wounded place. You will not be able to make your case if you are feeling the pain and wound of this long history. You need to speak clearly and in the moment.

RITA GROSS: How we speak about gender issues is critically important, and if we are speaking out of emotional turmoil, we're probably going to make the situation worse, not better. It's important to go through whatever it takes to get to the point where we can speak clearly and calmly, and not defensively. However, it can be hard to get to the point where that's possible.

LAMA PALDEN DROLMA: It's more being centered and grounded, and, like Rita was saying, working through our emotional reactivity so we can be heard more clearly. We can also model how to rest in the realization of the emptiness of self, and be assertive and clear and step forward simultaneously.

RITA GROSS: For me, what it took was seeing that my violent, angry, emotional outbursts were polarizing the situation. They might have provided a temporary relief for me, but they weren't doing anything to help anybody.

CHRISTINA FELDMAN: If women speak from a sense of need—needing approval or needing to belong—it's never from a sense of sufficiency. The more that women find that sufficiency within their practice, within themselves, they're not speaking from a place of need. Then there doesn't need to be anger and there's no need to be defensive, because sufficiency is not reliant upon approval or belonging or acceptance.

GRACE SCHIRESON: Still, even if we come from a place of sufficiency, and even if we're grounded in the realization of selflessness while we're being assertive, we're likely to encounter some reactivity in our audience. You need to be prepared for that. You do need to be prepared when you speak up on these matters, because no matter how careful we are there's going to be some reactivity or even an attack.

What hope do you see for resolving the issue of gender in Buddhism? Can you share some of your own inspiration?

LAMA PALDEN DROLMA: One thing I want to share is that high teachers are making corrections. For example, there were empowerments given in the Darjeeling area for a lot of Shangpa practitioners, my particular lineage. In the seating for the empowerments, the late Bokar Rinpoche put the non-Tibetan female lamas ahead of the male monastics. That was a big thing, and a statement to the monastic community. I think a lot of the rinpoches are seeing the inequality and wanting to remedy that—there's the wish for women to come forward.

GRACE SCHIRESON: As Westerners become more confident in the practice and in standing on their own two feet, they're willing to change things. To me this is the most encouraging point. For example, the ordination of bhikkhunīs was made possible because Westerners said, "We can change this. There's been some mistake in not allowing this tradition to continue or to be revived."

The same has been true in my tradition. The traditional chant that places us in the Buddhist family has no women's names in it. We've created a new chant that includes our women ancestors and it has been approved by the national organization of teachers. This group is made up of men and women who are acknowledging the mistake and saying, "We have the confidence now to add documents to the ones we inherited in our lineage. We have the confidence to correct these mistakes."

CHRISTINA FELDMAN: What is most inspiring to me is that I see around me a generation of sincere practitioners, women and men, who have actually reclaimed the possibility of awakening. I think this is one of the most extraordinary steps that this generation could ever have made.

RITA GROSS: One of the things I've changed in relating with these issues is that I'm no longer so interested in the outstanding role models like Yeshe Tsogyal, who would be very hard to emulate anyway. I'm interested in the notion that ordinary life is adequate for enlightenment. You don't have to be unusual and exotic and one in a thousand. That's not really the goal. The idea of just being oneself and becoming enlightened as one is has been a new take for me, and it is very refreshing. We really have everything we need, and all we need to do is work with that.

26

Monks, Nuns, and Yogis:
The Need for Full-Time Practitioners

ROBERT THURMAN

JUDY LIEF

JOSEPH GOLDSTEIN

What role have long-term, full-time practitioners—whether monastics, priests, mountain yogis, or forest yogis—played in the development of Buddhism? Are their activities essential to the continuation of an authentic Buddhist tradition?

ROBERT THURMAN: Monasticism has been an essential element in Buddhism since the beginning. However, I don't like to define a full-time practitioner only as someone who is a monastic or on retreat. I would say that the fate of Buddhism has depended historically on people who turn their lives toward enlightenment as their constant preoccupation. But that has not always been monastics or retreatants. There have been laypeople who have practiced the Dharma by not responding in anger to violence when people shouted at them or hit them or did something wrong to them. That is also full-time practice. Applying antidotes to the kleśas is a forceful practice.

Therefore, I don't think we should define full-time practitioners only as those in retreat. But having said that, it is true that historically people have needed to go on retreat to develop the ability to counter the kleśas. You need to withdraw, to be alone with the emotions and the mental functions and factors to gain a handle on them. Having done so, you are able to deal with the world in a full-time way.

JUDY LIEF: Part of the question hinges on the definition of practice. If we understand practice as bending the mind toward awakening and the present moment, then practice can take place in many guises. A certain number of people do need to disrupt their lives and dedicate themselves to realization as their full-time priority. But people can also dedicate themselves to Buddhist principles of compassion no matter what lifestyle they may have. Like Bob, I would not link practice solely with monasticism. There are many ways of going about it.

When I met my teacher, I dropped out and moved to where he needed me to be. Many people have done similar things when they were inspired, whether they went to live in a practice community or went to receive in-depth teachings from a particular teacher. A powerful component of any sangha are the people who transform their priorities dramatically, the people who turn their minds from the usual career path or materialistic values toward awakening.

JOSEPH GOLDSTEIN: There is another key reason why it is important for a certain number of people to dedicate their lives in a full-time way to practice, for at least some period of time: the wisdom that leads to awakening rests on the foundation of concentration. Most people need a secluded environment to develop concentration. That is one of the crucial things missing in the West now, given that our society and culture is so distracted. It may be wishful thinking to imagine that we can actually realize the depth of the teachings in the midst of such a lifestyle.

Historically, what role have intensive practitioners played in the practice of lay Buddhists?

JOSEPH GOLDSTEIN: Historically, the laypeople have relied on the intensive practitioners both for general life guidance and more specifically for meditation guidance.

ROBERT THURMAN: There is no question that without the bhikṣus, bhikṣuṇīs, and ordained lay men and women who followed the Vinaya, Buddhism would not have had the impact it did in Asia. They were developing a much deeper mental focus, and they were creating a higher lifestyle in those societies: greater self-restraint, greater focus, and greater wisdom. Aside from the effect of their formal teaching, they created a vibe that emanated from their institutions that completely changed the quality of the society.

Laypeople depended on the foundation provided by the ascetics. However, the laypeople's way of practicing the religion was through developing generosity, morality, and patience, more than developing concentration and wisdom. In fact, there became too great a duality between the monks and nuns developing the concentration and wisdom part and the laypeople working more on the moral interaction level, relying on the vibes emanating from the monks and nuns.

JUDY LIEF: Over time, the monastic establishment separated itself from lay society in a very elitist way. Different teachings were given to laypeople than were given to monastic people. The special teachings were held out for the special people, and the other people were left with a more superficial, moralistic side of Dharma.

Also, in terms of the monastic Sangha, the women are at the bottom of the heap. So much religious exclusivity and sexism has been linked with the monastic approach that it has been quite harmful to at least 50 percent of Buddhists, who are looked down upon as taking care of the mundane world, in contrast to males, who are devoted to higher matters.

What opportunities exist today for Westerners to devote themselves full-time to practice and study of the Dharma?

JOSEPH GOLDSTEIN: Overall the opportunities for intensive practice do seem to be limited. There are few places where people can devote themselves full-time to practice. We are just now at a stage of development of Buddhism in the West where the need for more long-term practice places is becoming apparent.

JUDY LIEF: We are not without opportunities, though. Zen communities offer programs where one can spend a year or two in residence. Some of the Tibetan sanghas offer community residency options, and there are three-year retreat programs in Europe and the US. IMS offers longer-term practice facilities and the Shambhala community has a regular schedule of *dathün*s, which are month-long meditation sessions. Opportunities for intensive practice seem to exist in all the traditions—maybe not lifelong situations, but definitely lengthy, intensive practice and study opportunities.

But is it sufficient to have places where people can practice for a month or a year or several years, or do we need opportunities for people to practice for a decade or more?

ROBERT THURMAN: It is hard to get people to realize that long-term practice is extremely important, not only because it benefits the practitioner but also because it benefits the entire society. It counteracts consumerism and violence. Institutions that foster long-term practice are crucial if we are to make headway in dealing with society.

On the other hand, Joseph's point about the gradual seeding that has taken place is very well taken. You can't just drop out with an untutored mind and expect to get a result in solitude. You need to be aiming in the right direction, so that you can use the solitude in a creative way.

Do we need institutions that can create a cadre of Western Buddhists who are deeply knowledgeable about Buddhism, as well as deeply practiced?

JUDY LIEF: In fact, we have some strong features in our society that were not present in some of the traditional societies. For example, we have many more literate people. We also have many publications and books from all traditions, and we also have many university programs.

ROBERT THURMAN: And we have more women.

JUDY LIEF: Yes, we have more women, best of all. [laughs] We also have many schools of Buddhist studies that offer in-depth training on the academic and intellectual side. We have institutions like Naropa University and various retreat centers that create alternative value systems. It is now becoming more widely known that there are other ways to obtain education and training besides the "get your credential and get a bunch of money" approach. Buddhist communities are creating the critical mass for supporting practice in all its styles, from retreat to full engagement in the world and everything in between.

JOSEPH GOLDSTEIN: A key moment will be when there are a number of quite realized Westerners. At that point, the transmission of the teachings will really begin to take root deeply in our culture. For most of us, our teachers have been Asian, and even though we have many Western teachers, we don't put them in the same category as our original teachers. The deepening of realization among Westerners is going to have a tremendously significant impact.

My motivation for developing the forest retreat center at IMS has been to create a place where people can come to practice for however long it is fruitful for them to practice. My inner vision is that it would be great if we started to see some Western *arhats*—or the Mahāyāna or Vajrayāna equivalents—coming out of such a retreat center.

I don't see that happening unless there are places for long-term practice. There will be the occasional remarkable individual, but for most of us, realization is going to be the fruit of a lot of work over a long, long time. We need a place to do it and a place that will support that.

ROBERT THURMAN: It might be a good idea for people who want to do the long retreats to have degree programs associated with their intensive practice. Perhaps it could be an MA program or a psychology program like they have at Naropa or the California Institute of Integral Studies. They would take a couple of years of preliminary Buddhist education and language studies and then go into the retreat. The retreat would become the equivalent of fieldwork within the Western social setting. Then they come out with a psychology degree, for example, which they could use to become counselors.

Usually when someone is ready for a retreat, they just go into it and then they worry about how they will integrate into society when they come out. To overcome that obstacle, I would love to see a Buddhist university—or even a conventional university—create educational programs that would fit around long retreats. It would help retreatants before the retreat to make it more fruitful, and it would help them integrate into society after the retreat. They would be teachers, or PhDs or MAs, and they would have a livelihood that would fit with their attainment.

If long-term practice is important in achieving deep realization, what does that say about the lay practice that dominates in the West?

ROBERT THURMAN: We should be cautious about anyone considering themselves great practitioners, whether they are practicing on retreat or in lay life. The bodhisattva does not dwell upon the thought of being a bodhisattva.

Laypeople can practice and they should do retreats. And the ones who get really good will probably give up that stupid job making that stupid money, which someone else is going to inherit when they die anyway. In the meantime, though, giving gifts and supporting those who do long retreats, and acting in a restrained way—that is practice and should be understood to be so.

JUDY LIEF: I would go further than that. I don't think the lay path is second best. It is a valid path in and of itself. I call it back-and-forth practice: retreat time and engaging in the world time. In my own experience, this is the most powerful form of practice. Retreat time is a time to concentrate, to focus your mind, to study intensively. But until that is brought back into your world, it is not really tested.

It is easy to get caught up in your own sense of your own realization—until you go back home and you visit your parents and the whole thing crumbles. By holding the view of twenty-four-hour practice, we can utilize whatever we encounter as fuel for realization. If your mind flips over so that you actually are open to receiving teachings in the many forms that they exist throughout the world, it enriches the retreat experiences. In the same way, the retreat experiences enrich the interactions in daily life.

ROBERT THURMAN: I regret that I haven't spent more of my life on retreat. If I had developed the kind of concentration Joseph was talking about, I'm sure I would have been better at encountering the challenges outside of retreat. So I think it is good for laypeople to see that they could be doing something more and better in the way of intensive practice.

JUDY LIEF: But I think it is also important to get beyond the idea that there is a special time for practice, and that what's outside of that is nonpractice. It would be helpful to try to soften that boundary. Retreat is unquestionably a valuable thing, and all of us would like to figure out ways in our lives to do more of it. Nonetheless, the attitude that there are these special times and the rest is wasted time doesn't seem very helpful.

JOSEPH GOLDSTEIN: Two key questions arise from what we have been talking about. First, how much retreat time is necessary for laypeople to be able to carry its value over into their lives? We don't want to fool ourselves into thinking, "If I do one weekend a year, or one ten-day course a year, someday I am going to end up a buddha in this lifetime." It is possible, but unlikely. I have seen people who have come to several retreats a year over many years and deepened their practice a lot, but how much intensive practice is enough remains an important question.

The second question concerns what is needed during nonretreat time to support a level of awareness that will actually bring insight. We don't get a lot of support from our society. What could we do so that in our ordinary life we are actually using our practice to that end? One obvious answer is Dharma community. And what about people who are not living in community? How could they really bring community into their lives and practice in a meaningful way? I think it is a tremendous challenge.

To develop well-trained teachers, should we concentrate on developing monasteries, or are a variety of different forms appropriate?

ROBERT THURMAN: We should be developing monasteries.

JOSEPH GOLDSTEIN: We need both monasteries and other forms as well. The monastic form offers tremendous benefit and value, and brings with it a whole support structure. There are also many practitioners who for one reason or another are not drawn to the monastic form. We need to provide opportunities for them to deepen their practice as well. I see the whole range as being needed and valuable, from lay centers to monasteries.

JUDY LIEF: We also need academic centers, translation centers, research centers, and libraries. There are so many different—and vitally important—forms of community. Monasticism is certainly one of them, although it is certainly not an easy form to develop. It is also not a tremendously popular form at this point.

ROBERT THURMAN: We have to realize that in American culture a big obstacle to monasticism is the Protestant ethic—the idea that there is something wrong with people who are not doing something "productive." There's no free lunch and all that. There is a genuine block in people's minds about the virtue and the potency of monasticism; it is thought of as something wrong and backward.

JOSEPH GOLDSTEIN: The kind of cultural resistance seemed to be more of a factor when I was first starting practice. I remember hearing when I was in India, "You're just wasting your time there, why don't you come back and get a job?"

My sense is that this kind of resistance has now lessened. The difficulty today has more to do with a lack of appreciation for, and a lack of understanding of, renunciation. This is a huge obstacle for people, because in our society renunciation obviously doesn't have a great reputation. People are afraid of the renunciate lifestyle.

Traditionally, lay practitioners saw it as their role to support full-time practitioners. Is there an impulse today among lay practitioners to support the long-term practice of others?

JOSEPH GOLDSTEIN: In our organization people are quite generous when they are solicited for funds for scholarship programs. There are great resources available to support people in practice. It is just a question of both educating and asking; the money is there. I think there is a large enough pool of practitioners with resources to support long-term practitioners.

ROBERT THURMAN: Another key issue in this regard is the distance that can open up between the monastic and the lay community. In the Vinaya, the Buddha said that a monastic *vihāra* should not be more than seven stone-throws away from the marketplace. He was purposely distinguishing these abodes from distant forest retreat places.

JUDY LIEF: Exactly. That monastic model is different from the current Western model, which is more of a permanent retreat model, with little interaction with the lay community.

ROBERT THURMAN: Traditionally, the monks had to go to a lay family's house every day to get food. They would often give a talk or hang out at the house. Then the people would ask questions of the venerable monk or nun who had come to visit and have lunch. That free lunch was something that enabled there to be much more interaction between lay families and monks and nuns.

There were many elements of social wisdom in the Vinaya that allowed for there to be a lot of interaction between monastics and laypeople, without the monks or nuns losing their renunciation, and without the laypeople being deprived. Modern versions of all of these methods will slowly develop, but nevertheless at the heart of it is the need for more realized people. We have to have more arhats and more advanced retreat courses that give degrees to people who have put in the time. Then we will have a lot of enlightened people instead of a bunch of amateurs like me. Then the institutions will naturally be founded as a result of their activity.

27

Engaged Buddhism:
How Political Is the Dharma?

DAVID LOY

JOAN SUTHERLAND, ROSHI

MUSHIM IKEDA

Does Buddhism inevitably include some element of political engagement?

DAVID LOY: The Buddha emphasized that all he really taught was suffering (*dukkha*) and how to end it. But given the political context he lived in, the kinds of social and political dukkha that he could address were limited. The Western emphasis on social justice has helped us become more aware of the opportunities not only for socially engaged Buddhism but politically engaged Buddhism.

As we deepen our awakening, we realize that our own suffering can't be distinguished from the suffering of others. As we overcome our delusive sense of a separate self, we can no longer pursue our own well-being with indifference to the well-being of others.

JOAN SUTHERLAND, ROSHI: The results of practice can lead to political engagement. Over time, there tends to be a deepening of gratitude for the fact of existence, for what we speak of as interpermeation. That gratitude is not an emotion but a way of being, fundamentally, and its expression quite often occurs as generosity. The generosity then looks for ways to be helpful. That seems to be quite a natural, organic development with long-term practice.

MUSHIM IKEDA: Human interactions are inevitably political, so except for people living totally off the grid, they're going to have some level of political engagement. Even with just one other human being, political dynamics are at work because people have different needs and different ways of strategizing to fulfill those needs.

JOAN SUTHERLAND, ROSHI: One of the offerings we can make to the world at large is the practices that have developed within Buddhism, and one of these practices is to ask questions rather than make statements. Approaching political engagement as a series of questions and explorations is very different from approaching it with position papers or assumptions that you already know what something means.

DAVID LOY: Politics in the broad sense involves engagement with lots of people, most of whom are not interested in Buddhist practice. We have to acknowledge that we're dealing with many different types of ego and ego-based institutions. Buddhists like to emphasize being in the here and now and we want to focus on the process rather than a goal. But if we get involved in politics, it's because we're trying to achieve something. That can give one a future orientation that tends to lose the here and now.

There's always going to be some tension between thinking in terms of means and ends—causality—and acting out of an emptiness that has nothing to gain and nothing to lose. The challenge of political involvement for Buddhists is not sacrificing one because we're so completely focused on the other.

Many a Buddhist practitioner would say that they go on retreat or sesshin because they want quiet time, a respite from the world where they can work with their own mind. If that space becomes politicized, they may no longer feel it is a refuge for them.

MUSHIM IKEDA: I have to laugh when people say they would like to live in a temple or monastery because they want to be alone and meditate all the time. In any community, virulent tensions will arise because of individual differences. Human beings are going to have conflict, and conflict generates a lot of noise, both internally in the mind and externally in the environment. As an example, I heard about one residential community where the kitchen staff got into an acrimonious and lengthy debate about whether there should be one large bottle of Tabasco sauce kept in the condiments area or small bottles at each table.

JOAN SUTHERLAND, ROSHI: I can understand the desire for the silence and the space to relax and to begin to see things more clearly, but the dichotomy between that and the Tabasco sauce wars is illusory. Neither can exist in isolation, and if one part of our practice is about a deepening experience of spaciousness, the other part is about embodying that in the world. It's the old form and emptiness thing, and if you fall too far on one side or the other, something is missing.

You have to do the difficult work of getting tossed back and forth between the quiet, spacious world and the active, lively world until it doesn't feel like you're being tossed anymore, until you find something underneath that contains both the stillness and the activity, no matter what the circumstance. The more we rest in that and emerge from that in our activities, the less there is a sense of losing something because we're including the other and the more there is a sense that practice is one whole thing we can gladly work with.

DAVID LOY: It's important to distinguish Dharma practice on the personal level—where we work on our own transformation—from political activities. Practice is what enables us to see the connections between personal transformation and social transformation.

JOAN SUTHERLAND, ROSHI: The tensions we're talking about can be tremendously creative if we're willing to hang out with them and be uncomfortable. In Japan during World War II, for example, Zen became involved with imperialism. It was a horrible period in the history of Zen, and for a while in the postwar period, people in Zen didn't want to get involved in politics. Then, a few decades later, a movement began toward becoming politically engaged. But it was now an engagement that benefited from the lessons of World War II. Staying alert to how time and circumstances and people are changing is tremendously important.

If acting politically is a natural outgrowth of Dharma practice, what kind of actions would it be skillful for a Buddhist to take? Is it skillful to join in protest movements in the name of Buddhism or a Buddhist organization?

DAVID LOY: The more groups, religious and otherwise, that join in such demonstrations, the more effective they would be in showing breadth of support. So from that side, I don't see a problem. The issue arises if one is going to represent a particular sangha or not, and how does one decide that? Would the Buddhist teacher make that decision? Would it be a democratic process on the part of the group, requiring a 51-percent vote?

JOAN SUTHERLAND, ROSHI: We went through a process in Santa Fe, and for us it was very important that we had a meeting where everybody had a chance to say what they wanted. I felt very strongly about supporting the Occupy movement. It seemed to be doing exactly what Buddhists have always done, which is to bear witness. Occupy was saying: Hey, there's a serious problem here; people are really suffering, and we need to pay attention to that. That was about as pure a Buddhist message as I could imagine.

On that basis, I put the question to the community. At the meeting, some people had what I thought was an important concern—that we not engage in the kind of us-and-them and sometimes aggressive or violent rhetoric that was occurring in some places.

We decided we would participate in Occupy Santa Fe once a week. There was no coercion or obligation, and whoever wanted to come would show up for an hour on Wednesday mornings, bringing warm clothes and groceries to share. We'd just sit—no banner, no tent, no literature—meditating on tarps on the ground, and when we left, we'd haul out some garbage.

DAVID LOY: Your meditation practice was undoubtedly having an impact on the way Occupy was developing. Buddhism does have something to offer in that situation in its emphasis on nonviolence and avoiding abusive rhetoric.

Some sanghas have forums, usually online, where people have presented strong political views with an implicit sense that there's prior agreement with them by the rest of the sangha.

JOAN SUTHERLAND, ROSHI: The important question is, what is the culture of your community? If persuading people politically is congruent with that culture, okay, but if people are being made uncomfortable by it, you've got a cultural problem and that's what you need to address.

DAVID LOY: I don't see this issue as significantly different from whether to take a banner to a street demonstration. Ultimately, it's up to the members to decide what kind of boundaries they want to set around their political action.

JOAN SUTHERLAND, ROSHI: Saying that supporting a candidate is an expression of my bodhicitta is one thing, but saying that it is therefore also an expression of everybody's bodhicitta is a cultural problem.

The prevalence of anger in politics scares a lot of Buddhists. How do practitioners work with that anger?

DAVID LOY: Fundamentally, anger is a kind of energy, and the issue is whether we understand this energy and how to use it wisely. If it's understood in a dualistic way, the self-righteousness of an ego that's attacking somebody else, it's very dangerous. But one could also understand anger within the larger context of love. Can we have a politics based not on anger but on love? That, of course, fits in well with the Buddhist emphasis on compassion and nonduality, and realizing that we're not separate from other people. But there is still a role for the energy that gets expressed as anger, such as when people who should be held in a loving situation are being abused or taken advantage of.

Although we in the Occupy movement may be saying, "We are the 99 percent," it's not as though we are trying to promote the interests of the 99 percent by destroying the 1 percent. From a Buddhist standpoint, the emphasis is on realizing that what we're working toward is ultimately going to benefit everyone.

JOAN SUTHERLAND, ROSHI: I agree that ferocity and fearlessness are important qualities. But I've noticed that when I get angry it's often because I'm taking a break from sorrow. The sorrow is almost unbearable and it can be easier to be angry.

We have a practice of meeting our broken hearts with the great broken heart of the world, which of course is the First Noble Truth. We look to see what's possible when we're not fleeing from that sorrow into anger or self-righteousness or numbness. As for ferocity and fearlessness, questioning becomes crucial, because if you're going to be fierce and assertive and all of that great stuff, it makes a big difference if you don't believe you're right. What the Dharma offers is that the most we can aspire to is our best guess— and that's subject to change, depending on new information.

MUSHIM IKEDA: A good practice question for the Dharma students I work with, many of whom are strong social justice activists, would be: Can I just be purely in that anger over the incredible injustices in the world, over the people who are getting chewed up and spat out by the machinery of our society every single day, without any trace of aggression?

DAVID LOY: The key here is whether the anger arises within a larger container of nondualistic love, in which we're not taking sides by pursuing the well-being of one group of people at the cost of another group of people. From a Buddhist perspective, the love or compassion we're talking about obviously does include what is called the 1 percent.

Chögyam Trungpa Rinpoche talked about compassion including both "yes" and "no." Saying "yes" is accommodating, but saying "no"—clearly identifying what is wrong and unjust—is also compassionate.

JOAN SUTHERLAND, ROSHI: On the "no" side of compassion, if we're holding other people accountable for their actions, we have to be sure we're holding ourselves accountable too.

One of the ways we can do that is with a rigorous inquiry when we are working for change. When we feel anger about something we think must not stand, we need to ask whom we are trying to make comfortable? There might be an element of "I'm trying to make myself comfortable because I just can't bear that things are like this," which is very human. But we need to be aware to what extent our activities are motivated by a genuine sense of wanting to help those who are suffering and to what extent our motivation is wanting to feel more comfortable ourselves.

Is it skillful for Buddhism to be associated with a particular political position, or does that limit our ability to help as many people as possible, including people with different political beliefs?

JOAN SUTHERLAND, ROSHI: I would urge us to be humble. We need to listen to a lot of different voices, and not just because we happen to stumble upon an important conversation. We need to seek out voices we might not ordinarily run into in our lives. There was a discussion in the larger Buddhist world about whether it was right to have a Buddhist presence for the cadets at the Air Force Academy in Colorado Springs. Interestingly, this conversation did not include the people at the academy who are actually involved in living the questions every day.

MUSHIM IKEDA: If I am strongly allied publicly with a particular political position, I'm immediately going to be perceived as the opposition by those who have different values and political beliefs, and my chances for being heard are going to decrease accordingly. Hardening around a particular political stance, as Joan wisely pointed out, might be valid for us today but not meet our needs tomorrow.

DAVID LOY: Social justice is not a traditional Asian Buddhist concept. It developed in the Abrahamic tradition, goes back to the prophets, and ultimately depends upon the duality between good and evil. When the prophets challenged the rulers for oppressing poor people, that shows the positive side of good versus evil. The negative side is that one of the main causes of evil in our world has been our effort to get rid of evil. We try to separate good and evil, when the reality is that they're two sides of the same coin: we feel good about ourselves when we're fighting against evil, which means we have to find something evil to fight against. George W. Bush and Osama bin Laden were fighting the same holy war of good versus evil, but what one thought was good the other thought was evil, and vice versa. Ironically, the result was much greater evil.

The Buddhist emphasis is not on good versus evil but on wisdom versus delusion. Buddhism raises all kinds of questions about what really makes people happy. Just because those in the 1 percent have piles of money doesn't mean they can escape dukkha. One of the wonderful things about Buddhism coming to the West is that our concern for social justice is supplemented by the Buddhist insight of making sure we're not just caught up in vainly trying to satisfy the greed and negativity of our egos.

28

Where Do We Go from Here?
New Generations of Buddhists

SUMI LOUNDON KIM ▪ **ZOKETSU NORMAN FISCHER**
ROD MEADE SPERRY ▪ **IRIS BRILLIANT**

The Buddhists in North America referred to as "convert Buddhists"—those who did not inherit it as a part of their ethnic background—are largely baby boomers. Are enough younger people coming up through the ranks to sustain healthy Buddhist communities?

SUMI LOUNDON KIM: The next generations of Buddhists make up a very small proportion of the current self-named Buddhists. I'd estimate that less than a fifth of all convert Buddhists are under forty.

I don't think that's going to grow too significantly over the coming decades, so the Buddhist community is going to shrink considerably. But it's still going to be large enough to sustain well-established groups long into the future. Communities will also be very well-funded, because the baby boom Buddhists are going to generously donate their life savings to their favorite Dharma center. The traditions that have taken root in America will not die with the baby boomers.

ZOKETSU NORMAN FISCHER: If you're talking about people who take vows and who are loyal members of sanghas, in that case, what Sumi said applies. But if you change the framework and count all the young people who've been influenced by Buddhism; been to Buddhist centers and meditated; who are in dialogue with their friends about Buddhist ideas, concepts, and values; who are hooked into websites that are at the nexus of popular culture and Buddhism, you may end up with a very different picture.

Younger Buddhists aren't necessarily following the model of their parents' generation by becoming a Zen priest or a committed Vajrayāna practitioner or what have you. Instead, they're attending retreats, going to Dharma centers, even establishing eclectic meditation groups on their own. They're putting together a unique package for their lives. If you look at it that way, you see a very large flowering of Buddhism in the culture of the next generations.

At the San Francisco Zen Center, there are young people who spend significant time there before they move on. They may not be counted in the Buddhist community *per se*, because they're not formally affiliated with any center, but the practice has had a tremendous influence on their lives. As they get older and settle down, they will naturally join groups, which at this point are too expensive for them and filled with older people.

ROD MEADE SPERRY: It may be healthy for Buddhism to evolve haphazardly into new shapes that probably won't look like exactly like the shapes we have now. Everything that ever happens in the Dharma is an innovation at first—each new sect is an innovation. To some it may be heresy, but for others it's what works for them in their time and place.

What we're going to see is new forms of Buddhism that are viable and work for whoever comes next. As the saying goes, when the student is ready, the teacher appears. I've also found that when the student is ready, the Sangha appears. People end up finding their own sangha or create their own sangha. They see a need that isn't being served and say, "You know what? I'll start a sitting group." In the future we'll have the old established communities, but we will have a lot of others too, started by people who are innovating based on their own inspiration.

IRIS BRILLIANT: I think socially engaged Buddhism is a strong driving force for younger people. Many people my age are very political, and many of them are taking an interest in Buddhism or going on retreats. As a result, Buddhism is being integrated into movements such as the environmental, antiracist, and LGBTQ movements. People are using practice in a way that is deeply intertwined with social justice. Practice is used not only as a way to become more centered but as a tool to become a more grounded activist.

SUMI LOUNDON KIM: I'm not sure we can characterize the next generation of Buddhist or Buddhist-influenced people based on one model alone. It appears to me that there will probably be a split of populations. There will be young people who take a fairly traditional approach to Buddhism, because they're looking for a religion and everything that comes with that. On the other side, you'll have the Buddhist-influenced or meditation-influenced people who may not self-identify as Buddhists or be part of what we would generally call Buddhist communities.

Is it fair to say that those who came to Buddhism in the sixties and seventies were trying to leave their culture and create another one, and that the new generations of practitioners have a different relationship to culture?

ZOKETSU NORMAN FISCHER: My generation felt the Vietnam War demonstrated the corruption of our whole society and way of life. We thought Asian society was much better, so we thought let's be Buddhist, let's be Tibetan, let's be Thai, let's be Japanese.

The new generation doesn't seem to hold that concept. It's pretty obvious now that everybody is screwed up, East and West. The younger people I meet are aware of that, and also aware that values come from their own heart. It's not a matter of Asia or the West. They're looking for whatever will help cultivate the good intention in their heart. As hard as the sixties people tried their best to be Japanese or Tibetan, it obviously didn't really happen.

IRIS BRILLIANT: In the youth retreats I went on at Spirit Rock, the teachers tried to make Buddhism accessible to everyone. They made the practice seem culturally neutral and emphasized the universal nature of the human experience. Most of the anecdotes in Dharma talks were about the teacher's personal life. The focus was definitely on the Dharma itself, but it was relateable to a broader framework of life in today's world. For example, they suggested we text message each other every time we sit, as a way of encouraging each other.

ZOKETSU NORMAN FISCHER: That's great!

IRIS BRILLIANT: So instead of shying away from technology and taking an extremist route, they emphasized that we should try to function within mainstream culture, embrace technology, and try to integrate it into our practice, which is definitely a new, and very American, thing.

SUMI LOUNDON KIM: Buddhism was, for Norman's and my parents' generation, very much counterculture. Now Buddhism is more what we'd call "alternative," in the sense of being outside the mainstream but acceptable. It's clear that there is still a need for young people to step outside mainstream American culture. Perhaps they already feel like they're outside of the mainstream and they're looking for something that feels like home, or perhaps they're just looking for some perspective.

In either case, there is a turning away of some kind. Often kids have grown up in very comfortable situations, and they begin to feel turned off by materialism, and Buddhism has something to say about that. They are willing to step into Buddhism as another point of view to critique mainstream America. To that extent, Buddhism is not fully integrating into the mainstream yet.

ZOKETSU NORMAN FISCHER: The Dharma is always going to manifest in many different ways. It needs conservatives, innovators, and dabblers. That's the fabric of the Dharma. Even in "deeply Buddhist" cultures, there are people who aren't practitioners who do something to uphold the monastics or take part in something cultural that makes them feel connected to the Buddhist culture.

ROD MEADE SPERRY: I see lots of interesting contemporary manifestations of Dharma reflected in contributors to my website. Their expression of Dharma is a healthy mix of reverent and irreverent. It could be street art influenced by the Dharma, Dharma tattoos, a death-metal band making music inspired by the Dharma. They're finding their own modes of expression, but they are not knocking down the old guard, either; they're adding to it, assimilating it into the way they live. Instead of *thangkas*, they have thangka tattoos.

We're not people who relate to images of tranquility. We never had it. It's not the society we grew up in. Tranquility may be something we're going for, but that's not what's going to connect with us. We see the New Age as just marketing. That's why we go for the oldest, most classic expressions of the Dharma, and add a new spin on them.

The web is a wonderful model for how the Dharma is evolving. It's an incredible gift of skillful means. It allows people to contribute in the way that they can contribute. We see so many new blogs and websites that are not run by teachers. Practitioners run them; young people who want to talk about Dharma, to be part of it, run them.

IRIS BRILLIANT: Young people are coming to Buddhism for a myriad of reasons. There's no single reason, but their reasons tend to be profound and important. Yet they are very interested in retaining their individuality rather than just becoming a certain Buddhist identity. That's one of the more interesting phenomena occurring right now.

ZOKETSU NORMAN FISCHER: When the Dharma is allowed to flower and express itself in so many different ways, it becomes something more people realize they can enter into. It's not just for holy people. It's for regular people like me, or irregular people like me.

It seems that many young people today are less interested in particular traditions. Will the future take the shape of a kind of pan-Buddhism or will people gravitate to specific traditions eventually?

ROD MEADE SPERRY: The teachers who interest me are those who find a confluence of their primary practice with something else. There can be modes of teaching that include various traditions without watering the traditions down. As time goes on, you'll see more of that.

SUMI LOUNDON KIM: I agree that there are going to be syncretists, who will bring together elements from within the overall tradition, like Zen and Vipassanā, or bring something from outside, like punk, into Zen. There will also be people who settle into one path, once they do a bit of searching. There is something appealing about the integrity of a tradition that has liturgy, cosmology, ethics, and practices that have been developed over the centuries so that they work together to transform a person. In the wake of globalization and the dissolution of tradition, there will be people who will seek the roots that come with a tradition.

IRIS BRILLIANT: Most of the people I know who are interested in Buddhism are open to all of the traditions and are eager to learn about them. But it seems a lot of people put together their own hodgepodge of ideas and facets, which allows them to have something they make their own. Many people are only interested in sitting a little bit every day, learning a bit about the Dharma, maybe going on retreat. They're usually willing to go on any style of retreat.

I'm really interested in learning more about the Dharma itself, its history and its teachings. But I'm also excited when any group of young people wants to get together and learn just about the techniques of meditation. It's great to know that people are taking the initiative to become more clearheaded, even if they're doing it in a secular and detached way. That's immensely beneficial for them and those around them.

Will the tension between the popular, simpler forms and the traditional forms continue into the next generations?

ZOKETSU NORMAN FISCHER: It's complex, and it will change over time. People at the so-called popular end of the spectrum—secular meditators, people with Buddhist tattoos, people who are merely turned on by something they heard on Oprah—in my experience actually have respect for the tradition and an appreciation for the need for deeply committed practitioners.

In addition, as you get older, your views generally change and you become more conservative. Many people who have nipped at the edges of the Buddhadharma will see the need for a more coherent community and more committed practice. It may turn out that the Buddhist movement is something very broad, lively, and multifarious, but that as people who participate in the movement get older—into their fifties and sixties—they may find themselves having a more narrow focus and more conservative practice regimen, if they can find good teachers who will validate and understand the experience they've had over their lifetime.

What do the Buddhists of today need to do to ensure that the Buddhism of tomorrow is more diverse, and therefore continues to grow, in spite of the eclipsing of the baby boom?

IRIS BRILLIANT: I agree with Sumi that the focus on retreats is a little too heavy, so it would be good if it were easier for people to start their own sitting groups, maybe inviting one teacher to support them and give Dharma talks. The Internet is another wonderful resource for people to connect with practice, including having more talks available for download. Young adult retreats are another great way of getting more young people involved. The people on my young adult retreat became very close-knit and have stayed in touch afterward. And I can't say it enough: it's critical that the Dharma become more affordable.

SUMI LOUNDON KIM: Affordability is a key issue. A lot of the young people tell me they started on a Goenka retreat. Why? Because it was free. I have to say, though, that this complaint bothers me a little, because a lot of Dharma centers do offer scholarships. Having worked on the administrative side of a Dharma center, I know that the retreat fees barely cover expenses. On the other side, there can be an expectation in the younger generation that they'll be supported. There's not as much nitty-gritty, I-will-do-what-it-takes-to-do-this-retreat attitude that I saw in my parents' generation, most of whom had nothing either. Maybe my generation and the one after it don't want to work as hard to get into a retreat.

ROD MEADE SPERRY: I've been the beneficiary of sanghas that have gone out of their way to offer scholarships. It's important to let people know that if they want to put something in the *dana* box after sitting, that's good, and if not, that's OK too. It's also important to let people know that a retreat has a suggested charge, but if you can't afford it, you are still welcome. I know that creates difficulties, but it's a real gesture toward inclusion.

IRIS BRILLIANT: I'd also add that if you're talking about being more inclusive of young people, it's important to be unafraid to discuss issues that young people tend to face, such as sexuality and sexual orientation.

Obviously, it can be tricky. How do you talk to minors about sex on a Buddhist teen retreat without getting in trouble with their parents? But there are ways to talk about sex, drugs, stress in school, and the pressure to succeed. These issues can often be lost when young people are just part of the crowd of adults. If there were places for open discussion about what they are going through, that would draw more young people into the practice. They'd see it as relevant to their lives.

SUMI LOUNDON KIM: I agree. It seems like the examples in talks of challenges people face, as well as the casual discussions at centers, have to do with things like menopause, caring for elderly parents, or what to do with your investments. Dharma talks and articles and postings that address young people's issues would make the teachings stick with them.

How could centers approach these issues in a way that would be useful?

IRIS BRILLIANT: Having more younger teachers, people in their twenties and thirties, would help. I had one assistant teacher at Spirit Rock who was considerably younger than the other teachers, and just knowing that she had started to practice at my age, and wasn't that much older than me, made me feel so much more comfortable.

In general, teachers could try to push themselves a bit beyond their comfort zone. I don't think every teacher should be forced to talk about issues specifically related to young people, but it's important for teachers to know what the issues are and do their best to address them in an appropriate way.

The older generation of teachers often simply proclaims the Dharma, with less of the dialogue that Norman was talking about earlier.

ZOKETSU NORMAN FISCHER: We learned that style from Asian teachers, or Western teachers who were very close to Asian teachers. It's a style that came from an authoritarian, feudalistic culture, and it worked well in that culture. Now the generations are shifting, and it's obvious that's not workable. This presents a challenge, because the Dharma is not make-it-up-as-you-go-along. There's something that must be learned, and there is tradition, but that tradition has to be delivered clearly in dialogue. If you're a young person going to a retreat and people are talking about aging and menopause, that's not skillful teaching. When there are young people in the room, we older teachers are going to have to listen and be challenged and changed.

IRIS BRILLIANT: In addition to trying to lessen the heavy authority role that seems to come with a lot of teachers, one of the things that makes people want to come back, especially on teen retreats, is when they make close bonds with their peers, and then stay in touch and check in with one another.

Trying to foster areas in which young people can meet other young people who are as dedicated as they are and are willing to support one another would help a lot. It helps to find young leaders who are willing to rally people together. Having a great teacher isn't quite enough. You really need people your age.

If you have more workshops directly focused on how the Dharma can help you do more effective social action, which will draw a younger and more diverse crowd and help to demonstrate a broader focus.

SUMI LOUNDON KIM: This broader focus includes redefining the very idea of a Dharma teacher. There are a lot of young people thinking about roles not just as Dharma teachers in the traditional way, but as chaplains in hospices and hospitals, even in the military. Dharma practice may be married with quite a range of professions, roles, and causes. We're in a pioneering phase. It's a little daunting, but we are stumbling toward a path.

Contributors

Ven. Ajahn Amaro is a bhikkhu in the Thai forest tradition and the abbot of Amaravati Buddhist Monastery in southeast England.

Guy Armstrong is a member of the Spirit Rock Teachers Council and a guiding teacher of the Insight Meditation Society.

Geoffrey Shugen Arnold, Sensei, is the head of the Mountains and Rivers Order and abbot of the Fire Lotus Temple in Brooklyn, New York.

Harvey Aronson, PhD, MSW, is a psychotherapist in private practice and a Buddhist meditation teacher. He is the author of *Buddhist Practice on Western Ground.*

Ezra Bayda teaches at the Zen Center of San Diego. His most recent book is *The Authentic Life: Zen Wisdom for Living Free From Complacency and Fear.*

Jan Chozen Bays, Roshi, is a pediatrician and coabbot of Great Vow Zen Monastery in Claskanie, Oregon. She is the author of *Mindful Eating* and *How to Train a Wild Elephant and Other Adventures in Mindfulness.*

Patricia Dai-en Bennage is the abbess of Mt. Equity Zendo in Pennsdale, Pennsylvania. She practiced Zen in Japan for twenty-three years and trained at the NiSodo women's monastery in Nagoya.

Ven. Bhikkhu Bodhi is an American Theravāda monk, writer, and activist. His translations include *The Buddha: A Translation of the Majjhima Nikaya* and *The Connected Discourses of the Buddha*. He is the cofounder of Buddhist Global Relief.

Iris Brilliant is a Buddhist practitioner who has participated in teen and young people retreats organized by the Buddhist Peace Fellowship and also attended young people retreats at Spirit Rock Meditation Center.

Elizabeth Callahan completed a traditional three-year Vajrayāna retreat and studied with and interpreted for Khenpo Tsultrim Gyamtso Rinpoche. Her translations include the Ninth Karmapa's *The Ocean of Definitive Meaning* and Jamgon Kongtrul's *Treasury Knowledge*.

Francisca Cho is a translator and associate professor of Buddhist studies at Georgetown University. Her publications include *Everything Yearned For: Manhae's Poems of Love and Longing* and *Embracing Illusion: Truth and Fiction in the Dream of the Nine Clouds*.

Georges Dreyfus is Jackson Professor of Religion at Williams College. He was a monk for fifteen years in the Geluk tradition of Tibetan Buddhism and was the first Westerner to receive the *geshe* degree.

Lama Palden Drolma was authorized as a lama by the late Kalu Rinpoche following her completion of a three-year retreat and has taught Vajrayana Buddhism since 1986. She is the founder of the Sukhasiddhi Foundation, based in Fairfax, California.

Christina Feldman is a guiding teacher in the Insight Meditation Society and cofounder of Gaia House in Devon, England. She is the author of *The Buddhist Path to Simplicity* and *Compassion: Listening to the Cries of the World*.

Gaylon Ferguson is associate professor of religious studies at Naropa University and an acharya in Shambhala International. He is the author of *Natural Wakefulness*.

Zoketsu Norman Fischer is founder of the Everyday Zen Foundation and a former abbot of the San Francisco Zen Center. A poet and writer, he is the author of *Training in Compassion: Zen Teachings on the Practice of Lojong* and *Taking Our Places: The Buddhist Path to Truly Growing Up.*

Gil Fronsdal has a PhD in Buddhist studies and trained in both the Insight Meditation and Soto Zen traditions. He is the primary teacher for the Insight Meditation Center in Redwood City, California.

Bhante Gunaratana is the founder abbot of the Bhavana Society and author of *Journey to Mindfulness: The Autobiography of Bhante G* and the classic *Mindfulness in Plain English.*

Ron Garry has a PhD in Indo-Tibetan Buddhism and completed a three-year Vajrayāna retreat. He is the translator of *Wisdom Nectar: Dudjom Rinpoche's Heart Advice.*

Joseph Goldstein is a former monk in the Burmese forest tradition and cofounder of the Insight Meditation Society and the Forest Refuge, both in Barre, Massachusetts. He is the author of *One Dharma*; *Insight Meditation: The Practice of Freedom*; and *Mindfulness: A Practical Guide to Awakening.*

Michael Grady is a guiding teacher at the Cambridge Insight Meditation Center and a senior teacher at the Insight Meditation Society.

Rita Gross is a scholar, writer, and dharma teacher in the community of Jetsun Khandro Rinpoche. Among her many publications are *Soaring and Settling: Buddhist Perspectives on Contemporary Social and Religious Issues* and *A Garland of Feminist Reflections: Forty Years of Religious Reflection.*

Paul Haller is a Zen teacher and former abbot of the San Francisco Zen Center.

Sarah Harding is a Tibetan translator and lama in the Kagyü school of Vajrayāna Buddhism. Her translations include *Creation and Completion: Essential Points of Tantric Meditation* by Jamgon Kongtrul and *Lion's*

Gaze: The Special Teachings of the Wise and Glorious Sovereign by Patrul Rinpoche.

Zenkei Blanche Hartman is a senior dharma teacher at the San Francisco Zen Center. She was the abbess of SFZC from 1996 to 2003.

Steven Heine is professor of religion and history and director of Asian studies at Florida International University. His many publications include *The Zen Canon: Studies of Classic Zen Texts*; *The Zen Poetry of Dōgen*; and *The Kōan: Meaning and Metaphor.*

Mushim Ikeda is a Buddhist teacher, writer, and community activist. She is a core teacher at the East Bay Meditation Center in Oakland, California, a Buddhist community that emphasizes social justice and diversity.

Marlene Jones (d. 2013) was a founder of the Diversity Council at Spirit Rock Meditation Center. She also led retreats and programs there for people of color.

Sumi Loundon Kim is the Buddhist chaplain at Duke University and teacher for the Buddhist Families of Durham. She has published two anthologies about young Buddhists: *Blue Jean Buddha* and *The Buddha's Apprentices.*

Anne Carolyn Klein is a founding director and resident teacher at Dawn Mountain Tibetan Temple in Houston, Texas. She is a professor of religious studies at Rice University and author of *Heart Essence of the Great Expanse: A Story of Transmission.*

Jack Kornfield trained as a Buddhist monk in Thailand, India, and Burma. Returning to the United States, he cofounded the Insight Meditation Society and is a founding teacher at Spirit Rock Meditation Center. He has a PhD in clinical psychology and is the author of such classics as *A Wise Heart*; *After the Ecstasy, the Laundry*; and *Bringing Home the Dharma.*

Robin Kornman (d. 2007) was a translator, writer, and close student of the late Chögyam Trunpga Rinpoche. His major translation is of the Tibetan epic *King Gesar of Ling.*

Cyndi Lee is the founder of OM yoga and a longtime student of Gehlek Rinpoche. She is the author of *Yoga Body, Buddha Mind* and *May I Be Happy: A Memoir of Love, Yoga, and Changing My Mind.*

Taigen Dan Leighton is a writer and translator and the guiding dharma teacher at Ancient Dragon Zen Gate in Chicago. Among his books are *Zen Questions: Zazen, Dogen, and the Spirit of Creative Inquiry* and *Faces of Compassion: Classic Bodhisattva Archetypes and Their Modern Expression.*

Judy Lief was trained and empowered by Chögyam Trungpa Rinpoche as a teacher in the Buddhist and Shambhala traditions. She is the editor of many of Trungpa Rinpoche's books, including the three-volume set *The Profound Treasury of the Ocean of Dharma*, and is the author of *Making Friends with Death: A Buddhist Guide to Encountering Mortality.*

John Daido Loori, Roshi (d. 2009), was the founder of Zen Mountain Monastery and the Mountains and Rivers Order, where he served as the guiding teacher for almost thirty years. A holder of both the Soto and Rinzai Zen lineages, he was the author of numerous books, including *The Eight Gates of Zen* and *The Zen of Creativity.*

David Loy is a professor, writer, and Zen teacher in the Sanbo Kyodan tradition. His work focuses on the encounter between Buddhism and modernity, focusing on contemporary social and ecological issues. He is the author of *The Great Awakening: A Buddhist Social Theory, Money, Sex, War, Karma,* and *The World Is Made of Stories.*

Kamala Masters is one of the founders and teachers of the Vipassana Metta Foundation on Maui. She teaches retreats in the Theravāda tradition worldwide and is a guiding teacher at the Insight Meditation Society.

Elizabeth Mattis-Namgyel has studied and practiced for thirty years under the guidance of her teacher and husband, Dzigar Kongtrul Rinpoche. She spent six years in solitary retreat and serves as retreat master at Mangala Shri Bhuti's retreat center in southern Colorado. She is the author of *The Power of an Open Question*.

Guy McCloskey is the vice general director of the Soka Gakkai International movement in the United States.

Ken McLeod completed a three-year retreat on the guidance of the late Kalu Rinpoche. He translated *The Great Path of Awakening*, Jamgön Kongtrül's commentary on lojong, and is the author of *Wake Up to Your Life*. He is the founder of Unfettered Mind in Los Angeles.

Larry Mermelstein is the executive director of the Nalanda Translation Committee and an archarya in Shambhala International.

Yongey Mingyur Rinpoche is a teacher in the Karma Kagyu and Nyingma lineages of Tibetan Buddhism. He has authored two best-selling books, *The Joy of Living* and *Joyful Wisdom*, and founded the Tergar Meditation Community, an international network of Buddhist meditation centers.

Phillip Moffitt is a member of the Teachers Council at Spirit Rock Meditation Center and the founder of the Life Balance Institute. He is the author of *Dancing with Life* and *Emotional Chaos to Clarity*.

Mary Morgan is a member of the diversity committee and chair of the governance committee of San Francisco Zen Center. She is a Superior Court judge in San Francisco.

Reverend Shohaku Okumura is a Soto Zen priest and translator of the writings of Dōgen Zenji and Uchiyama Roshi. He is the founder and director of the Sanshin Zen Community, based in San Francisco.

Andrew Olendzki is senior scholar at the Barre Center for Buddhist Studies. He is a columnist for *Tricycle* magazine and the author of *Unlimited Mind*.

Frank Ostaseski is a leading voice on contemplative end-of-life care. He is founder of the Metta Institute, which offers education in end-of-life care, emphasizing the spiritual dimensions of dying.

Bhante Piyānanda is president and abbot of Dharma Vijaya Buddhist Vihara in Los Angeles.

Dzogchen Ponlop Rinpoche is a teacher in the Nyingma and Kagyu schools of Tibetan Buddhism. He is the founder of Nalandabodhi and the author of *Rebel Buddha: A Guide to a Revolution of Mind* and *Wild Awakening: The Heart of Mahamudra and Dzogchen.*

Charles Prebish is a leading scholar on the history and sociology of Buddhism in America. He is coauthor of *The Faces of Buddhism in America* and author of *An American Buddhist Life.*

Yvonne Rand is a meditation teacher and lay householder priest in the Soto Zen tradition. She is the resident teacher at Goat-in-the-Road in Mendocino County, California.

Reginald Ray is a scholar, Buddhist teacher, and spiritual director of the Dharma Ocean Society. He is the author of numerous books and audio sets, including *Indestructible Truth*; *Secrets of the Vajra World*; *Meditating with the Body*; and *Mahamudra for the Modern World.*

Marcia Rose is the founding teacher of the Mountain Hermitage and Taos Mountain Sangha Meditation Center. She is a regular visiting teacher at the Forest Refuge in Barre, Massachusetts.

Sharon Salzberg is a cofounder of the Insight Meditation Society and the author of such bestsellers as *Real Happiness, Love Your Enemies* (with Robert Thurman); *Loving-Kindness*; and *Faith: Trusting Your Own Deepest Experience.*

Grace Schireson is a clinical psychologist and dharma teacher in the lineage of Shunryu Suzuki Roshi. She is the founder and head teacher of the Empty

Nest Zen Group and the author of *Zen Women: Beyond Tea-Ladies, Iron Maidens, and Macho Masters*.

Miranda Shaw is associate professor of religious studies at the University of Richmond. She is the author of *Passionate Enlightenment: Women in Tantric Buddhism* and *Buddhist Goddesses of India*.

Marcia Schmidt is a writer and translator and the cofounder of Rangjung Yeshe Publications. She is the editor of *The Dzogchen Primer* and *Quintessential Dzogchen* and the author of *Confessions of a Gypsy Yogini*.

Bhante Seelawimala is a Theravāda monk from Sri Lanka and professor at the Graduate Theological Seminary in Berkeley. He is president of American Buddhist Seminary Temple in Sacramento and the Buddhist Vihara in Vancouver.

Richard Shrobe received dharma transmission from the late Korean Zen master Soen Sa Nim and is the guiding teacher of the Chogye International Zen Center in New York City. He is the author of *Elegant Failure: A Guide to Zen Koans* and *Don't-Know Mind: The Spirit of Korean Zen*.

Judith Simmer-Brown is an acharya in Shambhala International and professor of religious studies at Naropa University. She is the author of the classic *Dakini's Warm Breath: The Feminine Principle in Tibetan Buddhism*.

Rod Meade Sperry is the associate editor and web editor of the *Shambhala Sun*. He is the creator of the Buddhism and pop culture website The Worst Horse and editor of *A Beginner's Guide to Meditation*.

Myogen Steve Stücky (d. 2013) was central abbot of the San Francisco Zen Center from 2010 to 2013, when he stepped down because of ill health. He was also the guiding teacher of Dharma Eye Zen Center in San Rafael, California.

Ven. Ajahn Sumedho is the foremost Western disciple of the late Thai meditation master Ajahn Chah. He is founder of Amaravati Buddhist Centre, a Theravāda monastery in Hertfordshire, England.

Joan Sutherland, Roshi, is founder of the Open Source, a network of practice communities in the Western US emphasizing the confluence of Zen kōans, creativity, and companionship.

John Tarrant, Roshi, directs the Pacific Zen Institute, where he is developing on a new way of teaching koans for people with no experience of meditation. He is the author of *Bring Me the Rhinoceros and Other Zen Koans That Will Save Your Life* and *The Light Inside the Dark: Zen, Soul and the Spiritual Life.*

Robert Thurman is one of North America's best-known Buddhist leaders and authors. He is the Jey Tsong Khapa Professor of Indo-Tibetan Buddhist Studies at Columbia University, president of Tibet House–US, and a leading voice for Tibetan Freedom.

Bonnie Myotai Treace, Sensei, founded Hermitage Heart and the Bodies of Water Society. She teaches Zen at Gristmill Hermitage in Garrison, New York. Her writings include *Zen Moon: A Season of Zen Teachings.*

Ringu Tulku is a lama in the Kagyü order of Tibetan Buddhism and founder of Bodhicharya. He is the author of *Daring Steps* and *Path to Buddhahood.*

Mark Unno was ordained in the Shin Buddhist tradition and is the head of the department of religious studies at the University of Oregon. He is the author of *Shingon Reflections: Myoe and the Mantra of Lights*, as well as many studies, translations, and articles in both English and Japanese.

B. Alan Wallace is a Buddhist teacher, scholar, and translator, and the founder of the Santa Barbara Institute for Consciousness Studies. Among his books are *The Taboo of Subjectivity: Toward a New Science of Consciousness* and *Buddhism and Science: Breaking New Ground.*

Tenzin Wangyal Rinpoche is president and resident lama at Ligmincha Institute in Charlottesville, Virginia. Trained in both Bön and Buddhist Dzogchen, he is author of *Awakening the Luminous Mind, Healing With Form, Energy, and Light*; and other books.

Sojun Mel Weitsman, Roshi, is the abbot of the Berkeley Zen Center. He was ordained as a priest by Suzuki Roshi in 1969 and served as coabbot of the San Francisco Zen Center from 1988 to 1997.

Index

About Wisdom Publications

WISDOM PUBLICATIONS is the leading publisher of classic and contemporary Buddhist books and practical works on mindfulness. Publishing books from all major Buddhist traditions, Wisdom is a nonprofit charitable organization dedicated to cultivating Buddhist voices the world over, advancing critical scholarship, and preserving and sharing Buddhist literary culture.

To learn more about us or to explore our other books, please visit our website at www.wisdompubs.org. You can subscribe to our eNewsletter, request a print catalog, and find out how you can help support Wisdom's mission either online or by writing to:

Wisdom Publications
199 Elm Street
Somerville, Massachusetts 02144 USA

You can also contact us at 617-776-7416 or info@wisdompubs.org.

Wisdom is a 501(c)(3) organization, and donations in support of our mission are tax deductible.

Wisdom Publications is affiliated with the Foundation for the Preservation of the Mahayana Tradition (FPMT).

Also Available from Wisdom Publications

In the Buddha's Words
An Anthology of Discourses from the Pali Canon
Bhikkhu Bodhi
Foreword by His Holiness the Dalai Lama
512 pages | $18.95 | ebook $13.81

"It will rapidly become the sourcebook of choice for both neophyte and serious student alike."—*Buddhadharma*

Mindfulness in Plain English
Bhante Gunaratana
224 pages | $16.95 | ebook $12.35

"A classic—one of the very best English sources for authoritative explanations of mindfulness."—Daniel Goleman, author of *Emotional Intelligence*

A New Buddhist Path
Enlightenment, Evolution, and Ethics in the Modern World
David R. Loy
144 pages | $16.95 | ebook $11.99

"This is a manifesto of genuine spiritual freedom."—James Ishmael Ford, author of *If You're Lucky, Your Heart Will Break*

Sitting with Koans
Essential Writings on Zen Koan Introspection
Edited by John Daido Loori
Introduction by Thomas Yuho Kirchner
368 pages | $16.95 | ebook $12.35

"Required reading for those interested in how koans are used in Zen practice."—*Shambhala Sun*

Attention Revolution
Unlocking the Power of the Focused Mind
B. Alan Wallace
Foreword by Daniel Goleman
224 pages | $16.95 | ebook $12.35

"Indispensable for anyone wanting to understand the mind. A superb, clear set of exercises that will benefit everyone."—Paul Ekman, Professor Emeritus at University of California San Francisco, and author of *Telling Lies* and *Emotions Revealed*

Unlimiting Mind
The Radically Experiential Psychology of Buddhism
Andrew Olendzki
200 pages | $15.95 | ebook $11.62

"This book has the power to change how you see yourself and the world. It's a remarkable read for anyone interested in the human condition."
—Christopher K. Germer, author of *The Mindful Path to Self-Compassion*

Buddhism and Psychotherapy Across Cultures
Essays on Theories and Practices
Edited by Mark Unno
384 pages | $19.95

"Points toward a real integration of Buddhist thought into our culture, our lives, and our worlds."—Mark Epstein, author of *Thoughts Without a Thinker*

Blue Jean Buddha
Voices of Young Buddhists
Sumi Loundon
Foreword by Jack Kornfield
256 pages | $16.95 | ebook $12.35

"A bellwether anthology."—*The New York Review of Books*

The Sound of Silence
The Selected Teachings of Ajahn Sumedho
Ajahn Sumedho
Preface and Introduction by Ajahn Amaro
376 pages | $18.95 | ebook $13.81

"Ajahn Sumedho's warm, human, and reverently playful style illuminates so clearly the causes of our suffering and the possiblities of freedom. His words are a treasure-house of dharma understanding."—Joseph Goldstein, author of *One Dharma*

The Svātantrika-Prāsaṅgika Distinction
What Difference Does a Difference Make?
Edited by Georges B.J. Dreyfus and Sara L. McClintock
416 pages | $36.95

"A brilliantly riveting and scholarly tour-de-force."—Anne C. Klein, Rice University, author of *Path to the Middle*

A Heart Full of Peace
Joseph Goldstein
Foreword by His Holiness the Dalai Lama
128 pages | $9.95 | ebook $9.95

"In this short but substantive volume, Joseph Goldstein, who lectures and leads retreats around the world, presents his thoughts on the practice of compassion, love, kindness, restraint, a skillful mind, and a peaceful heart as an antidote to the materialism of our age."—*Spirituality & Practice*

Zen Questions
Zazen, Dogen, and the Spirit of Creative Inquiry
Taigen Dan Leighton
312 pages | $17.95 | ebook $13.08

"Taigen Dan Leighton's clear, accurate, and eminently useful book will save any serious Zen practitioner, or even a curious novice, years of wasted error, wrong turns, and plain old delusion."—Peter Coyote

The Zen Teaching of Homeless Kodo
Kosho Uchiyama and Shohaku Okumura
288 pages | $17.95 | ebook $11.99

"Kodo Sawaki was straight-to-the-point, irreverent, and deeply insightful—and one of the most influential Zen teachers for us in the West. I'm very happy to see this book."—Brad Warner, author of *Hardcore Zen*

Zen Women
Beyond Tea Ladies, Iron Maidens, and Macho Masters
Grace Schireson
Foreword by Miriam Levering
320 pages | $16.95 | ebook $12.35

"An exceptional and powerful classic with great depth, humor, and clarity."—Joan Halifax, abbess of Upaya Zen Center